CRITICAL ACCLAIM FOR
HELLO! BUDGET HOTEL GUIDES

"The best travel resource guides on the market for independent, budget-minded travelers."
—The Thrifty Traveler

"Classé may be the best thing for budget travelers—since Arthur Frommer. These are good. Very good indeed."
—The Times-Picayune

"Even the most ambitious books rarely devote as much space to listing accommodations. For sheer number of entries…the books can't be beat."
—The Wichita Eagle

"It's a great guide and one that we highly recommend."
—Paul Lasley and Elizabeth Harryman,
The Touring Company

"The hotels are customer-friendly and centrally located."
—Los Angeles Times

"This book is a dream. Not only does it list over 200 accommodations, all of them are well documented including addresses, phone numbers, credit cards, etc. …This book is definitely a winner."
—Shoestring Travel

"[For] cost-conscious travelers who are too old for hostels and dormitories, but don't care if the curtains match the bedspread."
—The Times-Picayune

"You'll find…cheap quarters in Margo Classe's *Hello France!*."
—Washington Post

"Extraordinarily useful."
—S

"What this book does is allow you the freedom of not making reservations until you get to Italy…"

—*Pasadena Weekly*

"I found a very acceptable hotel [in Paris]…comfortable, in a great location, was clean and offered breakfast and friendly service."

—*Joanne Gerber, French Government Tourist Office*

WHAT READERS ARE SAYING
ABOUT *HELLO!* BUDGET HOTEL GUIDES

"Thanks for writing your books. We found them useful a few times in Italy and Spain. Let us know whenever you have any new books coming out."

— *Anne Colon*

"We spent this past June in Italy and used your book for almost all of our accomodation choices. We were extremely happy with all of them. Thanks for all your hard work!"

—*Eric Brahm & Yvonne Wiebelhaus*

"I have recommended your book to a lot of people. Most of the travel books (other than Rick Steves) do not have the excellent type of information that you do and his are not nearly as extensive. You have been very helpful! Thank you again."

—*Maryellen Federico*

"Thanks to you and your book, I was able to book everything here and have faxes and e-mails with the needed info. Thank you for these wonderful publications. Since our daughter has been in France so many times and we plan to visit her again next summer, guess that I will need the hotel book for France also! Please let me know your site address again. (www.Hello Europe.com) Thanks for everything!"

—*Michel Puckett*

"I am happy to report that I am a purchaser of your great book regarding Italy. I have "dog-earred it to death in preparation for our trip next month. Again, thank you for your great book."
—*Mitch Harada*

"I just wanted to say that the hotel recommendations from *Hello Italy* worked out great. We stayed at the Pausania in Venice. Thanks for writing a great guide book."
—*Mike Frey*

"Thank you for your great guide *(Hello Italy) An Insiders Guide Italian Hotels!* We have just returned from 18 days in Italy where we had reservations in three hotels you recommended (Hotel Canal in Venice, Hotel Caschi in Florence and Hotel Primavera in Rome). I was so curious about the accuracy of your book that I visited two additional hotels you recommended (Hotel Lidomare and Hotel Amalfi) while staying in Amalfi. The rooms and terms were just as you had described , the locations were great, and the staff very friendly and helpful."
—*Mara and Charles Walter*

"I usually follow Frommer, Fodor, and Rick Steves, but I have a new leader, Margo Classé. It offers pricing, location, discounts available, directions, tips on reservations, packing, etc. Try it, you'll like it."
—*Mary Anna Bramberg*

"The book was worth the money! It did what it purported to do, namely get us into hotels for under $80 consistently. Most were around the $40-$50 range."
—*David Dingee*

"As a woman traveling alone, I was concerned about security as well as economy. I found your comments about the neighborhoods 'right on the money.' I never was disappointed in any of the hotels where I stayed."
—*Mary Redmond*

Hi Margo,
Just back from paris. Found your recommendations right on
target. Will always use your guides in the future.
—*Thanks, Mimi Greenberg*

Dear Margo Classé,
About your book — it is a very excellent book. You are doing a
very good job and I hope you become very successful, because
there is definitely a need for what you are doing. Keep up the
good work!!!!
—*Michelle Patterson*

Dear Ms. Classé,
I simply must write and tell you how glad I was to find your
book. We are happy to be saving money as most everything has
been under $100 per night.
—*Maryellen and Gil Federico*

Margo,
I have recommended your book. Your book was worth the two
hotels we stayed in!
—*Sincerely, Ken Mijeski*

Hello Margo,
I love what you have done. That is, pair travelers with smaller,
more intimate hotels with a personal touch. You have helped us
and so many others find the wonderful, small, intimate hotels that
really make the trip rather than a large impersonal "American"
hotel just like the ones here in the States.
—*Michel Puckett*

Margo,
I have had great fun marking places in your book. Your
descriptions are wonderfully thorough. I am so glad someone
is finally doing what you are doing.
—*Hebe Smythe*

Margo,

I love your book because you embrace one of my big requirements....clean!! And the other huge thing you added into some descriptions that helped me with the yeah/nay decision....'popular with students' which can often mean...late night kinds of folk..also was glad to see the designation 'quiet' or 'noisy' P.S. Thanks for all your hard work. I certainly can trust your recommendations in the future, which says a lot because there's so many 'guide books' out these days ya never know!

—*Andrea Egan*

Dear Margo,

I received the book yesterday and really enjoy reading it. So helpful.

—*Pizza Hair*

My companion and I just returned from our 2 week trip and we used your book to choose our hotels. I wanted to thank you and to tell you about our good experiences. I wanted you to know that we thought your book was WONDERFUL and would recommend it.

—*Kindest regards, Amy Soelzer*

Hi, Margo,

Got your book yesterday and haven't put it down – it's great.

—*Larry Handley*

Other Wilson Publishing travel guidebooks
by Margo Classé:

*HELLO FRANCE! A HOTEL GUIDE TO
PARIS & 25 OTHER FRENCH CITIES $50-$99 A NIGHT*
ISBN: 0-9653944-0-9
$18.95

*HELLO SPAIN! AN INSIDER'S GUIDE TO
SPAIN HOTELS $40-$80 A NIGHT FOR TWO*
ISBN: 0-9653944-2-5
$18.95

HELLO ITALY!

A Hotel Guide to
ITALY

Rome Venice Florence
& 23 Other Italian Cities

$50-$99
(45-90 Euros)
a Night

▶ *Centrally Located Hotels*
▶ *Restaurants* ▶ *Travel Tips*
▶ *Web Sites* ▶ *Packing & More*

Margo Classé

Wilson Publishing
Los Angeles, California

HELLO ITALY!
A Hotel Guide to
ITALY
Rome Venice Florence
& 23 Other Italian Cities
$50-$99 (45-90 Euro) A Night

By Margo Classé

Published by: **Wilson Publishing**
Tel: (323) 939-0821 Fax: (323) 939-7736
http://www.HelloEurope.com/
E-mail: margo@helloeurope.com
Order toll-free: (888) 663-9269

2nd Edition

Cover designed by Opus1design.com

Cover photographs by Tyrell Wilson

Map illustrations by Opus1design.com

Text designed by Opus1design.com

Edited by Brenda Koplin

reprinted by Central Plains Book Manufacturing
Manufactured in the United States of America

ISBN: 0-9653944-6-8
Library of Congress Catalog Card Number: 98-61454

While every care has been taken to ensure the accuracy and timeliness of the information in this guide, the author and publisher cannot accept responsibility for the consequences of errors or changes that may occur.

This book is dedicated to my husband, Tyrell Wilson, whose love, passion and support allow me to continue pursuing my dream and making it a reality.

Acknowledgments

This is my fourth book, and without the support and friendship of the following people, it would have been a much more difficult task.

Geovanni Brewer, my buddy who always rescues me from myself, shares my love of traveling and constantly gives me the freedom to release my stress.

My close friends Lillian Martin, Marvinia Anderson, Sheryl Carey, Christy Hervey, Jeff Fischgrund, Linnie Washington and Pamela Terry. Pamela, I owe you a special gratitude.

Esther Wilson, my adopted mom, for all her contributions.

As the new kid on the block to the book publishing world, I never would have come this far without the help of the following people in the media:

Millie Ball, travel editor, *New Orleans Times-Picayune*

Barbara Shea, travel writer, *Newsday*

Arlice Davenport, travel editor, *Kansas Wichita Eagle*

Pucci Meyer, travel editor, *New York Post*

Mary Orlin, travel news, CNN

Gary Lee, travel writer, *Washington Post*

Bill McCoy, executive editor, *Arthur Frommer's Budget Travel*

Shirley Davis, travel editor, *Quad-City Times*

Lucy Izon, syndicated travel writer

Eric Adler, *Shoestring Traveler*

Ava Plakins, executive editor, *Moneysworth*

Elaine Glusac, contributing editor, *American Way*

Paul Lasley and Elizabeth Harryman, Touring Company, KPCC

Don Schaffer, Drive Time, KSL

Jerry Reno, Drive Time, WHO

Location of Cities

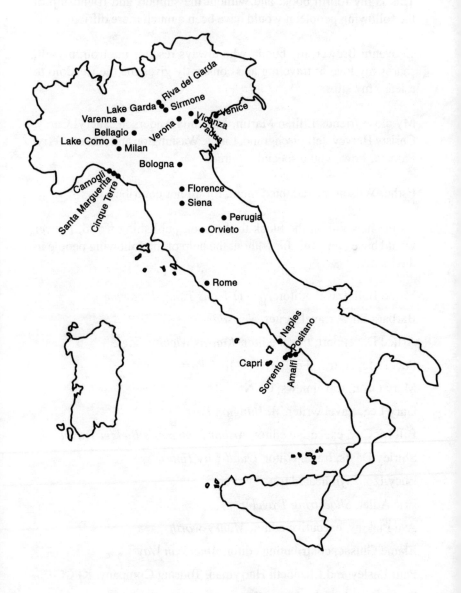

TABLE OF CONTENTS

TABLE OF CONTENTS

TO READERS OF MY BOOKS:

I traveled with my husband to 26 of the most popular cities in Italy, which took six consecutive weeks (no days off), to visit each of these hotels in person. This is no easy accomplishment. We worked hard to bring you an extensive resource guide on very clean, safe, inexpensive, centrally located charming hotels (with private bathrooms) in these 26 cities so that you would be able to have a more affordable, enjoyable vacation. The book is filled with lots of tips and information gathered from actual experience. Please take the time to read it so that you may benefit from it.

My husband, Tyrell, and I pay for all our expenses including the cost of publishing our own books. No hotel or restaurant pays us to be in our books. Any discounts I get are passed on to my readers. I have included my contact information in the front of the book and I encourage you to use it. However, if any details in this book are not correct or you experienced something beyond my control, please forgive me and have a good time.

INTRODUCTION

Many of us lead very structured lives. Most of our days include strict timelines, so when it is time for a vacation, I would think you would want a more relaxed schedule. You can accomplish this by planning your own vacation. Take charge of your trip, arrange your own day tours and have some fun at your own pace. Select your hotel by reading this book and making your own reservations. I have made it quite easy by doing all the research for you. All that is left for you to do is to decide what city you want to visit, what sites you want to see and how long you want to be in each city. Read about the cities you want to visit. Write, fax or e-mail the tourist offices of those cities and request information on day tours, maps and events.

My husband, Tyrell, and I are travelers who like to get the most for our money. We like the spontaneity and freedom of not being committed to a particular schedule. Thus the reason for this book. In our 10 years of traveling in Italy, I have put together a list of hotels that can be rented for an all-inclusive rate of $50 to $99 (some a little more than $99) a night for double occupancy (depending on the exchange rate). This means you can spend your money on the important things such as sightseeing, food, shopping and more food!

My criteria for selecting hotels are that they must be *very clean*, safe, inexpensive, centrally located and, above all, have a toilet and shower in the room. All the hotels listed in this book are family-run unless otherwise indicated and have at least one room with a toilet. For me, the sole purpose of a hotel room is to provide a *safe* place to sleep after an enjoyable day.

In October through November of 1998, I visited each hotel listed in this book in person in all 26 cities. *Many of the hotel owners agreed in writing to give my readers a discount when you show them this book (no copies or rip-out pages will be accepted) before (not after) you check into the hotel. (Please see "Tips on Hotel Accommodations" for more specific details on this subject.) I made a notation in each hotel listing where a discount is offered. Depending on the time of year, it ranges from about 5% to 10% or more per room. However,* all discounts go out the window when you arrive during Easter or any other major festivals that take place in the cities. (For a calendar of events, see Appendix V in the back of this book.) I have organized this book by listing the 26 Italian cities alphabetically. Most of our traveling through Europe is done by train, so I use the train station squares as my starting point in the listings for directions to the hotels. Hotels are listed alphabetically within each city, with street (mailing) address, phone and/or fax number, along with a brief description of the hotel. The Appendixes list information on packing tips, tourist offices in the U.S., using telephones in Italy, Italian phrases for checking in and a schedule of holidays and special events when hotels are crowded, so you can plan ahead.

What this book will *not* do is tell you about Italy, when to go, how to get there and what sights to see. That is what your favorite travel guide does. Also, you will not find information regarding youth hostels, dormitories, student accommodations and camping sites.

What this book *will* do is allow you the freedom of not making reservations until you get to Italy, and arm you with plenty of choices and information on inexpensive hotels, special discounts and directions to the hotels from the train station. It lists clean and safe hotels in Italy that are available at $50 to $99 a night for double occupancy (most of the time you have to add the value-added tax to the room rate and the meal). To avoid any misunderstandings, always confirm the rate and what it includes at the time you check into the hotel.

LAUNDRIES
The use of self-service laundries throughout our travels helps us tremendously because we pack light. I have tried to include locations of the various laundries for most cities listed in this book.

RESTAURANTS
This is a new addition to my series. When I was working on the Spain book, I met an American couple who had just arrived in Spain who suggested that I select one restaurant for each city. They explained how difficult it is when you arrive on your first day in a city and are looking for a decent restaurant. I decided that if I found a

restaurant I really liked, I would include it in the section. My criteria for selecting restaurants are that they must have great food, be clean, be moderately priced, have a friendly atmosphere and be family-owned. I also happen to be a lover of good local house wine. Hint: When visiting cafés, food and drinks cost less if you stand at a bar versus sitting at a table, and eating at an outside table might cost more than an inside table. (After a five-hour hike, I informed my girlfriend Marvenia of this fact and she stated she didn't care what it cost to eat, she was sitting down at a table.)

SUPERMARKETS
Take advantage of these well-priced markets that usually take major credit cards (some have a minimum purchase). I have tried to include locations of various supermarkets for most cities listed in this book. Buy your wine, cheese, fruit, candy and stock up on bottled water (that sells for three times as much on the street). If you are lucky enough to have a minibar in your room you can keep these items cold and have them later for midnight snacks. Sometimes I buy a pastry or two and keep the leftovers in the minibar for the following evening.

THE MOST IMPORTANT TIP OF ALL: If I could give you one piece of advice to follow, it would be this: Be extremely patient and polite with everyone you talk to. If you treat each person you meet with respect and exhibit the attitude that you know you are a guest in their country, hopefully you will never have any difficulties. I do not speak Italian, but I do know how to say "Thank you," "Good morning" and "Please." (See Appendix IV.)

BEFORE YOU LEAVE HOME

Please read your travel guide for all the basic information on what to do before you leave home. The following is intended to be used as additional advice only.

Anticipate hotels' busy times: Familiarize yourself with the schedule of local holidays, traditional events, fashion shows and religious celebrations in the cities you are planning to visit so that you know which times of the year hotels are likely to be especially busy. This will help you to decide whether you need to make advance reservations. If a public holiday falls on a Tuesday or Thursday, many businesses also close on the nearest Monday or Friday for a long weekend. For each city in this book, I have included the phone and fax numbers of the city's local tourist office. Take advantage of this and write or fax them prior to your leaving the States. Request that they send you information on the city, a detailed list of local events for the month you plan to visit the city, hotels and a map. Their information will be more detailed than what you will get from the tourist offices of Italy in your country.

ATM/Credit Cards: Confirm with your bank that your ATM/credit cards can be used in Europe and that they will be recognized by the Cirrus or Plus systems. Cirrus Network: (800) 424-7787; Plus System: (800) 843-7587. Call for a list of locations. Carry several cards from two or more different banks. Apparently demagnetization seems to be a common problem and ATMs have been known to eat the cards. Make sure the PIN code is numeric and not alphanumeric and is only four digits. If it is more than four digits, change it before you go. You may also want to arrange with your bank to have your daily withdrawal limits raised in the account attached to the ATM card before departing from home, since you incur a fee each time you do a transaction. Call your credit card company to let them know you will be in Italy using the card. I had been unable to use my card because the credit card company put a hold on it because they thought it was stolen. I found out when I called them from Europe. Get the lost/stolen phone numbers from your bank for all your ATM & credit cards. Most banks have call-collect numbers that you can use since 800 numbers do not work from Europe. Speaking of lost/stolen cards, make sure your bank offers the same protection on your ATM/Visa or ATM/MasterCard as regular credit cards because those cards are attached to your checking/savings account. If those cards get lost/stolen all your money in your checking account can be wiped out. Carry cash, traveler's checks and credit cards as a back-up because there could be computer glitches, or as I mentioned, your card could be eaten by the ATM. If by chance your card does gets eaten, report it immediately to your bank. I have heard stories where people did not report it to their bank, thinking the useless card and the unwritten PIN were safe, but found out the funds in their checking account were wiped out because of an inside job at the bank.

Books recommended: The following are convenient and handy for traveling and you should not leave home without them. **1.)** Your favorite travel guide; **2.)** *Hello Italy!* (this book); **3.)** *Eating & Drinking in Italian,* ISBN: 0-88496-437-X (this user-friendly guide is my first, best and only choice of menu readers because it alphabetizes the food and drinks and is compact. Its authors can be reached at e-mail: EatnDrink@aol.com) **4.)** *Italian: A Rough Guide Phrasebook,* ISBN: 1-85828-147-4; **5.)** *Thomas Cook European Timetable*, ISSN: 0952-620X, for train schedules (rip out the pages on Italy and you are ready to go).

Cellular phone: I never thought about doing this before but with today's inexpensive technology this is an affordable and sometimes quite necessary expense. For the first time, I rented an international cellular phone to take along with me. It was the best and most comforting thing I have ever done for myself on a trip. I move around a lot from town to town, hotel to hotel, and having the portable phone made it possible for my husband to keep up with my travels and eased his worries about my traveling all alone in a foreign country. My family and friends didn't have to struggle with broken Italian to reach me. It also made it quite convenient for me to keep in touch with home as well as make advance hotel reservations along the way. What was really great was being able to use it while I was on a seven-hour train ride. I didn't have a chance to make hotel reservations before leaving the last city, so I called while I was on the train. There are several companies in operation but I recommend Cellhire,

USA because of their low rates and excellent reputation. Cellhire, USA: (888) 476-7368 or **Web site:** http://www.CellHire.com/

Luggage: The amount of luggage you carry can make or break your trip. European hotels do not offer a lot of closet space. Also, there are no porters in these charming small hotels. My husband and I are in our late forties and we still travel a month or more at a time with only two bags each. Therefore, we do not require a lot of closet space. We use the Eagle Creek's *Cargo Switchback™ Plus* convertible suitcase & *Cargo SB Traveler*. These are bags that work together as a system. The *Switchback™* is a 2-in-1 modular system. The first is a 14x21x8 (14x23x8 w/wheels) suitcase that comes with an extension handle that allows it to roll on wheels; or it can be carried as a backpack or by hand-handle. This luxury of choices is very convenient when cobblestone streets sometimes makes it almost impossible to navigate the wheels. I can't say enough about these bags. I pulled, wheeled, banged and dragged (sometimes through pouring rain) these bags up and down stairs in train stations, cobbled streets and country roads in 26 cities throughout Italy. I stuffed them with my notes, brochures and information collected after visiting more than 500 hotels that tested the strength of the zippers and handles. The *Switchback™* has a day pack (12x16x5) that attaches (zips) to it. The second is the *Cargo SB* bag (21x13x8) that slips over the handle of the Switchback but can also be carried as a backpack or on the shoulder. The best feature about these bags is that they both meet the now revised specifications for carry-ons allowed on airlines. I also love their sidekick waist & shoulder bag. I wear it around my waist when I board the plane so the airline personnel don't count it as an extra bag. Then I use it as a shoulder bag when I arrive at my destination. It is roomy enough to hold my paperback book, umbrella, camera, flashlight, water bottle, etc. **Web site:** http://www.eaglecreek.com/ The use of self-service laundries throughout our travels helps us tremendously because we pack light. I have tried to include locations of the various laundries for most cities listed in this book.

Maps: Obtain a map of each city you are planning to visit. Having the map ahead of time will help you to familiarize yourself with the layout of the city as well as the location of the hotels. I cannot stress enough how important this information is because it also helps you to determine whether you can walk or should take the bus, train or taxi to the hotel. If you forget to pick up a map before you leave the States, you can always purchase one at the convenience stores located at the train stations. It amazes me when I hear tourists who don't speak Italian asking for directions. The time you spend getting lost will cost you more than an investment in a good map. Most travel guides suggest picking up a free map from the local tourist information centers located within the city. This is a great idea. However, given the hours of the tourist offices and the time of day that you may arrive in the city, this suggestion will not always be possible to follow. Besides, how will you find the tourist office? Numerous bookstores carry an abundance of information regarding traveling. I purchase some of my maps from MapLink at (805) 692-6777, fax: (800) 627-7768, (805) 692-6787 or **Website:** http://www.maplink.com/ and from Our Heritage/Maps of Italy: fax: (626) 332-0422; Website: www.initaly.com/ads/maps.htm/ Whatever map you decide to purchase, make sure it has an index to help you find the street you are looking for. Many streets in Italy have two names. When using a map to look up the street names, look up the second name of the street address first. If you can't find the name, then try the first name. I used Hallwag maps for Venice, Rome and Florence.

Packing: As a result of my years of traveling, I have compiled a packing list of seldom thought-of but very necessary items. (See Appendix I.) These items will make your trip more enjoyable and hassle-free. Most of these items are carried by your local favorite travel bookstore.

Precautions for safe travel: As an experienced traveler, I take certain precautions that I assumed everyone takes or knows about. I was wrong. I met people on my many journeys to Europe who shared their negative experiences with me on how they were pickpocketed. What surprised me was how simple it was for the thief. I don't consider any city in Italy including Naples to be as dangerous as New York City (where I was born and raised) or Los Angeles (where I currently live). But you must be aware of pickpockets. They have so many different scams that they use to distract you: making believe there is a bird dropping on your jacket; putting a newspaper or card-board up to your face; mother with the infant baby; simple bumping into you; watching you in a gift store to see where you put your wallet; person on a moped grabbing your bag and your arm with it; or just running up to you and grabbing your purse off your arm, etc. Pickpockets dress for the job in clothes ranging from the typical gypsy look to the elegant look of a well-dressed Italian tourist riding the bus on the way to the Vatican. Leave your valuables locked in your room or with the hotel management. Nowadays most hotels including 1-stars have safety boxes inside the room. If you are un-comfortable with that, then invest in a deluxe undercover wallet that is worn underneath your clothes. They come in different shapes and styles to be worn around your waist, shoulders, legs or neck. Buy whatever is comfortable for you but get one. Once I leave my hotel room there is never any reason for me to go into or open my deluxe undercover wallet because I also use *Eagle Creek's* wallet/purse that loops onto my belt to carry the estimated money I plan to use for the day, one credit card, a pen and a memo pad. Remember professional pickpockets are always watching where you reach for or put your money. If I underestimated the money I needed for the day, I replen-ish my funds from inside a stall in a ladies' bathroom and nowhere else. These items are carried by your local favorite travel store or Magellan's at (800) 962-4943. Check my Web site http://www.HelloEurope.com/ for a list of travel stores. I do not use fanny packs but if you want to use one, do not put anything of value in it. Use a separate wallet for your money and put all the unimportant items you will need for the day in the fanny pack, and put a small combination lock on the zipper. Do not assume because you have a fanny pack that it is safe from the pickpockets. *Make photocopies of all your important documents: airline ticket, passport, traveler's checks, credit card numbers and phone numbers of the credit card companies in case they are lost or stolen.* Make sure someone at home has the duplicate set of everything you photocopied. Remem-ber pickpockets also work airports.

BEFORE YOU LEAVE HOME

Train travel in Italy: My husband and I do all our traveling by train or bus. To make our train travel more efficient throughout the country, we use the *Thomas Cook European Timetable*, which is sold in most travel bookstores or you can order it directly from Forsyth Travel Library, tel: (800) FORSYTH in the U.S. or Canada. This is the best timetable available and is published on the first day of each month. It is worth its weight in gold because it can save you hours of standing on information lines at various train stations. Otherwise, you can visit Rail Europe's **Web site** at http://www.raileurope.com/ or call them at (888) 382-7245 or fax them at (800) 432-1329 or try FS (the Italian State Railroad) at **Web site** http://www.fs-on-line.com/ I use these numbers to get an idea of the cost, distance and time it takes to travel to each city's FS train station. Rail Europe also has an information-by-fax-on-demand system. The prices and information you get from contacting Rail Europe will help you to decide what type of rail pass you will need, if any. There are so many variations of passes that are sold by Rail Europe. The following is a brief summary of the different passes available for Italy. 1.) Eurailpass-a multicountry pass sold either as a consecutive days usage pass or flexipass, which is a certain amount of days in a time frame (1st class only). 2.) Eurail saverpass is the same as the Eurailpass but is cheaper if two or more people are traveling together on the same schedule (1st class only). 3.) Europass-a specified number of days for specific number of countries (1st class only). 4.) Europass saverpass-same as Europass but is cheaper if two people are traveling together on the same schedule (1st class only). 5.) Europass drive-combination rail/drive pass (1st or 2nd class). 6.) Italy rail card-a specified number of consecutive days in a month (1st or 2nd class). 7.) Italy flexi rail card-a specified number of days in a month (1st or 2nd class). 8.) Italy rail 'n drive pass-combination pass for train and car (1st or 2nd class). Most of the passes mentioned above are available for people under 26 at discounted prices and would include the use of 2nd class travel. If you decide on a rail pass, be sure to buy it from Rail Europe before leaving home; those available elsewhere cost more. Please note that whether you have a rail pass or not, reservations are mandatory on the Eurostar Italia (ES), EuroCity (EC), InterCity (IC), the Pendolino and EuroNight (EN) night trains. I usually go to the train station a day or two ahead to make my reservations for the next leg of my trip.

This cuts down on the stress of finding out that the departure times or seats you want are sold out, which has happened to me more than once when I waited to the last minute to make my reservation. Train information line in Italy (English language) Tel: 1478-88088. Hrs.: Daily 7am-9pm. However, once I get to Italy, I buy the FS "InTreno" which is the official train timetable that the train conductors use for information. The FS "InTreno" timetable came in quite handy for the Italian Riviera and Cinque Terre which is not covered by the Thomas Cook Timetable. This book also saved me precious time that would have been wasted waiting in information lines in Florence, Venice and Rome. The FS "InTreno"is available at newsstands inside the train stations for 8,000L.

Train tips:
1. Always purchase your ticket as soon as you know your departure time. Don't wait until the morning of departure, especially if you plan to catch a Eurostar Italia (ES), EuroCity (EC) or InterCity (IC). It doesn't matter whether it is 1st or 2nd class, always make reservations as soon as you are sure of your departure times, as these trains fill up quickly. This rule also applies to railpass holders. Be sure to bring your cable locks because ES, EC and IC have separate compartments for luggage. Many times you are too busy looking out the window to watch your luggage.

2. If a train ride is more than three hours and I am traveling with luggage, I always buy 1st class tickets if I am not using my 1st class rail pass. It is less crowded and allows me to spread out comfortably. The only time I use 2nd class on trips longer than three hours is if the train is a ES, EC or an IC. 2nd class is extremely comfortable.

3. When you look at the departure board at the train stations, it is not always easy to identify which train is yours. Here are some tips to assist you in assuring you catch the right train:
a. Using your timetable, look for the number of the train on the board.
b. The city you are going to may not be listed on the board. Look for the train's final destination.
c. Look at the departure time of your train. The trains are listed chronologically.

4. When using individual train tickets, make sure you stamp your ticket before you board the train, using any one of the convenient orange machines. Always check the ticket to make sure it got stamped. You'll get a hefty fine if you board the train without a stamped ticket.

5. When waiting on the platform to board your train, look for the display boards that may have diagrams of the layout of the train. These diagrams are quite useful. They will show you the direction the train is going and approximately where the 1st & 2nd class cars will stop at the train station. In the case of a ES, it will show you what part of the platform your assigned car will stop. (Check your ES ticket for the number of your car & pre-assigned seat number.)

6. When boarding a train without reserving a seat, make sure you sit in a non-reserve seat. Just look at the back of the seat or on the glass door (depending on the type of train you are boarding) for the words "non-reserve." I can't tell you how many times I've heard our fellow Americans get upset because they were not told that they were in the wrong seats until they were comfortably on their way.

7. When the train conductor comes by to stamp your ticket, always confirm with them that you are in the right car. Some trains split up their cars at certain train stops and will travel in different directions. There is nothing more frustrating than having yo grab your luggage because you found out at the last minute that you were in the wrong car. (I speak from experience.)

8. Don't forget to pack water, fruit peeler, towelettes, inflatable head pillow, book, toilet seat covers and snacks for long trips.

9. The great advantage of having a rail pass (& this book which gives you lots of choices on affordable hotels) is you can change your destination while you are on the train. I have done this several times. Example: I was on my way to Genoa and decided to go to Santa Marguerita at the last minute. I didn't have to worry about canceling my hotel reservation in Genoa because I didn't have one. I also knew that if for some reason I was unable to get a hotel room in Santa Marguerita, I could always use my pass to hop back on the train to Genoa.

BEFORE YOU LEAVE HOME

Europe by Air: This is another alternative for getting around Europe. This is a low-cost European air fare network that offers about 110 cities or more within Europe (and the Canary Islands) that can be connected by air for just $99 a ticket. However, tickets for these European cities can only be bought prior to leaving home and you must buy a minimum of three air passes at $99 each. The tickets are valid for 120 days and nonrefundable. Call, fax or e-mail them to have an information packet sent to you. *Europe by Air:* (888) 387-2479, fax (512) 404-1291 or **Web site:** http://www.europebyair.com/

TIPS ON HOTEL ACCOMMODATIONS

Addresses: On most streets, the numbers are even on one side and odd on the other side. But as always, there are many exceptions to this rule especially in Florence, Rome and Venice. Many streets in Italy have two names. When using the index of a map to look up the street name, look up the second name of the street address first. If you can't find the name, then try the street's first name. Many streets are called *Via* unless they have trees on them, then they are called *Viale*.

Air-conditioning: I know how important this feature is to many people. I specifically asked each hotel if they had air-conditioning in the hotel rooms and not just the hotel lobby. Each hotel that I list in this book as having air-conditioned rooms assured me that it is in the rooms. If you are reserving a hotel because the hotel has air-conditioned rooms, always ask what time the air-conditioning is turned on and off each day. Please keep in mind, the hotel may charge extra to use the air-conditioning and it may not be adjustable from your room.

Balconies *(balcone)*: I have included whether hotels have rooms with balconies because this is such a special feature. However, a balcony facing the street can be quite noisy at night even if the windows are double-paned. Don't forget to pack your earplugs. Also, please keep in mind that the sizes of the balconies vary from one foot to the size of a full terrace. A balcony is great to have when your traveling buddy needs to grab a smoke.

Bathroom facilities: One of the biggest complaints I hear about is the small bathroom size. Some bathrooms are so small, you can shower, brush your teeth and use the toilet all at the same time. I realize this is an adjustment but we should not compare European bathrooms in most 1, 2 and 3-star hotels to American-size standard bathrooms. We forget that some of the buildings that house these hotels are centuries old. Even when the hotel renovates the rooms, there isn't much left over for a full-size bathroom. The only thing that matters to my husband and me regarding a bathroom is that it is clean, private and has a shower, toilet and sink in it. Speaking of bathrooms, there is a difference in price between rooms with a bathtub and rooms with a shower. A room with a shower is cheaper than one with a bathtub. A room with a bathtub = *vasca da bagno*; without bathtub = *senza vasca da bagno*; with shower = *con doccia*; without shower = *senza doccia*. Do not assume anything when it comes to a bathroom in an Italian hotel room. Some rooms have a toilet and sink, or a sink only with no shower or toilet, or a shower but no toilet. I think you get my drift. Make absolutely sure of what you are getting. Use the convenient Italian phrases I have included in Appendix IV in the back of this book to confirm the facilities. *Towels:* Forget the size and softness of the towels you use back home. I have dried my body with stiff, hard, small towels in Italy. Also, Italian hotels do not have facecloths. I always pack mine. *Showers:* I haven't figured out why some showers don't have shower curtains on them. This inconvenience makes it impossible sometimes for two people to use the bathroom at the same time. If there are no shower facilities in your room, you might be charged an additional fee for the use of the hall shower.

Beds: A double bed *(letto matrimoniale)* is usually cheaper than twin beds *(due letti singoli)*. Be specific when requesting a room for two. Indicate whether you want *letto matrimoniale* or *due letti*. It is important when you ask to see the room that you also check the bed to make sure it is firm and not soft and lumpy.

Breakfast (*colazione*): Most hotels in Italy serve a continental breakfast at an extra charge unless otherwise specified in the hotel listing. The price ranges from 5,000 to 20,000 lire per person per day. Always check before turning it down. Sometimes you might luck out and get a buffet (Italian bread, cheese, eggs, ham, chocolate milk, juice, jam plus the basics), but normally it consists of *caffe latte* (coffee with hot milk) and a choice of Italian bread, toast or baguettes and awful canned juice. The bread is not always fresh and the coffee might be reheated from the day before. According to Italian law, breakfast in Italy is not supposed to be obligatory. However, most hotels will assume that you are having breakfast at their hotel and will automatically add the extra charge to your bill. Politely make yourself perfectly clear when you are checking into the hotel whether or not you plan to have breakfast in the hotel. The only time you have no choice is when they post signs on the wall stating that breakfast is included in the room rate and that the hotel room rate is the same whether you eat breakfast or not. Then the only choice you have is not to take the room. Breakfast is usually served from 7:30am to 11:00am. Many budget hotels do not have an area where they can serve breakfast, so be prepared for them to serve breakfast in your room. Confirm the serving time with them and what the meal consists of and where they serve it. Tyrell and I prefer to enjoy our breakfast at the local café, with the conversation of Italians on their way to work as the background, at half the price the hotel will charge. *Note:* Half-board means room plus breakfast and one other meal. Full-board means room plus breakfast, lunch and dinner.

Buildings: Don't get discouraged by an unimpressive entrance or lobby as you enter a building to your hotel. You can walk through the most magnificent lobby and your room can be small and drab or you can walk through a shabby entrance of a building, take the elevator to the hotel and when the doors open, you will be pleasantly surprised at how cheerful your room looks.

Car parking: If there is parking available at the hotels, assume there will be an additional daily charge for the convenience (about 30,000L a day).

Checking in: Never pay for a room in advance for more nights than you will need. You may not always get your money back. Never check into a room without seeing it first, and remember to check the bed. If they refuse to show you the room, politely leave. If a hotel is holding your deposit for a room but you know in advance that you will be arriving after 1700 hrs. (5:00pm), contact the hotel immediately. The hotel is within their rights to give away your room after that time, regardless of the fact that they have your money. **If you made advance reservations, please remember to pack and bring your hotel confirmation with the person's name on it along with you.**

Checking out: 11:00am is the normal checkout time in Italy. Do not assume you have the right to leave your luggage in the hotel's care while you finish your day. Not all hotels have this service, and keep in mind they are not responsible for lost or stolen property. I have offered to pay them to hold my luggage. They usually accept my offer. When departing the hotel, always make sure you get a receipt marked "paid in full." If you plan to leave very early in the morning, **I recommend paying the hotel bill the night before**. This relieves the stress of trying to catch that early-morning train or bus and allows time to clear up any discrepancies or misunderstandings regarding the final bill.

Children: I have included in the hotel listings at what age the hotel starts to charge for children. The general rule is most of the time hotels will charge for children if they require an additional bed in the room. Always confirm before you make a reservation to see if you can have your children in the room at no charge or at least 50% off the extra-person price.

Closet space: Please see **Luggage** in chapter "Before You Leave Home."

Credit cards: Hotels and restaurants prefer cash over credit cards. Because I personally visited each hotel, I have indicated wherever possible whether the hotels take credit cards or cash. Do not let them intimidate you into paying cash, which some may try to do (unless, of course, they are willing to give you a cash discount). I listened to one hotel manager ask a tourist, "Don't you have any lire?" when there was a sign hanging on his wall next to the desk stating "Credit cards accepted." The young lady said "No" and whipped out her credit card. Also, more than once when I tried to pay my hotel or restaurant bill by credit card, the portable credit card machines the Italians use to process the cards did not always work properly the first time. It was embarrassing in the beginning because they made me feel that the problem was with my card and not their machine. I would offer to pay by cash, but then I started insisting that they try again and again. Several hotels and restaurants had to swipe my card in their portable machines almost 10 times before it worked. I met other Americans who experienced the same thing.

Discounts on hotel rooms: Many of the hotel owners agreed in writing to give my readers a discount if you show them this book. I made a notation in each hotel listing where it applies. Depending on the time of year, it ranges from about 5% to 10% or more per room. I included a name wherever possible. If I did not give an amount, it is because they did not state how much they would give. It could be given in the form of a free breakfast. Discounts are a sore subject for the Italians. They do not like giving them. Please do not be surprised if they give you a distasteful look when you ask for one. Do not let them intimidate you. (Sometimes this is easier said than done.) If you arrive at the hotel and are having problems getting your discount, you can always try asking the hotel manager to contact me via fax (323) 939-7736 and request to have the written form I received from the hotel authorizing the discount. This may not always work and I may not be around but it's worth a try. Also disregard all discounts when it comes to national holidays or festival celebrations.

Eating in hotel rooms: Management frowns upon eating in the rooms. If you plan to do this type of activity (which I am guilty of), don't leave gingerbread crumbs in the room as evidence. Please be neat and use paper towels as coasters and napkins.

Elevators: I know a hotel elevator is an important feature to some people. Using the elevators in most 1, 2 and 3-stars hotels can be an experience in itself. Elevators come in different sizes in these small family-owned hotels. Most of them have elevators that are just big enough for one person. The elevators can be so small that sometimes my husband goes up with the bags and I'll either wait for the elevator to come back or take the stairs. This is another reason why I advise people to pack light because porters are nonexistent in these hotels.

E-mailing & faxing hotels: Please see Appendix III for the specifics & tips on making hotel reservations via e-mail & fax. Also, see hotel reservations in this section and Appendix III.

English: Where I indicate in the listings that limited English is spoken at a hotel, this means they speak enough English to confirm what type of room and bathroom facilities you want. Use the Italian phrases in Appendix IV to help you with hotel reservations.

TIPS ON HOTEL ACCOMMODATIONS

Exchange rate: I quoted the hotel room rates in Italian lire (L) and euro (E). I used the exchange rate of 1,500 Italian lire per US dollar ($US). To convert lire to dollars, divide the number of lire by 1,500L. Example: 100,000L divided by 1,500L = $67. For euro, I used the exchange rate of 1,950 Italian lire per each euro. From 1/01/99-12/31/01, the euro will be used only in noncash transactions, such as traveler's checks and credit card purchases. On 1/01/02, euro notes and coins will be introduced into circulation and will coexist with the currencies of the 11 EMU countries until 6/30/02. After 7/01/02, only the euro will be accepted as legal tender for the EMU countries. If you call Thomas Cook Foreign Exchange at (800) 287-7362 and ask for the exchange rate for the Italian *lire* or the euro, they usually give you lower rates than the ones you receive when you are in Italy. Thomas Cook's rate could be 1,450 lire per dollar but when you arrive in Italy you could get an exchange rate of 1,550 lire. You can order foreign currency from International Currency Exchange at **Web site:** http://www.foreignmoney.com/ or call (888) 842-0880 East Coast or (888) 278-6628 West Coast; or from Thomas Cook at **Web site:** http://www.thomascook.com/ or call (800) 287-7362. **Web sites** to determine current currency exchange rates: http://www.olsen.ch/cgi-bin/exmenu/pathfinder/ or http://www.xe.net/currency/

Floors: Usually Americans call the ground floor the first floor, but the Italians call it *piano terreno* (ground floor). In Italy the first floor (*piano primo*) is our second floor. I have followed the Italian convention in this book. In the addresses for the hotel listings where it states "2nd flr.," it means 2 floors above the ground floor. The ground floor is noted by a "T" on the elevator panel.

Handicapped access: This is a new feature I have added to my books. I have noted in the individual hotel listings which hotels have handicapped-access rooms and how many they each have. The problem with trying to identify these rooms in small family-owned hotels in Europe is that there are different interpretations of a handicapped-access room. The hotel or the hotel room may have a couple of steps in front of the door and/or the bathroom may be large enough for a wheelchair but without safety bars inside. I ate at one restaurant in Santa Marguerita that stated they had handicapped access. I watched as three of their waiters literally carried the wheelchair up the stairs. The occupant didn't seem to mind at all but others might not be so understanding. When you make your hotel reservation, please confirm with them that the handicapped-access room will accommodate your needs.

Handwashing clothes in the rooms: The washbasin sink is supposed to be for washing your hands or brushing your teeth. However, I am guilty of using it to soak my clothes. (Just pack a sink stopper with you.) But be careful. Although hotel management frowns upon washing clothes in the rooms, what they really dislike is the water dripping on the furniture or carpet. Use common sense and make sure you put the clothes away before your room gets cleaned. I always pack a portable clothesline with some clothes pegs. The hotels want and expect you to use the self-service laundries. I have tried to provide information on laundries in most of the cities.

Hotel ratings: I think the rating system is misleading. It has nothing to do with the charm or the quality of the hospitality. The hotel's star rating can be based on things like the percentage of rooms with full baths, the size of the bathrooms, reception area or breakfast room and whether the hotel has an elevator or TVs. The only difference between a 1-star hotel and a 2-star hotel could be that the 2-star has an elevator, a restaurant or a bar. The difference between a 3-star and a 4-star may be that the 3-star doesn't have separate bathrooms for men and women in their restaurant. The number of rooms that an establishment has can also determine whether it is a 2-star or 3-star hotel. The higher the star the more the hotel has to pay in taxes. The ratings are allocated once only, unless the hotel requests a reassessment. None of this information should matter to you as much as your specific room. Some hotels have no rating because the hoteliers have never asked the government to rate them. Do not place any importance on the rating system; I stayed in 2-star hotels that were nicer and better equipped than 3-star hotels.

Hotel reservations: All the travel guides advise you *never* to arrive in Italy during the summer without reservations and that your reservation should be in writing with a deposit. They are absolutely correct. However, I am a risk taker and have never had a problem getting a room with a shower and toilet at my price point. The trick is to arrive in the city early in the morning when yesterday's guest will be checking out. Pull out your phone card and start calling the hotels listed in this book. It takes a lot of courage to arrive in Italy without reservations, especially during Easter and the Christmas week, the busiest times of the year when room rates jump. So make sure you are up for it.

To make reservations ahead of time from the United States, do it during the Italian business day when the owner/manager is available to give you a discount. (For time differences between the U.S. and Italy, see Appendix III in the back of this book.) You may have to fax them three or four times before you get a confirmation or a response back from them. If you don't hear back from them it doesn't always mean they don't have a room. I can't express the level of frustration I experience when I try faxing requests for friends of mine. The hotel's reasons for not responding vary: reservation is too far in advance for them to take seriously, they are too busy to respond or they just don't feel like responding. On the other hand it could be because you didn't put your country of origin and/or the proper telephone fax number for them to respond back to. I was told by numerous hotels that Americans are the only group of people who do not do this on their request for reservations. There is no magic formula for dealing with these small family-owned hotels. You must be persistent and constantly follow up. Make it a point to confirm about three to ten days before your arrival date. Make sure you get a written confirmation of the agreed-upon arrangements. Examples: bath or shower, toilet, balcony, number of people (if children, what is the cutoff age), which floor, front or back of hotel, extra charge for air-conditioning, room number, with or without breakfast and total cost per night (including the service charge and tax). You may still have to insist upon these same arrangements when you arrive at the hotel, but it is a lot easier when you have a copy of the written confirmation with you. I cannot emphasize this enough. **If you made advance reservations, please remember to pack and bring your hotel confirmation with the person's name on it along with you. Also, always ask what is the hotel's cancellation policy. If you have to make any changes in**

your reservations be sure to fax the hotel with the changes. **Do
not rely upon a verbal confirmation of your change. Try and get
a confirmation from the hotel indicating the new changes. I cannot stress this enough.** A sample of a hotel fax form has been pro-
vided for you at the back of this book. (You can adjust the size of the
form by going to my **Web site:** http://www.HelloEurope.com/) A
useful Web site on the Internet for translating English into Italian:
http://babelfish.altavista.digital.com/cgi-bin/translate?urltext= Obvi-
ously, it is a lot easier to confirm reservations via fax and with a
credit card, but many of the smaller, inexpensive, family-run hotels
do not accept credit cards. They usually require you to mail one night's
deposit (usually a foreign-currency draft). Contact your bank or call
Thomas Cook Foreign Exchange at (800) 287-7362 or International
Currency Exchange at (888) 842-0880 East Coast or (888) 278-6628
West Coast to purchase an international draft. Mailing a deposit may
present a problem if you decide to cancel your reservation because
getting the deposit back may not always be a pleasant task. Keep in
mind, Italy has the worst reputation for delivering and receiving mail.
The U.S. Postal Service doesn't include Italy in its "Global Priority"
overseas mail program. If you choose to make reservations in writing before you leave the United States, try to include an International
Reply Coupon (found at post offices), which saves the hotel return
postage and will almost guarantee a response. Never pay for a room
in advance for more nights than you need. You may not always get
your money back. Please check the section on bathroom facilities
and the Italian phrases in Appendix IV in the back of this book for
specific types of rooms and facilities. *Tip:* If there are no English-
speaking staff members at the hotel, refer to Appendix IV or to your
Italian travel phrase book and fax or repeat the phrases regarding
accommodations. Also, familiarize yourself with military time and
calendar days. *Example:* Arrival time 4:00pm is 1600 hours and June
7-15, 2000 is 7/6/00 to 15/6/00. (To find out how to call or fax from
the United States to Italy, see Appendix III.)

Hotel room payment: There are still some hotels left in Italy that do
not accept credit cards. Payment is on a "cash only" basis. These
hotels usually offer greater value than the others. This means they
are usually booked far in advance. If you plan to stay at these hotels
without making reservations, get there early in the morning!!

TIPS ON HOTEL ACCOMMODATIONS

Hotel room rates: All rates for the rooms have to be displayed in a prominent place. Look for the rate chart either by the entrance or near the reception desk. The staff doesn't always offer their cheapest room at first. Make sure the rate quoted includes the city tax. The city tax (per room, per night) is normally included in the quoted price for the room. Always get the total price of the room including the city tax before registering. According to Italian law, the room rate chart should also be posted on the back of your hotel room door. If it is not posted, you can ask why. Regardless of the reason, the hotel cannot legally charge you more than the maximum rate shown in the display that is either on the back of your hotel door or at the front desk. If they do, you can tell them that you will send a letter of complaint about the extra charge either to the address that is stamped on the display or local municipal office. You can find out the correct address from the tourist office. The Italian government is very strict and will issue steep fines to hotels that gouge tourists.

You might notice that some of the rooms are cheaper than what I quoted. It seems the biggest complaint of travelers is that guidebooks are out of date by the time they are used, so I quoted a little higher to keep pace with increases. Also, the *minimum* rate quoted for a hotel room usually applies to one or all of the following: off-season, the smallest room, one large double bed, a room with no shower or toilet or no phone or TV. You can assume it will be missing something. Of course, the *maximum* rate means that the hotel room has everything the hotel offers or it is the room's rate for high season. In the hotel listings, rates are shown with a hyphen (-), indicating a range. *Example*: "75,000-200,000L pp" could mean the hotel has rooms for either 75,000 lire or 200,000 lire per person depending on the season, or it means the hotel has several choices that range from 75,000 to 200,000 lire per person. Single = 1 person; double = 2 people; triple = 3 people; quad = 4 people; pp = per person.

Hotel room service: I found out the hard way that the Italians do not change the towels every day. (Forget about the sheets.)

Hotel safes: I did not include whether a hotel has a room safe or not because I still don't trust them. I have heard too many stories about people having negative experiences with safes whether they stayed at a 5-star or a 3-star hotel. As a matter of fact, I think I feel more secure in a smaller 2-star hotel because the management recognizes the residents, the staff is usually smaller, visible, and has been with the hotel longer than the staff of the larger hotels.

PP: Per person

Size of hotel rooms: I would like to say up front that in some rooms, if you stretch your arms out to the sides you could almost touch most of the walls of your rooms. Even in the better hotels, rooms are usually on the small size by American standards. Many of these hotels are located in buildings that are centuries old and in many cities it is against the law to remodel these buildings. As long as the room is clean, has a comfortable bed, a private toilet and shower and is at the right price, we grab it. Many of these hotel rooms do not offer a lot of closet space, so please keep that in mind when you pack.

Streetside vs. rooms in the back: Rooms that face the street may offer you more light and interesting views but this is usually accompanied by lots of noise which may force you to keep your windows closed at night. Not a great idea if it is a hot night and the hotel doesn't have air-conditioning. Rooms that face the back are likely to be quieter but darker.

Telephone and faxing hotels: Please see Appendix III for how to call and fax hotels in Italy.

Useful Web sites & information:

Around the World Travel: (800) 590-7778 or
http://www.atwtraveler.com/
eTravel Tips: http://www.etravel.org/
Europe Travel: http://www.eurotrip.com/
Shoestring Traveler: http://www.stratpub.com/
Traveling Smart E-mail: cuber@dragonflyerpress.com
Travel Abroad: http://www.transabroad.com/
http://www.beaumonde.net/
Information on discount airfares, accommodations, hostels & rental cars, bus, train information, embassies, visas, health and road safety, backpacking, currency conversion, Internet: cybercafes, laptop hook-ups, meeting travelers, study & live abroad.

Air travel
Alitalia: (800) 223-5730 or http://www.alitalia.com/
American: (800) 433-7300 or http://www.aa.com/
Continental: (800) 525-0280, (800) 231-0856 or http://www.flycontinental.com/
Delta: (800) 241-4141 or http://www.delta-air.com/
New Frontiers: (800) 677-0720
Northwest: (800) 225-2525, 0142669000
TWA: (800) 892-4141 or http://www.twa.com/
United: (800) 538-2929 or http://www.ual.com/
USAir: (800) 428-4322 or http://www.usairways.com/
Tower Air: (800) 348-6937 or http://www.towerair.com/
Frommers: http://www.frommers.com/hottest/airfare/
Best Fares: http://www.bestfares.com/
Lowest Fares: http://www.lowestfare.com/
Cheap Tickets: http://www.cheaptickets.com/
Travelscape: http://www.travelscape.com/
Aviation Internet Resources: http://www.airlines-online.com/
Rules of the Air: http://www.1travel.com/
Aviation Internet Resources: http://www.airlines-online.com/
eTravel Tips: http://www.etravel.org/
Euro Flight Pass: (888) 387-2479 or http://www.europebyair.com/

Airports in Europe
http://www.airwise.com/airports/euroboard.html/

Cars
Auto Club of Italy: http://www.aci.it/
Auto Europe: (800) 223-5555 or http://www.autoeurope.com/
Avis Rent-a-Car: (800) 331-1084 or http://www.avis.com/
Europe by Car: (800) 223-1516 or http://www.europebycar.com/
Europcar: (800) 800-6000 or http://www.europcar.com/
Hertz: (800) 654-3001 or http://www.hertz.com/
Kemwel: (800) 678-0678 or http://www.kemwel.com/
Kilometers between places: http://www.iti.fr/

Cellular phone
Cell Hire: (888) 476-7368 or http://www.CellHire.com/

Credit cards & money
American Express: (800) 843-2273 or http://www.aexp.com/
Cirrus Network: (800) 424-7787. Call for a list of locations.
Currency Converter: http://www.oanda.com/
International Currency Exchange: (888) 842-0880 East Coast, (888) 278-6628 West Coast, or http://www.foreignmoney.com/
MasterCard: (800) 999-0454 or http://www.mastercard.com/atm/
Plus System: (800) 843-7587. Call for a list of locations.
Thomas Cook Foreign Exchange: (800) 287-7362 or http://www.thomascook.com/
Universal Currency Converter: http://www.xe.net/ucc/
Visa: (800) 336-8472 or http://www.visa.com/
World Cash: (800) 434-2800 or fax (800) 434-2822
Worldwide Currency Converter: http://www.olsen.ch/

Culture
http://www.culturekiosque.com/

Customs, embassies, tourist office & warnings
Italy Tourist Board: http://www.italiantourism.com/
Embassy of Italy: http://www.emb.org/
U.S. State Dept. warnings: http://www.travel.state.gov/travel_warnings.html/
Travel laws & protection: http://www.nolo.com/ChunkCTIM/ctim.index.html#1/

Cyber cafes
http://www.netcafeguide.com/
http://www.cybercaptive.com/

USEFUL WEB SITES

Hotels in Italy
http://www.vacanzeonline.it/
http://www.saritel.interbusiness.it/TPHOTEL/
http://www.italyhotels.it/
http://www.venere.it/home/italy.html/
http://www.hoteldirect.com/
http://www.room-service.co.uk/ITALY-BROCH/italy.html/
http://www.lodgingintuscany.com/
http://www.bookeurohotels.co.uk/

Italian sculpture
http://www.thais.it/SCULTURA/

Italy
Italy Tourist Board: http://www.italiantourism.com/
Italy Tourist Webguide: http://www.itwg.com/
Italy Tourist Web Guide: http://www.masternet.it/
Italy Travel info: http://www.travel.it/
Italy Fever: http://www.italyfever.com/
World Travel: http://www.wtgonline.com/navigate/world.asp/
Planet Italy: http://www.planetitaly.com/
Untours in Italy: http://www.untours.com/italian.htm/
Italy tour: http://www.italiatour.com/
http://www.city.net/countries/italy/
http://www.travel-italy.com/
http://www.piuitalia2000.it/
http://www.traveleurope.net/
http://www.initaly.com/
http://twenj.com/

Language
Language Translator: http://babelfish.altavista.digital.com/cgi-bin/
translate?urltext=
Travel Language Home Page: http://www.travlang.com/
Web Italian Lessons: http://www.june29.com//Italian/

Maps
MapLink: (805) 692-6777 or http://www.maplink.com/
Maps of Italy/Our Heritage: http://www.initaly.com/ads/

Newsletters & magazines
Independent Traveling: http://www.footloosetravel.com/

USEFUL WEB SITES

International Travel News: http://www.intltravelnews.com/
Italian Traveler: (800) 362-6978 or (201 535-6572
Journey Woman: http://www.journeywoman.com/
Shoestring Travel: http://stratpub.com/
Travel Abroad: http://www.transabroad.com/
Travel Books Reviews: http://members.aol.com/travbkrev/
recentreviews2.html/

Trains
Rail Europe: (888) 382-7245 or http://www.raileurope.com/
Italy Rail Information: http://www.fs-on-line.com/
Italy Rail Information: http://www.amicotreno.com/
Eurostar: http://www.eurostar.com/

Travel clothes & necessities
Magellan's Travel Supplies: (800) 962-4943 or http://
www.magellans.com/
(Don't forget to check my packing list at the back of this book.)
Packing Tips: http://www.oratory.com/travel/index.html/
TravelSmith: (800) 950-1600 or http://www.travelsmith.com/
Universal Packing List: http://www.henricson.se/mats/upl/

Travel insurers & medicine
International SOS Assistance: (800) 523-8662 or
http://www.intsos.com/
Travel Insurers: Access America (800) 284-8300
                   Carefree Travel (800) 323-3149
                   Travelex (800) 228-9792
Travel Medicine: (800) 872-8633 or http://www.travmed.com/

Weather
http://www.weather.com/
http://travel.epicurious.com/travel/
http://www.usatoday.com/weather/

Wilson Publishing (my Web site)
(888) 663-9269 or http://www.HelloEurope.com/

World Clock
http://www.timeanddate.com/worldclock/

AMALFI
Amalfi Coast, zip code 84011
Area code 39, city code 089

Orientation: Charming seaside resort town set in a wide cleft in the cliffs of the Amalfi coastline. It makes a great base for exploring the most beautiful coastline of Italy. Whether you arrive by sea or bus, you will start from **Piazza Flavio Giovia** near the water. To reach the **Piazza Duomo** (main square), from the water, pass through the arched portal and enter the village. Amalfi's one street runs north from the water and continues as **Via Lorenzo d'Amalfi** to the central Piazza Duomo (on your right), it then leads you uphill from the Duomo and becomes **Via P. Capuano**. Most of Amalfi is made up of narrow alleys and stairways. Be prepared for the hotels in Amalfi to ask you for half-board rates in the summer season. If you are unable to find affordable lodging in this area, try nearby Sorrento.

Amalfi's Tourist Information Center (AAST)
Corso Repubbliche Marinare 27. **Tel:** 089-871107. **Fax:** 089-872619. Hrs.: Mon.-Sat. 8am-2pm. With your back to the water, walk along the waterfront to your right, located next to the post office.

Low season Jan. 4-May, Oct.-Dec.; high season June-Sept.; Easter, Christmas & New Year's.

Hotels
AMALFI: Via Pastai 3. **Tel:** 089-872440 **Fax:** 089-872250. **Web site:** http://www.starnet.it/hamalfie. **E-mail:** hamalfi@starnet.it (40 rms., all w/toilet & bath or shower.) 75,000-135,000L (38-69E) single; 95,000-195,000L (50-100E) double; 120,000-280,000L (62-144E) triple; 160,000-370,000L (82-190E) quad. Breakfast (7:30-10:30am) is included in the rates & can be served in the room but can be deducted to reduce room price. Breakfast is served on the veranda in warm weather. Visa, MC, AX, DC. English spoken (Carmela), direct-dial phones, satellite TV w/English channel, charming hotel w/ nicely furnished bright airy rms., #406 w/view of Amalfi, #315 & 316 are hidden away in the garden, 10 rms. w/balconies but no views, central heating, rooftop terrace w/magnificent view overlooking the

town, quiet location, wonderful citrus garden, bar, restaurant with veranda, elevator, 7 flrs., garage parking (20,000-25,000L per day). The hotel is constantly renovating. Their new reception will face the main street in year 2000. They offer half-board rates required Aug./ Sept. *5% rm. discount when you show owner/manager Carmela Lucibello or staff this book.* Carmela is wonderful and will work with you on your budget. Call her and see if she has something to fit your budget. Walk up the main street, past the Duomo, continue uphill, turn left at the meat market (look for hotel sign) up a flight of steps to the hotel.

LIDOMARE: Largo Piazza Piccolomini 9. **Tel:** 089-871332. **Fax:** 089-871394. (15 rms., all w/toilet & bath or shower.) 65,000-85,000L (33-44E) single; 115,000-155,000L (60-79E) double; 180,000-200,000L (92-103E) triple; 220,000L (113E) quad. Breakfast (7:30-10:30am) is included in the rates & can be served in the room but can be deducted to reduce room price. Visa, MC, AX, DC. Limited English spoken (Maria), satellite TV w/English channel, 13th-century hotel w/antiquish furnished large comfortable pretty rms., nice floors, #41, 42, 43, 36, 44 & 34 have balconies w/sea views, #55 has a small balcony w/view of the square, #56 w/balcony but no view, #34 has a huge terrace, most w/view of the water, double-paned windows, minibars, central heating, air-conditioned, bar, no elevator, 2 flrs. *5% rm. discount when you show owner/manager Maria Camera or staff this book.* Located in Piazza Piccolomini through the passageway across from the Duomo. Take a left up the stairway into the Piazza.

MARINA RIVIERA: Via P. Comite 9. **Tel:** 089-871104/871024. **Fax:** 089-871351. (30 rms., all w/toilet & bath or shower.) 145,000-175,000L (74-90E) single; 195,000-215,000L (100-110E) double; 250,000L (128E) triple. Breakfast (7:30-10am) is included in the rates & can be served in the room but can be deducted to reduce room price. Visa, MC, AX, DC. Limited English spoken (Antonio), direct-dial phone, TV, wonderful beautiful hotel w/nicely furnished comfortable large airy rms., lots of character & ambiance, all the rooms have terraces, beautiful sea views & bathtubs, #56 is a corner rm., 10 rooms have a jacuzzi, 6 rms. have handicapped access, minibars, central heating, air-conditioned, spectacular panoramic view from terrace, bar, restaurant, elevator, 3 flrs., free parking. *5% rm. discount when you show owner/manager/chef Antonio Gargano or staff this book.* Hotel is cut into the side of a hill going down to the water. Located at the east edge of town. With your back to the water dock, walk (10-minute) along the waterfront to your right, past the tourist office & the post office around the cliff to the hotel. (Closed Nov.-Feb.)

The following hotels were closed when I got to Amalfi so I was unable to get updated information.

FONTANA: Piazza Duomo.**Tel:** 089-871530. (17 rms., 14 w/toilet & bath or shower.) 75,000-85,000L (38-44E) single; 100,000-125,000L (51-64E) double. Rooms overlook the marina or Piazza Duomo.

RESIDENCE: Via Repubbliche Marinare 9. **Tel:** 089-871183. **Fax:** 089-873070. (27 rms., all w/toilet & bath or shower.) 150,000-185,000L (77-95E) double. Breakfast (7:30-10:30am) is included in the rates. Visa, MC, AX, DC. Wonderful hotel w/comfortable rms., all rms. have balconies that face the sea, higher flrs. are better, dramatic staircase, elevator. (Closed Oct.-April.) Located on the waterfront in front of the dock.

RESTAURANT
Please check page 20 for my criteria for selecting restaurants.

AMALFI: Via Pastai 3. **Tel:** 089-872440. Hrs.: Dinner only 7:30-9pm. Approximately 25,000L pp for a 3-course meal including service charge. Visa, MC, AX, DC. The pasta is homemade. If you decide to eat at this hotel, please let me know if I missed a good meal. *Show owner/manager Carmela Lucibello this book and she will give you a complimentary limoncello.* I didn't have to a chance to eat here. The smell coming from the kitchen was so good with Carmela's mother in the kitchen, I thought I should mention the restaurant. Located on the 5th floor of the hotel with a wonderful view. Outside terrace is open in warm weather.

BELLAGIO
Lake Como, zip code 22021
Area code 39, city code 031

Orientation: A charming pretty village surrounded on three sides by Lake Como. Walk through the steep narrow medieval streets, beautiful gardens and up and down lots of steep, steep steps.

Bellagio's Tourist Information Center
Piazza Chiesa 14. **Tel/Fax:** 031-950204. **Web site:** http://www.fromitaly.net/bellagio/ **E-mail:** prombell@tini.it Hrs.: Mon. & Wed.-Sat. 9am-12pm; 3-6pm. Open every day April-Oct. These hours are not etched in stone. Located near the church.

Low season March 21-April, & Sept. 27-Oct. 24; mid-season May, June 21-July 18, high season July 19-Sept 19.

Hotels
All the hotels listed here are within a five-minute walk from the waterfront.

EXCELSIOR SPLENDIDE: Via Lungo Lago Manzoni 28. **Tel:** 031-950225. **Fax:** 031-951224. (47 rms., all w/toilet & bath or shower.) 120,000-185,000L (62-95E) double; 140,000-220,000L (72-113E) triple. Prices vary greatly depending on the season. Buffet breakfast (7-9:30am) at 16,500L pp is not obligatory. Visa, MC. English spoken (Lorena), direct-dial phone, some rms. have satellite TV w/English channel, charming old-style bldg. w/quaint old-fashioned furnished comfortable large rms., #36, 37 & 38 are the best rms., #33 has a magnificent view, some rms. w/views of the lake, 3 rms. w/balconies, bar, waterfront restaurant, pool, elevator, 4 flrs. They offer half- and full-board rates. The hotel is not family-owned but is managed by Claudio & Lorena Moneta. *10% rm. discount when you show manager Lorena Moneta or staff this book.* Located opposite Bellagio's charming lake in the center of town. (Closed mid-Oct.-mid-March.)

GIARDINETTO: Via Roncati 12. **Tel:** 031-950168. (13 rms., 11 w/toilet & bath or shower.) 75,000L (38E) single; 105,000-115,000L

(54-60E) double; 140,000L (72E) triple. Breakfast (8-10:30am) at 13,500L pp is not obligatory. Cash only. English spoken (Eugenio & Laura), charming unusual hotel w/simply furnished airy bright comfortable interesting rms. which vary in size, 7 rms. w/balconies, intimate lobby w/fireplace, double-paned windows, #18 (balcony), 7 (huge) & 9 are the best rms., #14 is nice w/balcony, #19 has a private bathroom in the hall, central heating, huge vine-covered garden/terrace where you can picnic, quiet location, bar, no elevator, 2 flrs. Owned/managed by Eugenio & Laura Ticozzi. Located around the corner from the tourist office. (Closed Nov.-Feb.)

ROMA: Salita Grandi 6. **Tel:** 031-950424. **Fax:** 031-951966. (27 rms., 16 w/toilet & bath or shower.) 70,000-90,000L (36-46E) single; 97,000-110,000L (50-56E) double; 120,000-160,000L (62-82E) triple; 180,000-190,000L (92-97E) quad. Breakfast (8-10am) is included in the rates & cannot be deducted but can be served in the room (2,500L extra pp). Breakfast is served on the terrace in warm weather. Visa, MC, AX, DC. English spoken (Claudio, Isabelle & Carla), simply furnished nice-size airy bright rms., 10 rms. w/balconies, #42 (balcony & view) & 44 are the best rms., the rms. on the 5th fl. are without private bathroom facilities but have great views of the lake, central heating, bar, restaurant w/terrace, elevator, 6 flrs. They offer half- and full-board rates. *5% rm. discount when you show owners/managers/brothers Claudio & Rony or staff this book.* (Closed Nov.-Easter.)

SUISSE: Piazza Mazzini 8/10. **Tel:** 031-950335. **Fax:** 031-951755. (10 rms., all w/toilet & bath or shower.) 105,000-115,000L (54-60E) single; 140,000-150,000L (72-77E) double. Buffet breakfast (7-10am) at 16,500L pp is not obligatory. Breakfast is served on the garden terrace in warm weather. Visa, MC, DC. Limited English spoken (Ms. Christina), TV, basic hotel w/simply furnished rms., 3 rms. w/balconies & 3 w/terraces, hardwood flrs., #6 (balcony w/view) & 5 are the best, #7, 16 & 18 have views of water, central heating, bar, restaurant, no elevator, 3 flrs. *10% rm. discount when you show owner/manager Guido Sancassani or staff this book.* They offer half- (85,000-95,000L pp) and full-board (115,000-125,000L pp) rates. (Closed Dec.-Feb.)

Hotel in Pescallo

Located in the tiny village on the eastern side of Bellagio. I suggest you taxi to this hotel from the main waterfront.

PERGOLA (La): Piazza Porto 4. **Tel**: 031-950263. **Fax:** 031-950253. (8 rms., 4 w/toilet & bath or shower.) 135,000-160,000L (69-82E) double. Call for family rates. Buffet breakfast is included in the rates & is served on the terrace in warm weather. Visa, MC, AX. English spoken (Marilena), waterfront charming ancient hotel w/old-fashioned elegantly furnished large to huge rms., some rms. w/views of the lake, #4 is one of the best rms. w/a huge terrace & a wonderful view of the water, #5 (view of the parking lot but shares the same terrace as #4 & has a bathroom), #7 (bathroom & view of water), 8 (bathroom & view), 12 (bathroom), central heating (all rms. by '99), tranquil location, bar, waterfront restaurant closed Tues., free parking. Marilena plans to renovate the hotel by the end of '98 to include all bathrooms. I hope she keeps the hotel's old-world charm. For the good 20-minute walk to this hotel from the main waterfront (ferry stop), look for the 1st set of steep stairs on your right on Salita Gennazzini, take the steps up to the main road, cross the main road, look for the sign "Village of Pescallo," continue to walk up the 2nd set of steep stairs and then down the steps, make a right on Salita Cappucini, follow the road around which becomes Via Sfondrati, then Via Pescallo, you'll pass the hotel on your left. (Closed Nov.-March.)

BOLOGNA
Emilia Romagna, zip code 40121
Area code 39, City Code 051

Orientation: Bologna is the capital city and the heart of the region of Emilia Romagna. It makes a great base to visit Parma, Ravenna, Rimini and Ferrara. A very expensive city that is also known as the home of the oldest university and the one of Italy's greatest food towns. Renaissance architects worked very hard to distinguish this city from other cities in Italy. It is not a city filled with tourists only Italians. Bologna's high season is opposite of the more popular Italian destinations like Rome, Florence and Venice. The historic center of Bologna is quite small and is perfect for walking around. The **Bologna Centrale train station** is located in **Piazza Medaglie d'Oro** on the edge of the city center. To walk (20 minutes) to the historic center of Bologna, turn left from the train station, cross the street, walk down **Viale Pietramellara** toward **Piazza XX Settembre**, turn right onto **Via Indipendenza** (wide busy shopping street) which runs off Piazza XX Settembre (bus station) with the **Parc Montagnola** on your left, walk straight down Via Indipendenza toward the center of town to the intersection of **Via Ugo Bassi** on the right and **Via Rizzoli** to the left and the 13th-century **Piazza Maggiore** (the hub of the city) right in the middle with **Piazza Nettuno** at its edge. Piazza Maggiore is the cultural and social center of downtown Bologna. Or you can catch bus #25 to Piazza Maggiore. It might be better to taxi to the hotel if you have a lot of luggage.

Bologna Tourist Information Centers
Web sites: http://www.provincia.bologna.it/ or http://www.comune.bologna.it/ **1.)** Piazza Medaglie d'Oro, Stazione Ferroviaria. 40121. **Tel:** 051-246541. **Fax:** 051-251947. Hrs.: Mon.-Sat. 9am-7pm, closed Sun. & holidays except trade fair days. Located near the main exit to the street. **2.)** Piazza Maggiore 6. (Palazzo Comunale) **Tel:** 051-239660. **Fax:** 051-231454. Hrs.: Mon.-Sat. 9am-7pm and Sun. & holidays 9am-1pm. Next to the pharmacy in the square. **3.)** Guglielmo Marconi Airport, Borgo Panigale. **Tel/Fax:** 051-6472036. Hrs.: Mon.-Sat. 9am-1pm & 2-4pm. Closed Sun. & holidays. Make sure you fax the tourist office and request a current schedule of the fairs and congress meetings.

BOLOGNA

Low season June-Aug. & Dec. 15-Feb. 28; high season March-May, Sept.-Dec. 14 & all fairs & congress meetings.

Hotels near the train station
This area is only a 20-minute walk from the center of Bologna.

ATLANTIC: Via Galliera 46. **Tel/Fax:** 051-248488. **Fax:** 051-251538. (22 rms., 10 w/toilet & bath or shower.) 90,000-125,000L (46-64E) single; 120,000-195,000L (62-100E) double. Call for triple rates. Buffet breakfast (7:30-10am) is included in the rates & cannot be deducted. Visa, MC, AX, DC. Limited English spoken, direct-dial phone, TV, basic modern hotel w/simply furnished comfortable small bright rms., no atmosphere, bar, no elevator, 4 flrs., parking (13,000L per day). Owned/managed by Ognibene & Capatti. From the train station, turn left and walk down Viale Pietramellara toward Piazza XX Settembre. Turn right on Via Galliera which runs off Piazza Settembre. Hotel is about 2 1/2 blocks down on Via Galliera.

DONATELLO: Via Indipendenza 65. **Tel/Fax:** 051-248174.
Web site: http://www.hoteldonatello.it/ (38 rms., all w/toilet & bath or shower.) 155,000L (79E) single; 205,000L (105E) double; 250,000L (128E) triple. Check for low season prices. Buffet breakfast (7-10am) is included in the rates & cannot be deducted but can be served in the room. Visa, MC, AX, DC. English spoken, direct-dial phone, TV w/English channel, modern hotel w/nicely furnished comfortable rms., #409 has 2 bathrooms (1 w/a bathtub), hair driers, double-paned windows, central heating, air-conditioned, elevator, 5 flrs. Look under orientation for walking directions. The same family manages Hotel Accademia, a centrally located lower-price hotel not reviewed in this book. **Tel:** 051-232318. **Fax** 051-263590.

MARCONI: Via Marconi 22. **Tel:** 051-262832/235041. (46 rms., 26 w/toilet & bath or shower.) 85,000L (44E) single; 95,000-115,000L (50-60E) double; 150,000L (77E) triple; 170,000L (87E) quad. No breakfast is served. Cash only. English spoken (Louisa), basic hotel w/simply furnished rms., no atmosphere, noisy location, no elevator, 3 flrs. Turn right from the train station, cross the street, walk down Viale Pietramellar, turn left onto Via Giovanni Amendola which becomes Via Marconi after you pass through Piazza Martiri.

Hotels in the Historic Center

These hotels are in the historic center of Bologna's old city. Many are near Piazza Maggiore, the social square of the old city. Lots of shops, restaurants, tourists and medieval monuments.

APOLLO: Via Drapperie 5. **Tel/Fax:** 051-223955. (14 rms., 4 w/ toilet & bath or shower.) 75,000L (38E) single (no toilets); 112,000-140,000L (57-72E) double; 165,000-185,000L (85-95E) triple; 210,000-220,000L (108-113E) quad. No breakfast is served. Visa, MC, AX. Limited English spoken (Nadia), direct-dial phone, nice hotel w/simply furnished large rms., nice atmosphere, #12, 9, 3 & 7 have bathrooms, no elevator, 3 flrs. Located on a tiny street off Piazza Maggiore in a energetic, colorful neighborhood. Lots of local shops and markets. Catch bus from train station to Piazza Maggiore. With your back to the tourist office in Piazza Maggiore, walk straight ahead about 2 blocks toward Via Drapperie. (Closed 20 days in Aug.)

CENTRALE: Via Zecca 2, 3rd fl. **Tel:** 051-225114. **Fax:** 051-235162. (25 rms., 20 w/toilet & bath or shower.) 90,000L (46E) single; 155,000L (79E) double; 200,000L (103E) triple. Breakfast (8-10am) at 11,500L pp is not obligatory & can be served in the room. Visa, MC, AX. English spoken (Gionair), direct-dial phone, satellite TV w/English channel, old palace turned into a business bldg. w/nicely furnished modern comfortable large rms. & modern bathrooms, top-floor rms. have views of the historic center, #26 & 27 are the best rms., central heating, air-conditioned, double-paned windows in front, noisy location, bar, elevator, 2 flrs. Owned/managed by Werther Guizzardi. Right in the middle of all the shopping and sightseeing. (My husband and I stayed in rm. #14 which overlooks the main street and there happened to be an incredible basketball celebration taking place on it one night.) Located close to Piazza Maggiore and the two towers. Turn left from the train station, walk down Viale Pietramellara toward Piazza XX Settembre, turn onto Via Indipendenza which runs off Piazza Settembre with the Parc Montagnola on your left, walk straight down Via Indipendenza toward the center of town, at Piazza Maggiore turn right onto Via Ugo Bassi, turn left onto Via Zecca. You can also catch bus #25 to Via Ugo Bassi.

DUE TORRE: Via Usberti 4. **Tel:** 051-269826. **Tel/Fax:** 051-239944. **E-mail:** h2torri@iperbole.bologna (14 rms., all w/toilet & bath or shower.) 85,000-215,000L (44-110E) single; 145,000-315,000L (74-162E) double; 170,000-400,000L (87-205E) triple; 220,000-420,000L (113-215E) quad. Children under 5 free. Buffet breakfast (7-11am) is included in the rates & can be served in the room but can be deducted to reduce room price. Visa, MC, AX, DC. English spoken (Michele), direct-dial phone, TV, wonderful charming hotel w/nicely furnished comfortable large rms., small new bathrooms, rooms vary in size & decor, #104, 106 (terrace) & 105 are the best rms., lots of character & ambiance, mini-bars, double-paned windows, ceiling fans, air-conditioned, management pays a lot of attention to detail making you feel like you are at home, quiet location, bar, no elevator, 4 flrs., parking (35,000L per day). They offer half-board (40,000L pp.) and full-board (60,000L pp) rates. *10% rm. discount or free breakfast when you show owner/manager Cristina Malaguti or staff this book.* For directions, see Hotel Palace. From Via Montegrappa, turn right onto Via Usberti. You can also catch buses #25, 21 or 20 to the hotel.

PALACE: Via Montegrappa 9/2. **Tel:** 051-237442. **Fax:** 051-220689. (113 rms., 108 w/toilet & bath or shower.) 153,000-171,000L (78-88E) single; 203,000-239,000L (104-123E) double; 248,000L (127E) triple; 302,000L (155E) quad. Breakfast (7-11am) is included in the rates & can be served in the room (6,500 extra pp) but can be deducted to reduce room price. Visa, MC, AX. English spoken, direct-dial phone, satellite TV w/English channel, 16th-century renovated modern palazzo w/nicely furnished comfortable rms., most rms. w/ minibars, 4 rms. w/terraces, hair driers, elevator, 5 flrs.,parking (28,000L per day). The hotel has 5 rms. w/o bathrooms, TVs & phones for 135,000L. You have to ask about these rooms. They don't promote them. This hotel is not family owned. Turn left from the train station, cross the street, walk down Viale Pietramellara toward Piazza XX Settembre, turn right onto Via Indipendenza which runs off Piazza Settembre with the Parc Montagnola on your left, walk straight down Via Indipendenza toward the center of town, turn right onto Via Montegrappa which is one block before you get to Via Ugo Bassi at Piazza Maggiore. (Closed Aug.)

TOURING: Via Mattuiani 1/2. **Tel:** 051-584305. **Fax:** 051-334763. **Web site:** http://www.hoteltouring.it/ **E-mail:** hoteltouring@hoteltouring.it (40 rms., 38 w/toilet & bath or shower.) 125,000-205,000L (64-105E) single; 220,000-325,000L (113-167E) double; 260,000-400,000L (133-205E) triple; 300,000-460,000L (154-236E) quad. Children under 10 free. Buffet breakfast (7-9:30am) is included in the rates & cannot be deducted but can be served in the room (6,500L extra pp). Breakfast is served in the garden in warm weather. Visa, MC, AX, DC. This hotel is a combination of two (renovated & old) hotels into one basic plain hotel. The lower rates are for the 8 nicely furnished comfortable rooms on the 1st floor that have not been renovated. Rooms #101-108. The rest of hotel's description applies to the higher price rms. English spoken (Rita), direct-dial phone, satellite TV w/English channel, nicely furnished, #438 (family rm. w/view) & 224 are the best rms., all the rooms on the 4th fl. have terraces, rooftop garden terrace w/wonderful view of rooftops, double-paned windows, central heating, air-conditioned, bar, elevator, 5 flrs., parking (30,000-35,000L per day). *10% rm. discount when you show owner/manager Stegani Stagni or staff this book.* They offer half- and full-board rates with a nearby restaurant. Look under orientation for walking directions to Piazza Maggiore. From Piazza Maggiore, walk down Via Archiginnasio through Piazza Galvani to Via Mattuiani. (35-minute walk.)

Hotels near the university area
A very pleasant part of the city away from the hustle and bustle of the historic center. Lots of students, affordable restaurants and bars.

ROSSINI: Via Bibiena 11. **Tel:** 051-237716. **Fax:** 051-268035. (19 rms., 12 w/toilet & bath or shower.) 80,000-110,000L (41-56E) single; 115,000-165,000L (60-85E) double; 150,000-210,000L (77-108E) triple. Breakfast (8am) at 8,500L pp is not obligatory. Visa, MC, AX. English spoken, direct-dial phone, 12 rms. w/TVs, charming renovated monastery hotel w/simply furnished nice-size rms. w/big desks & lights, hotel attracts a lot of academics, 2 rms. have handicapped access but there are 3 steps, central heating, courtyard, bar, no elevator, 3 flrs. Located near Piazza Verdi, the university's main Piazza. From the train station, take bus #50 to Piazza Verdi, turn right down Via Bibiena. (Closed 10 days in July or Aug.)

SAN VITALE: Via San Vitale 94. **Tel:** 051-225966. **Fax:** 051-239396 (17 rms., all w/toilet & bath or shower.) 110,000-150,000L (56-77E) double; 155,000-195,000L (79-100E) triple; 195,000-235,000L (100-121E) quad. No breakfast is served. Cash only. English spoken (Daniela Po' & Valerio), direct-dial phone, wonderful charming hotel w/nicely furnished comfortable bright rms., 3 rms. w/double-paned windows, central heating, quiet location, nice street garden/terrace, no elevator, 3 flrs. Owned/managed by Daniela Po' & Valerio. Located at the eastern edge of the city, about a 10-minute walk to the center of town. Catch bus #32 to San Vitale.

MONEY
Banca Napoli: Via Farini 12. **Tel:** 051-239971. Hrs.: Mon.-Sat. 8:30am-1:15pm. 2:45-3:45pm. The rates are pretty good.

LAUNDROMATS (Lavanderia)
Daily: 9am-10pm. 13,000L for 14 lbs. of wash, dry and soap. Self-service.

Wash & Dry: Via Petroni 38B.
Lava & Lava: Via Irnerio 35B.
Onda Blu: Via San Donato 4.
Onda Blu: Via Saragozaa 34A/B.
Lavanderia: Via Sauro 16. Bring clothes early in the morning and pick up in the late afternoon.
Acqua Lavasecco: Via Todaro 4. Mon.-Fri. 8am-1pm. 3-7pm. Sat. 8am-12:30pm. Dry cleaning services.

RESTAURANT
Please check page 20 for my criteria for selecting restaurants.

DANIO: Via San Felice 50/A. **Tel:** 051-555202. Hrs.: Tues.-Sun. Lunch 12-3pm; dinner 7-11pm. Visa, MC, AX. Cover charge 3,500L pp. A full dinner complete with a liter of house wine and dessert will cost about 50,000L for two people. Wonderful little local restaurant that serves great food & homemade desserts. Menu changes every day. The *pollo arrosto* which is only served once a week is succulent. Most of the clientele consists of single working men. They have a no-smoking room which is rare in Italy. Owned/managed by Franco

& Pina (husband & wife team). Franco moved from Italy to Boston and back to Italy again. Franco works the room while Pina makes her fresh pasta in the kitchen. Ask which pasta is homemade. Franco also raises ostriches on his land close to Naples on his time off. *Show owner/waiter Franco or son/waiter Fabian this book and they will give you a complimentary limoncello.* Franco & Fabian speak English. From Piazza Maggiore, take Via Ugo Bassi, which becomes Via San Felice once you pass Via Guglielmo. Restaurant is on left side of the street.

CAMOGLI (House of Wives)
Italian Riviera, zip code 16032
Area code 39, city code 0185

Orientation: A small classic Mediterranean-looking fishing village that climbs uphill from the water. From the train (bus stop) station, turn right and then walk down the very steep stairs that take you to the main avenue Via Garibaldi, which is a colorful charming street for a stroll. It is hard to get lost in this very small village. Catch either a 5-minute train ride or 30-minute bus ride from Santa Marguerita.

Camogli's Tourist Information Center
Via XX Settembre 33r. **Tel/Fax:** 0185-771066. Hrs.: Mon-Sat. 9am-12pm and 4-6pm; Sun. 9am-1pm. Later hrs. in summer. (Not etched in stone.) Located across the street to the right of the train station about 2 blocks up on the left side of the street.

Hotels
AUGUSTA: Via P. Schiaffino 100. **Tel/Fax:** 0185-770592. (12 rms., all w/toilet & bath or shower.) 70,000-90,000L (36-46E) single; 90,000-130,000L (46-67E) double; 110,000-170,000L (56-87E) triple; 130,000-190,000L (67-97E) quad. Children under 8 free. Breakfast (7:30-10:30am) at 11,500L pp is not obligatory. Visa, MC, AX, DC. English spoken (Giacomo), direct-dial phone, satellite TV w/English channel, wonderful charming hotel w/simply furnished comfortable large rms., #10 has a balcony, central heating, bar, restaurant, no elevator, 1 flr. *10-15% rm. discount (except in Aug.) when you show owners/managers Giacomo & Lara Polverino or staff this book.* They offer half-board rates. They will give you information on the hiking trails, boats and buses to explore the area. Located at the opposite end of the town from the train station. With your back to the train station, turn right on Via XX Settembre which becomes Via Schiaffino. Hotel is on the right-hand side. 15-minute walk. Taxi 13,000L.

CAMOGLIESE (La): Via Garibaldi 55. **Tel**: 0185-771402. **Fax:** 0185-774024. (16 rms., all w/toilet & bath or shower.) 105,000L (54E) single; 125,000L (64E) double; 150,000L (77E) triple; 160,000L (82E) quad. Visa, MC, AX, DC. No breakfast is served. English spoken

CAMOGLI

(Mario), direct-dial phone, satellite TV w/English channel, wonderful charming hotel w/nicely furnished comfortable nice-size rms. & nice bathrooms, tiled flrs., #16b & 14 (balcony) are the best rms. & have views of the water, #4, 5 & 18 have balconies & views of the water, also #3 has view of the water, great quiet location, central heating, double-paned windows, no elevator, 2 flrs. *10% rm. discount when you show owners/managers Mario & Stefania or staff this book and pay in cash.* Perfect spot to relax and appreciate the natural beauty of this fishing village. With your back to the train station, look across the street for the hotel's blue sign at the top of the stairs. Take the steep stairs down to the hotel, 5 minutes. (Closed Nov.)

CAPRI
Area code 39, city code 081, zip code 80073

Orientation: Located three miles off Sorrento's peninsula is the beautiful island of Capri. All ferries and hydrofoils dock at the **Marina Grande** which is located at the base of Capri. You can reach Capri town several ways. Walk the very, very steep **Via Marina Grande** (30 min.) uphill and follow the signs to **Piazza Umberto I** (the heart of Capri town); or catch the funicular (1,800L pp + luggage charge) which connects Marina Grande port with Piazza Umberto (every 15 min.); or catch a taxi. There are buses (1,800L pp) just to the right of the tourist office at Marina Grande that will also take you to Piazza Umberto or directly to **Piazza Vittori**, the center of Anacapri. From Capri town, an Anacapri bus will also take you to Piazza Vittori. Many of these hotels listed in this chapter can be found on **Web site:** http://www.capriweb.com/Capri/hotels/zona5.html/

Capri's Tourist Information Centers (AACST)
Capri Web site Online: http://www.capri-island.com/index.html/
1.) Marina Grande. **Tel:** 081-8370634. Hrs.: Mon.-Sat. 9am-8pm. Longer hrs. in high season. As you exit the ferry, it is on the walkway before you hit the main dock. **2.)** Piazza Umberto I, 80073. **Tel:** 081-8370686. Hrs.: Mon.-Sat. 9am-1pm. 3:30-6:45pm. Located in center of Capri under the big clock. The tourist offices have 2 kinds of maps for Capri, a free one and one that costs 1,600L. Ask for the free map unless you need the better map to find your hotel.

Low season Jan. 4-Jan. 14, March 15-March 31-April 20, 1st week of May & Nov. 1-Dec. 22.

Hotels in Capri Town
I suggest you taxi to the hotels unless you don't have a lot of luggage. If you decide to walk or catch a bus to your hotel, there are uniformed men at the shuttle service next to the taxi stand at Marina Grande (13,500L per bag) or Piazza Umberto (7,000L per bag) to handle your luggage.

CAPRI

Hotel near the Marina Grande
BELVEDERE: Via Marina Grande 238, 80070.
Tel/Fax: 081-8370345. **Fax:** 081-8378822.
Web site: http://www.caprionline.it/hotels/h.belvedere/
E-mail: h.belvedere@capri.it (13 rms., all w/toilet & bath or shower.)
70,000-100,000L (36-51E) single; 125,000-185,000L (64-95E)
double; 170,000-240,000L (87-123E) triple; 220,000-260,000L (113-
133E) quad. Breakfast (8-10am) at 11,500L pp is not obligatory &
can be served in the room. Breakfast is served on the terrace in warm
weather. Visa. English spoken (Francesco), direct-dial phone, charming hotel w/simply furnished nice-size comfortable rms., nice flrs.,
the higher the fl. the better the view, #3 a large rm. w/huge terrace is
perfect for a family, #9 (wonderful), 10, 11 & 14 (private) have terraces, #8 & 12 have balconies, all rms. have views of the sea, small
terrace to relax, bar, no elevator, 3 flrs., free parking. *10% rm. discount or free breakfast when you show owner/manager Francesco
Ruocco or staff this book.* As you exit the ferry, turn right past the
taxi stand & bus stop, walk up the curved road, turn right onto Via
Marina Grande. (Closed Jan. 6-March 31 year 2000 only.)

Hotels near the Piazza Umberto
BELSITO: Via Matermania 9/11, 80073.
Tel: 081-8370969/8378750. **Fax:** 081-8376622.
E-mail: hbelsito@mbox.caprinet.it. (13 rms., all w/toilet & bath or
shower.) 80,000-135,000L (41-69E) single; 135,000-235,000L (69-
121E) double. Call for triple & quad rates. Breakfast (8-10am) is
included in the rates & cannot be deducted but can be served in the
room (6,500L extra pp). Visa, MC, AX, DC. English spoken (Lilliana),
18th-century renovated villa w/simply furnished nice-size bright airy
rms., the lower rates are for rooms w/o views, rooms #22-27 all have
balconies & magnificent views, #27 is a corner rm., #28 & 29 w/
balconies but no views, 6 rms. w/minibars, bar, spectacular panoramic
view from restaurant & rooftop terrace, lots of greenery, no elevator,
1 fl. They offer half-board rates which are required in July & Aug.
From Piazza Umberto, take Via Botteghe Fuortovado which becomes
Via Croce to Via Matermania.

CANASTA: Via Campo Teste 6, 80073.
Tel: 081-8370561/8378298. **Fax:** 081-8376675.

Web site: http://www.caprionline.com/canasta/
E-mail: canasta@capri.it (17 rms., all w/toilet & bath or shower.) 180,000-235,000-295,000-335,000L (92-172E) double. Call for triple rates. Rooms range in price from standard to superior. You have to ask for the lower-priced rooms. Breakfast (6am-12:30pm) is included in the rates. Visa, MC, AX. English spoken (Eleanor), direct-dial phone, satellite TV w/English channel, wonderful beautiful romantic hotel w/elegantly furnished comfortable rms., all rms. have balconies, hair driers, minibars, #23 standard room w/bathtub, balcony & wonderful sea view, #14 & 15 are standard rooms, #25 & 24 are superior large rooms which have automatic balcony shutters that open from the bed to a magnificent view, patio garden, no elevator, 2 flrs. Owned/managed by Eleanor. From Piazza Umberto, take Via Botteghe Fuortovado, turn right when you see the yellow canopy hotel sign for Hotel Floridiana which becomes Via Cerio, turn left onto Via Campo Teste. 20-minute walk w/luggage. (Closed Jan. 15-Easter.)

FLORIDIANA: Via Campo Teste 16, 80073. **Tel:** 081-8370166. **Fax:** 081-8370434. (36 rms., all w/toilet & bath or shower.) 165,000-320,000L (85-164E) double. Call for triple, quad & suite rates. Buffet breakfast (7-10:30am) is included in the rates but can be deducted to reduce room price. Visa, MC, AX. If you are lucky enough to arrive in Capri in low season this hotel is affordable because the lower rates are for low season. English spoken, direct-dial phone, satellite TV w/English channel, magnificent charming romantic hotel w/nicely furnished comfortable pretty nice-size rms., rooms vary in size & decor, minibars, pool, all the amenities of a 4-star hotel at 3-star prices, many w/views, central heating, bar, spectacular panoramic view from restaurant w/terrace, elevator. *Room discount when you show owner/manager Lucia Esposito or staff this book.* For directions, see Hotel Canasta. (Closed Nov. 15-March 15.)

PRORA: Via Castello 6, 80073. **Tel/Fax:** 081-8370281. (8 rms., all w/toilet & bath or shower.) 115,000-135,000L (60-69E) single; 215,000L (110E) double; 280,000-320,000L (144-164E) triple; 420,000L (215E) suite. Breakfast (8-10am) is included in the rates & cannot be deducted. Cash only. English spoken (Giovanna), wonderful charming hotel w/pretty rms., direct-dial phone ('99), nice flrs., all the rms. have magnificent views, #20 (terrace w/view) & 11 (2 windows, terrace w/view & private bathroom in the hall) are the best rms., #14 has terrace w/view, bathtub & minibar, #16 has minibar, family room suite includes a petite kitchenette, #19 & 18 w/o terraces, central heating, no elevator, 2 flrs. Walk up the stairs from the main bus stop in Capri, turn immediate right, continue straight to hotel.

STELLA MARIS: Via Roma 27, 80073. **Tel:** 081-8370452. **Fax:** 081-8378662. **Web site:** http://www.emmeti.it/welcome/ campania/capri/alberghi/maris/index.de.html/ (10 rms., all w/toilet & bath or shower.) 70,000-85,000L (36-44E) single; 95,000-135,000L (50-69E) double. Call for triple & quad rates. Breakfast (8-10am) at 22,500L pp is obligatory in July & Aug. & is served in the room. Visa, MC, DC. English spoken (Rosaria), direct-dial phone, basic hotel w/simply furnished nice-size rms., 3 rms. w/balconies, #12 great view, some top-floor rms. have views of the sea, small rooftop terrace w/view that you share w/the hotel's laundry, noisy location, central heating, no elevator, 2 flrs. *Room discount when you show owner/manager Rosaria or staff this book and pay in cash.*

Hotels near the Marina Piccola
From Piazza Umberto, take Via Roma which takes you into Via Marina Piccolo. I suggest you taxi to these hotels.

QUATTRO STAGIONI: Via Marina Piccola 1a, 80073. **Tel:** 081-8370041. (12 rms., all w/toilet & bath or shower.) 95,000-115,000L (50-60E) single; 165,000-205,000L (85-105E) double. Call for triple rates. Breakfast (8-10:30am) at 11,500-21,5000L pp is not obligatory in April, May & Oct. Breakfast is served on the terrace in warm weather. Visa, MC. English spoken, direct-dial phone, wonderful charming hotel w/nice-size pretty rms., #9, 10, 11 & 12 have garden/ terraces, #1, 2 & 3 have sea views, #13-16 are perfect for college students, mosquito screens on the windows, restaurant (summer), garden, terrace w/wonderful view, central heating, no elevator, 2 flrs. They offer half- and full-board rates. *10% rm. discount when you show owners/managers Anna Salvia & family this book in April, May or Oct.* Hotel is located outside Capri. Catch bus from Marina Grande port to Anacapri. Ask bus driver for stop: Due Golfi. Walk to your left down Via Marina Piccola to hotel. (Closed Nov.-March 20.)

The following hotels were closed when I got to Amalfi so I was unable to get updated information.

TOSCA: Via Dalmazio Birago 5, 80073. **Tel/Fax:** 081-8370989. **Web site:** http://www.caprionline.com/latosca/ **E-mail:** h.tosca@capri.it (11 rms., 7 w/toilet & bath or shower.) 70,000-90,000L (36-46E) single; 95,000-140,000L (50-72E) double; 140,000-188,000L (72-96E) triple; 165,000-215,000L (85-110E) quad. Breakfast (8-10:30am) at 13,500L pp is not obligatory & can be served in the room. Visa, MC. English spoken (Etore & Michele), direct-dial phone, wonderful charming renovated villa w/simply furnished large airy bright rms., #47 & 50 are the best rms., many of the rms. have small terraces that face the sea, 5 rms. w/terraces, rose & jasmine garden/courtyard, double-paned windows, central heating, bar, no elevator, 1 fl. *5% rm. discount when you show owner/manager Ettore Castelli, Michele Tine (American wife) or staff this book.* Walk up the stairs from the main bus stop in Capri, turn immediate right, walk past Hotel Prora, when you get to the fork, bear left down the road onto Via Birago, stay straight on the road to hotel. 15-min. walk. (Closed Nov.-Feb.)

AIDA: Via Birago 18, 80073. **Tel:** 081-8370366. (9 rms., 8 w/toilet & bath or shower.) 150,000-180,000L (77-92E) double. Cash only. Wonderful charming renovated villa w/simply furnished large airy comfortable rms., garden. For directions, see Hotel Tosca. (Closed Oct.-March.)

Hotels in Anacapri (above Capri)

Anacapri's Tourist Information Center
1.) Via Giuseppe Orlandi/Piazza Vittoria, 80071. **Tel:** 081-8371524. Hrs.: Mon.-Sat. 9am-3pm. Longer hrs. in season. Located off Piazza Vittoria as you get off the bus. There are buses just to the right of the tourist office at Marina Grande port that will take you to Piazza Vittoria, the center of Anacapri.

BIANCAMARIA: Via Giuseppe Orlandi 54, 80071. **Tel:** 081-8371000. **Fax:** 081-8372060. (25 rms., all w/toilet & bath or shower.) 165,000-195,000L (85-100E) single; 195,000-215,000L (100-110E) double. Call for triple rates. Breakfast (8-10am) is included in the rates & cannot be deducted but can be served in the room (11,500L extra pp). Visa, MC, AX, DC. English spoken (Biancamaria), direct-dial phone, TV, wonderful charming hotel w/simply furnished airy bright comfortable pretty rms., all 10 rms. w/balconies are w/o sea views, #41 & 40 have balconies, garden, some rms. face the sea, elevator, 3 flrs. Catch bus from Marina Grande port to Anacapri, located close to Piazza Vittori. (Closed Nov.-March.)

CAESAR AUGUSTUS: Via Giuseppe Orlandi 4, 80071. **Tel:** 081-8373395. **Fax:** 081-8371444. (56 rms., all w/toilet & bath or shower.) 150,000-200,000-220,000-450,000L (77-103-113-231E) double. Call for triple, quad & suite rates. Rooms range in price from standard, medium to superior. You have to ask for the lowest-priced rooms available. Breakfast (8-10:30am) is included in the rates but can be deducted to reduce room price. Buffet breakfast can be served in the room at extra cost of 6,500L pp. Breakfast is served on the terrace in warm weather. Visa, MC, AX, DC. English spoken (Franco & Savastano), direct-dial phone, wonderful charming hotel w/beauti-fully furnished comfortable rms., rooms vary in size & decor de-pending on the rate, #304 lower-priced room w/fabulous view, #318 has huge terrace, 52 rms. w/balconies, 30 rms. have handicapped access, central heating, 6 rms. w/air-conditioning, garden, pool, so-larium terrace w/wonderful panoramic view, bar, elevator, 3 flrs., free parking. I didn't even want to look at the deluxe suites because I thought the standard rooms were wonderful. The hotel has about 20 rooms that you can get at the lower rates. Located on the edge of a cliff. Catch bus from Marina Grande port to Anacapri. Ask bus driver for hotel stop: Via Giuseppe Orlandi off Piazza Vittori. (Closed Nov.-March.)

IL GIRASOLE: Via Linciano 47, 80071. **Tel:** 081-8372351. **Fax:** 081-8373880. **Web site:** http://www.ilgirasole.com/ **E-mail:** ilgirasole@capri.it. (24 rms., all w/toilet & bath or shower.) 55,000-105,000L (28-54E) single; 95,000-185,000L (50-95E) double; 140,000-260,000L (72-133E) triple; 160,000-260,000L (82-133E) quad. The lower rates are for cash only. Children under 12 free. Buf-fet breakfast (8-10am) at 11,500-21,500L pp is not obligatory & can be served in the room (6,500L extra pp). Breakfast is served in the garden in warm weather. Visa, MC, AX. English spoken (Angela), direct-dial phone, satellite TV w/CNN, wonderful charming hotel w/ nicely furnished pretty rms., #1, 12 & 13 have sea views, #8 & 9 share a terrace, #1 & 2 share a terrace. They are renovating the hotel so the room numbers might change, minibars, hair driers, nice flrs., central heating, air-conditioning (summer '99 & cost extra), garden, laundry services, pool w/solarium, fabulous peaceful location, no elevator, 1fl. Owned/managed by Arnaldo, Silvana & Angela Orlando. Arnaldo also manages a restaurant where you can get American breakfasts and good home-cooked Italian food for dinner. If you call ahead from the Marina Grande port, they'll pick you up (20,000L for 2) and take you to the hotel door. The taxi will only take you as far as the footpath & you'll have to walk the rest of the way w/your luggage. Or you can catch a bus from the Marina Grande to Anacapri, get off at Piazza Capril, the last bus stop. Walk down the path, you'll see the hotel sign with a red arrow on your left, cross the road & up the 3 steps, walk down the pathway, you'll come to a fork, walk straight down Via Linciano to #47. (Closed Feb.)

LORELEY: Via Giuseppe Orlandi 12, 80071. **Tel:** 081-8371440. **Fax:** 081-8371399. (16 rms., all w/toilet & bath or shower.) 90,000-95,000L (46-50E) single; 120,000-165,000L (62-85E) double; 155,000-180,000L (79-92E) triple. Call for quad rates. Breakfast (8-10:30am) is included in the rates & can be served in the room but can be deducted to reduce the room price. Breakfast is served on the terrace in warm weather. Visa, MC, AX. English spoken (Luigi), direct-dial phone, wonderful charming hotel w/comfortable large bright airy pretty rms., nice flrs., #12 w/balcony & sea view, #18 & 16 have balconies but no sea views, terrace w/wonderful panoramic view, #11 w/balcony is perfect for family, central heating, no elevator, 2 flrs., free parking. Catch bus from Marina Grande port to Anacapri, located close to Piazza Vittori. (Closed Nov.-March.)

SAN MICHELE DI ANACAPRI: Via Giuseppe Orlandi 1/3, 80071. **Tel:** 081-8371427/8371442. **Fax:** 081-8371420. (59 rms., all w/toilet & bath or shower.) 175,000-255,000L (90-131E) double. Children under 7 free. Buffet breakfast (7:30-10am) at 16,500L pp is obligatory & can be served in the room (4,500L extra pp). Breakfast is served on the terrace in warm weather. Visa, MC, AX, DC. English spoken (Norma), direct-dial phone, satellite TV w/English channel, wonderful charming hotel w/nicely furnished comfortable large bright airy rms., #112, 114-116, 118, 119, 219 & 221 have terraces w/sea views, #211, 212 & 214 have balconies w/sea views, all the 2nd fl. rooms have balconies & all the 1st fl. rooms have terraces, some rms. have handicapped access, hair driers, garden, solarium terrace w/wonderful panoramic view, central heating, bar, restaurant, Olympic pool, elevator, 3 flrs., free parking. *5% rm. discount when you show owner/manager Franco Coppola or staff this book.* They offer half- and full-board rates. For directions, see Hotel Caesar Augustus which is across the street from Hotel San Michele. (Closed Nov.-March.)

RESTAURANTS
Please check page 20 for my criteria for selecting restaurants.

FLORIDIANA: Via Campo Teste 16, 80073. **Tel:** 081-8370166. **Fax:** 081-8370434. Hrs.: Lunch 12-2:30pm & dinner 7-9:30pm. Visa, MC, AX. Delicious homemade food including pastas & desserts. Ask for Pepe, the waiter who speaks English and is wonderful. He came up with the recipe for Pepe's cake (lemon, white chocolate & almonds). Restaurant w/spectacular panoramic view from terrace.

BELSITO: Via Matermania 9/11, 80073.
Tel: 081-8370969/8378750. **Fax:** 081-8376622.
E-mail: hbelsito@mbox.caprinet.it Lunch 12-3pm & dinner 7-9:30pm. Visa, MC, AX. Restaurant (wood burning oven) w/spectacular panoramic view from terrace. *Show Lilliana this book and she will give you a complimentary after-dinner drink.* I did not get a chance to eat here but the food smelled so good, I think I missed a good meal. Friends of mine ate here and said it was delicious. If you eat here, please let me know what you think of the food.

CINQUE TERRE (5 Lands)
Area code 39, city code 0187, zip code 19016

Orientation: Cinque Terre are the five individual neighboring old-fishing villages perched in the coastal cliffs above the sea. Because of their remoteness, these villages have managed to retain their old-world charm without the trappings of tourism. Cinque Terre has one of the most beautiful coastlines in Italy. As you depart from Santa Margherita, the villages consist of **Monterosso Al Mare** (the largest, most developed, most expensive & least attractive), **Vernazza** (the prettiest), **Corniglia** (great coastline views), **Manarola** (captivating), and **Riomaggiore**. The villages are linked together in minutes by a local train and five hours by a wonderful strenuous footpath. It is best to arrive by train unless you park your car in Monterosso's parking lot. Out of the five villages, Monterosso is the only one with the sandy beach and many hotels in all price ranges. The others have plenty of rooms (*affitta camere*) in private homes. You can look for signs posted on houses; ask at the bars or some of the locals who are hanging around at the water. Sometimes the *affitta camere* may turn out to be a fully equipped apartment w/kitchen. Try to call ahead if you arrive in the winter. The major difference between a hotel room and an *affitta camere* in a private house is that they may not change your towels or clean your room every day. My husband and I arrived in Vernazza at 10pm without hotel reservations and the locals were yelling up to the open windows asking about empty rooms for us. We soon realized that everyone in town knew each other and which homes had the empty rooms.

Cinque Terre Tourist Information Center
The only office in Cinque Terre is located at Via Fegina 38, Monterosso. **Tel:** 0187-817506. **Fax:** 0187-817528. Located directly under the train station. Hrs.: April-Oct. Mon.-Sat. 10am-12pm & 4-6pm. Sun. 10am-12pm.

High season: June 15-Sept. 15 and Easter week.

Monterosso Al Mare
Hotels to the left of the train station
AGAVI: Via Fegina 30. **Tel:** 0187-817171. **Fax:** 0187-818264. (8

rms., all w/toilet & bath or shower.) 100,000L (51E) single; 150,000L (77E) double; 200,000L (103E) triple. No breakfast served. Cash only. English spoken (Hilary), wonderful charming hotel w/nice-size bright airy rms., some w/balconies & views, #4, 5, 6 & 7 face the front & have views of the water but are noisy in high season, #1 & 8 are in the back with no views but are quiet, minibars, central heating, no elevator, 1 fl. The hotel is located close to the train station. The local trains run from 6am-11:30pm, after that time only transport trains run at night so it is fairly quiet. Call the hotel only during the daytime because no one answers the phone at night. Tel: 0187-/801665 is Hilary's mother's number. With your back to the train station when you exit, turn left down the main road Via Fegina, hotel is 1/2 block down your left.

PASQUALE: Via Fegina 4.
Tel: 0187-817477/817550. **Fax:** 0187-817056.
Web site: http://www.pasini.com/ **E-mail:** pasquale@pasini.com (15 rms., all w/toilet & bath or shower.) 135,000L (69E) single; 195,000L (100E) double; 240,000L (123E) triple; 270,000L (138E) quad. Buffet breakfast (8-10am) is included in the rates & cannot be deducted. Visa, MC, AX, DC. English spoken (Felicita & Marco), direct-dial phone, satellite TV w/CNN, beautiful hotel w/modern nicely furnished comfortable airy bright rms., all rooms w/view of the sea, double-paned windows, hair driers, central heating, air-conditioned, bar, restaurant, no elevator, 4 flrs. Great location. Owned/managed by Pasini family who also own Hotel Villa Steno. They offer half- (40,000L extra pp) and full-board (70,000L extra pp) rates at their restaurant or a restaurant close to the hotel. With your back to the train station when you exit, turn left down the main road on Via Fegina, continue through the tunnel, hotel is on the left side before you start walking up the main road.

SOUVENIR: Via Goberti 24. **Tel:** 0187-817595. (12 rms., all w/ toilet & bath or shower). 100,000L (51E) single; 150,000L (77E) double. This hotel looked wonderful but there was no one around to talk to when I came by. It is a 3-star so how bad can it be? It is surrounded by greenery and trees. If you stay here, please let me know what you think. With your back to the train station when you exit, turn left down the main road on Via Fegina, continue through the tunnel, as Via Fegina becomes Via Roma, stay on the main street, look for the hotel's yellow sign in front of Hotel Jolly.

VILLA STENO: Via Roma 109.
Tel: 0187-817028/818336. **Fax:** 0187-817056.
Web site: http://www.pasini.com/ **E-mail:** steno@pasini.com (16 rms., all w/toilet & bath or shower.) 135,000L (69E) single; 195,000L (100E) double; 240,000L (123E) triple; 270,000L (138E) quad. Buffet breakfast (8-10am) is included in the rates & cannot be deducted. Breakfast is served on the terrace in warm weather. Visa, MC, AX, DC. English spoken (Matteo), direct-dial phone, satellite TV w/CNN, wonderful renovated villa w/modern nicely furnished comfortable bright airy rms., 12 rms. w/balconies, private gardens & fabulous views, #10 & 16 w/no views & no balconies are the cheapest at 175,000L, bar, no elevator, 2 flrs., lots of steep stairs surround the hotel, free parking but call to reserve a space. They offer half- (40,000L extra pp) and full-board (70,000L extra pp) rates at a restaurant close to the hotel. Owned/managed by Pasini family who also own Hotel Pasquale which is located near the waterfront. The hotel is about a ten-minute walk from the station at the top of the old town. With your back to the train station when you exit, turn left down the main road on Via Fegina, continue through the tunnel, as Via Fegina becomes Via Roma, stay on the main street, as you pass the bank on your left, look for some steep stairs taking you up to the black gate of the hotel, keep walking to the top of the stairs. 25-minute walk from the train station. Taxi 15,000L. (Closed Nov.-March.)

Hotels to the right of the train station
BAIA: Via Fegina 88. **Tel:** 0187-817512. **Fax:** 0187-818322. (30 rms., all w/toilet & bath or shower.) 195,000-235,000L (100-121E) double; 260,000-280,000L (133-144E) triple; 320,000L (164E) quad. Buffet breakfast (8-10am) is included in the rates & cannot be deducted but can be served in the room (6,500L extra pp). Visa, MC, AX. English spoken (Katruscia), direct-dial phone, TV, comfortable rms., 11 rms. w/balconies, #12, 16, 32, 36 & 22 are the best rooms w/balconies facing the water & worth every penny, central heating, double-paned windows, bar, waterfront restaurant, no elevator, 4 flrs. They offer half-board rates. Owned/managed by Tony Cella, although Tony's

ex-wife was at the reception desk helping me. Located near the station facing the beach. With your back to the train station when you exit, turn right down the main road on Via Fegina. (Closed Nov.-Feb.)

VILLA ADRIANA: Via IV Novembre 23. **Tel:** 0187-818109. (51 rms., all w/toilet & bath or shower.) 93,000-100,000L (48-51E) single; 158,000-165,000L (81-85E) double. Buffet breakfast (7:30-9:30am) is included in the rates & cannot be deducted. Visa, MC. English spoken (Clare), direct-dial phone, simple two-building hotel w/comfortable airy bright small rms. & large bathrooms, half the rooms w/balconies & views of the hills, tranquil location, chapel, bar, restaurant, 2 elevators, 3 flrs., free parking but hotel doesn't offer security for the cars. They offer half- and full-board rates. The hotel is not family-owned but is managed by the Catholic church. It was originally built as a retreat for nuns and priests which explains the abundance of single & double rooms but no rooms for triple or quad. 11pm curfew. No key is given for the front door. Located on the edge of town. With your back to the train station when you exit, turn right down the main road on Via Fegina, when you get to the fork with the public telephone on your left, turn right at the fork onto Via IV Novembre, hotel is up the hill on the left. (Closed mid-Nov.-mid-March.)

Hotel in Vernazza
SORRISO: Via Gavino 4, 19018. **Tel:** 0187-812224. **Fax:** 0187-821198. (19 rms., 8 w/toilet & bath or shower.) 90,000L (46E) single; 165,000L (85E) double; 245,000L (126E) triple; 320,000L (164E) quad. Breakfast is included in the rates but can be deducted to reduce room price. Cash only. English spoken (Paolo), combination of two hotels, rustic hotel w/11 basic simple rms., & a renovated home w/7 rms., 3 rms. w/balconies, central heating, bar, restaurant, elevator in only 1 of the bldgs. They are the only hotel in the village. Owner Paolo tries to act reserved but he can be as cuddly as a teddy bear. Walk under the train station to the hotel. (Closed Nov.-March.)

Rooms in Vernazza
CAMERE ANNA-MARIE: Via Carattino #64, 19018. **Tel:** 0187-821082. 120,000L (62E) double. Cash only. Limited English spoken, basic simple rms. This was the first time my husband and I had tried an *affitta camere*. The room on the top floor has a separate

shower on the roof. This was a new experience for us. Later she moved us to a renovated cave w/room & private bathroom which was great.

CAMERE DA FILIPPO: Via A. Santo 62, 19018. **Tel:** 0187-812244. (15 rms., some w/toilet & bath or shower.) 110,000L (56E) double; 135,000L (69E) apts. Cash only. Ask at the Blue Marlin bar located at Via Roma 43. **Tel:** 0187-821149.

GIANNI: Piazza Maconi 5, 19018. **Tel:** 0187-821003. I tried to talk with the woman who owns the rooms over the restaurant she also owns, but she refused to show me any of them.

Hotels in Manarola
CA' D'ANDREAN: Via Discovolo 101, 19010. **Tel:** 0187-920040. **Fax:** 0187-920452. (10 rms., all w/toilet & bath or shower.) 100,000L (51E) single; 125,000L (64E) double; 169,000L (87E) triple. Breakfast (8am) at 10,500L pp is not obligatory & can be served in the room. Breakfast is served in the garden in warm weather. Cash only. English spoken (Simone), direct-dial phone, wonderful charming hotel w/modern furnished comfortable nice-size bright rms. & large bathrooms, 5 rms. w/terraces, #4 was quite nice, central heating, beautiful garden w/lemon trees, bar, quiet location, no elevator, 3 flrs. Owned/managed by Morio, Simone Rolland and Simone's charming mother. From the train station, turn right after tunnel, walk up the very steep hill. 10-minute walk. No taxis. (Closed Nov.)

MARINA PICCOLA: Via Discovolo 38, 19010. **Tel:** 0187-920103. **Fax:** 0187-920966. (10 rms., all w/toilet & bath or shower.) 130,000L (67E) single; 150,000L (77E) double. Breakfast (8:30am) at 16,500L pp is not obligatory. Visa, MC, AX, DC. English spoken (Jan), direct-dial phone, nice cozy charming hotel w/modern furnished bright comfortable small rms., most w/views, #7 is the best rm., #2 is quite large, 3 rms. w/terraces, 5 rms. w/minibars, central heating, bar, waterfront restaurant w/veranda & terrace around the corner (closed Tues.), no elevator, 4 flrs. They offer half- and full-board rates. From the train station, walk through the tunnel to the left, follow the main road, you'll see the hotel's blue & white sign on the right. (Closed Nov.)
If you find yourself without hotel accommodations, you can call the

following people in Manarola or Riomaggiore. Make sure you ask to see the room before agreeing to pay the fee.

Apts/Rooms in Manarola
Inn "Da Baranin: Via Rollandi 35/a, 19010. **Tel/Fax:** 0187-920595. **E-mail:** baranin@5terre-vacanze.com 110,000L double. Call for family rates. English spoken (Sara Barani).

Apts/Rooms in Riomaggiore
Roberto & Luciano Fazioli: Via Colombo 94, 19017. Riomaggiore. **Tel:** 0187-920587. **Tel/Fax:** 0187-920904. **Cell:** 0368-442051. Hrs.: 9am-1pm & 2-8pm. Roberto & Luciano have lots of apts. & private rooms for rent all over town. Cash only. English spoken (Roberto), 2 deluxe apts. including kitchen facilities and bath near the port for 65,000-85,000L (33-44E) pp: (1) for 4 people w/marina view & (1) for 2 people; 2 basic apts. including kitchen facilities and bath in the historic center for 45,000-55,000L (23-28E) pp; (1) apt. for 4 people & (1) for 5 people; 6 rooms including private baths in a 17th-century building in the historic center for 45,000-55,000L (23-28E) pp; (4) rms. for 2 people, (1) rm. for 3 people & (1) rm. for 4 people; 3 rooms with bathrooms & showers outside of the rooms in a hilltop villa with a large terrace, table & chairs overlooking the ocean & vineyards for 45,000-50,000L (23-26E) pp; (2) rms. for 2 people & (1) rm. for 3 people. Make sure they don't try to book you into their unacceptable hostel-type apt. w/kitchen & bathroom. It is located near the port and can accommodate up to 7 people (usually young travelers and backpackers). Prices for this hostel are about 35,000-40,000L pp. *10% rm. discount when you show managers Roberto or Luciano Fazioli this book.* I met with Luciano, who is wonderful and very accommodating. He says he has a room for everybody's pocket. The Fazioli family are natives of Riomaggiore going as far back as their great-grandparents. They also participate in local traditions such as grape growing, wine making and selling the local but very popular Cinque Terre wine. With your back to the train station, bear to the right around the stone wall through the well-lit tunnel, exit the tunnel onto Via Columbo. Walk up the hill, look on the left side for a green & white striped canopy.

Anna Michielini: Via Colombo 143, 19017. Riomaggiore. **Tel:** 0187-920411. **Fax:** 0187-920411. **E-mail:** cammichi@tin.it
Anna has lots of fully equipped apts. for rent for about 50,000L (26E) pp. Cash only. Examples: a 3rd fl. apt. w/2 double bedrooms, living room w/2 more beds, kitchen & bathroom; a 2nd fl. apt. w/2 double bedrooms, kitchen & bathroom; a 1st fl. one-room apt. w/double bed, a corner equipped w/kitchen & bathroom (shower & toilet). Every apt. has central heating, satellite TV w/English channels (BBC, CNN, NBC). Anna will give you a discount if it is a group of more than 4 people or you are staying for at least a week. With your back to the train station, bear to the right around the stone wall through the well-lit tunnel, exit the tunnel onto Via Columbo. Anna is not licensed so it is better to call Anna first to let her know you are coming and definitely ask to see the room. I didn't meet Anna or see any of the apts. She faxed me all the above information.

RESTAURANT
Please check page 20 for my criteria for selecting restaurants.

IL CONTROVELACCIO: Via Colombo 237, Riomaggiore. 19017. **Tel:** 0187-920820. Hrs.: mid-June-Oct. 12-10:30pm; Nov. to mid-June 12-3pm & 7-9:30pm & closed Thurs. Visa, MC, AX, DC. Wonderful decor to match the sea. Mara & Mara speak English. Some of the best pastas in Italy have been served at this restaurant. If you love pasta w/pesto or pasta w/black olives, this is the place for you. Cinque Terre wine, soft bread and homemade pasta. Our base was Vernazza; my husband and I ate lunch here. Lunch was so good, we caught the 5-minute train ride back to the restaurant to have dinner the same night. *Show both Maras this book and they will give you a complimentary limoncello.* With your back to the train station, bear to the right around the stone wall through the well-lit tunnel, exit the tunnel onto Via Columbo.

FLORENCE (Firenze)
Tuscany, zip code 50123
Area code 39, city code 055

Orientation: Santa Maria Novella (SMN) train station is Florence's main train station which is located on the northwestern edge of central Florence in the Piazza Stazione. It adjoins **Piazza Santa Maria Novella.** The city is split by the **Arno** river. The **Piazza Duomo** (world-famous cathedral) is on the north (right) side of the river and the **Palazzo Strozzi** is on the west. **Oltrarno** (location of the **Pitti Palace**) is south of the river. It is about a 10-15-minute walk from the train station to the center (Duomo) of town. With your back to the train station, take **Via Panzani**, then left on **Via Cerrentari** to the center of Florence. **Via Calzaiuuoli**, the most popular shopping street, runs south from the Duomo to the romantic **Piazza Signoria** and the Arno. Running parallel to Via Calzaiuuoli on the west is **Via Roma** which becomes **Via Por Santa Maria**. Sectioned between the two is **Piazza Repubblica** (a busy cafe & shopping square). From Piazza Signoria, take **Via Vacchereccia**, turn left for two blocks to the **Ponte Vecchio** (old bridge). The Arno river has eight bridges crossing it but the Ponte Vecchio is the most celebrated and visited, with its many jewelry shops lining both sides of the bridge. Cross over the Ponte Vecchio into Oltrarno. Florence is a delightful city which can easily be managed by foot. It is a short walking distance to most of the hotels but the sidewalks are so crowded most of the year you'll feel like a sardine with a suitcase. Also, it is very difficult wheeling your suitcase over cobblestone streets.

Finding street addresses: There is a double-address system in Florence. Remember the following when you are looking for accommodations in Florence: Addresses of residences and hotels are in black or blue numbers on the front of the buildings usually with an "N" (*nero* = black/blue); addresses of commercial establishments are in red or brown numbers usually with an "R" (*rosso* = red). There is no connection between these two systems of addresses. The city is trying to eliminate this system and change everything to black. Until they succeed keep your eye on the black/blue numbers when looking for accommodations. I was able to find every hotel without any problems using the Hallwag map for Florence. (See maps in index for more information on purchasing maps.)

TRANSPORTATION TO AND FROM AIRPORT
The SITA bus goes to and from Florence's **Amerigo Vespucci (Peretola)** airport (8,000L pp) to the main bus terminal on Via Santa Caterina Siena 15R, located right next to the train station. To reach the SITA bus station from the train station, exit by track #5, cross Via Luigi Alamanni, turn left, and a right onto Via Santa Caterina Siena. The ATAF city bus service also has line #62 (every hr.) to and from Florence's **Amerigo Vespucci (Peretola)** airport for a 30-min. ride (2,000L pp) to Santa Maria Novella (SMN) train station. Taxi from the airport (15 min.) costs about 35,000L.

Firenze Tourist Information Centers (APT)
1.) Via Cavour 1R. **Tel:** 055-290832/290833. **Fax:** 055-2760383. 3 blocks north of the Duomo. Hrs.: Mon.-Sat. 8:30am-7:15pm; Sun. 8:30am-1:45pm; Shorter hours in low season. Sun. 8:15am-1:45pm. **2.)** Via A. Manzoni 16R., 50121. **Tel:** 055-23320/2346284. **Fax:** 055-2346286. Hrs.: Mon.-Sat. 8:30am-1:30pm. **3.)** Comune di Firenze. Located just outside the SMN rail station at the local bus stop in a covered area. Exit by track #16. Hrs.: Daily 8:15am-7:15pm. Shorter hours in low season. **Tel:** 055-212245. **Fax:** 055-2381226. **4.)** Borgo Santa Coce 29/R **Tel:** 055-2340444. **Fax:** 055-2264524.

Low season Nov.-Feb.; high season March-June, Sept.-Oct., Christmas & New Year's, fashion shows. Please keep in mind July, Aug. & Sept. attract lots of mosquitoes.

Many of the hotels can make arrangements for you to park your car even if they don't offer private parking at their hotel. Also, always ask the hotel manager about getting advance ticket reservations to the Uffizi Gallery.

Florence hotels listed alphabetically

FLORENCE

Hotels east of Santa Maria Novella train station

A good area if you are using Florence as a base and need to be close to the train station. The nights are quite noisy because of traffic and the station area does attract lots of hookers at night. A 20-minute walk to the San Lorenzo Central Market and Il Duomo.

ABACO: Via Banchi 1, 2nd fl. **Tel:** 055-2381919. **Fax:** 055-282289. (7 rms., 6 w/toilet & bath or shower.) 75,000-106,000L (38-54E) single; 100,000-130,000L (51-67E) double; 135,000-155,000L (69-79E) triple; 170,000-180,000L (87-92E) quad. Children under 3 free. Breakfast (8:15-10am) at 11,500L pp is not obligatory & can be served in the room. Visa, MC. English spoken (Bruno & Simona), direct-dial phone, TV, nice hotel w/simply furnished large rms., wood-beam ceilings, #7 & 1 are the best rms., #6 is huge w/bathroom, you can use his refrigerator to store your food, fans, central heating, double-paned windows, bar, laid-back student atmosphere, coin operated laundry machine, no elevator, 3 flrs., garage parking (35,000L per day). *Free breakfast when you show owner/manager Bruno Serratore or staff this book.* With the train tracks at your back, exit to the left near track #16, cross the street to McDonald's, cross the street to Piazza Unita Italiana, continue onto Via Panzani to where it intersects Via Tornabuoni and Via Banchi.

AUSONIA/RIMINI: Via Nazionale 24, 3rd fl.
Tel: 055-496547. **Fax:** 055-474014.
Web site: http://www.firenze.net/kursonia/
E-mail: kursonia@firenze.net (11 rms., 6 w/toilet & bath or shower.) 95,000-120,000L (49-62E) single; 150,000-170,000L (77-87E) double; 205,000-225,000L (105-115E) triple; 250,000-280,000L (128-144E) quad. Children under 4 free. Buffet breakfast (7:30-10am) at 13,500L pp is not obligatory & can be served in the room (6,500L extra pp). Visa, MC. English spoken (Paola & Celeste), direct-dial phone, nice hotel w/simply furnished bright airy rms., #5 (bathroom) & 7 (sink only) are the best rms., central heating, rooms facing the street have double-paned windows although the rooms in the back are very quiet, laundry services available, small outside terrace, elevator, 3 flrs. They offer half- and full-board rates with a restaurant near the hotel. *5% rm. discount in high season & 15% rm. discount*

in low season when you show owner/manager Paola Angelini or staff this book. E-mail computer service available. Managed by the same owners as the hotel Kursaal. (The hotel Ausonia e Rimini is the inexpensive side of the hotel Kursaal.) With the train tracks at your back, exit to the left near track #16, cross the street to McDonald's which is near the corner of Via Nazionale.

AZZI: Via Faenza 56, 1st fl. **Tel/Fax:** 055-213806. (12 rms., 3 w/ toilet & bath or shower.) 50,000-75,000L (26-38E) single; 70,000-125,000L (36-64E) double; 87,000-145,000L (45-74E) triple; 100,000-170,000L (51-87E) quad. Children under 12 free. Breakfast (7:30-10:30am) at 7,500L pp is not obligatory & can be served in the room. Breakfast is served on the garden/terrace in warm weather. Visa, MC, AX, DC. English spoken (Valentino & Victorio), eccentric 16th-century hotel w/old-fashioned furnished comfortable large rms., #4 (bathroom), 5 & 8 are the best rms., #3 & 7 have bathrooms, charming sunny terrace w/a view, central heating, most rms. have double-paned windows, noisy location, ask for a room away from the noise, bar, no elevator, 1 fl., parking (27,000L per day). Bohemian-style atmosphere which makes it popular among students, musicians and artists. *15% rm. discount or free breakfast when you show owner/manager Sandro Berti or staff this book.* Same family manages Hotel Paolo & Hotel Anna which are not reviewed in this book. Both hotels have no private bathrooms. With the train tracks at your back, exit to the left near track #16, continue past the taxi stand, cross the island, cross the street, turn left, make the 1st right onto Via Bernardo Cennini, 2nd right to Via Faenza.

BERKLEYS: Via Fiume 11, 3rd fl. **Tel:** 055-2382147. **Tel/Fax:** 055-212302. (9 rms., all w/toilet & bath or shower.) 85,000-125,000L (44-64E) single; 105,000-165,000L (54-85E) double; 170,000-210,000L (87-108E) triple; 190,000-220,000L (97-113E) quad. Breakfast (8-10am) is included in the rates & cannot be deducted (only in low season) but can be served in the room (4,000L extra pp). Visa, MC. English spoken (Catia), direct-dial phone, simply furnished pretty rms., #6 (balcony), 1 & 9 (TV) are the best rms., #5 (balcony) is perfect for a family, central heating, some rms. have double-paned windows, located on the top floor in the bldg., elevator, 1 fl. The hotel is getting all new furniture in 1999. *10% rm. discount when you show owner/manager Catia Andreoli or staff this book.* To avoid the crowd on Via Nazionale, with the train tracks at your back, exit to the left near track #16, continue past the taxi stand, cross the island, cross the street, turn left, make the 1st right onto Via Bernardo Cennini, 1st right to Via Fiume. (Closed 1 wk. in Aug.)

BURCHIANTI: Via Giglio 6. **Tel/Fax:** 055-212796. (12 rms., 6 w/ toilet & bath or shower.) 90,000L (46E) single; 135,000-155,000L (69-79E) double; 190,000L (97E) triple; 220,000L (113E) quad. Children under 5 free. Breakfast (8-9am) at 6,500L pp is not obligatory & can be served in the room (6,500L extra pp). Cash only. Limited English spoken (Rela), 16th-century old palazzo w/beautiful historic decor which gives you a nostalgic feeling, antique furniture mixed with prefabricated shower stalls, #6, 5 & 3 have no bathrooms but you feel like you are rooming with the artists because of the lovely frescoed walls & ceilings, central heating, terrace, no elevator, 1 fl. *Free breakfast when you show owner/manager Rela Burchianti or staff this book.* With the train tracks at your back, exit to the left near track #16, cross the street to McDonald's, cross the street to Piazza Unita Italiana, continue onto Via Panzani to Via Giglio.

CASCI: Via Cavour 13. **Tel:** 055-211686. **Fax:** 055-2396461. **Web site:** http://www.venere.it/firenze.casci/
E-mail: casci@pn.itnet.it (25 rms., all w/toilet & bath or shower.) 105,000-135,000L (54-69E) single; 135,000-185,000L (69-95E) double; 170,000-245,000L (87-126E) triple; 200,000-300,000L (103-154E) quad. Buffet breakfast (7:30-9:30am) is included in the rates & cannot be deducted. Visa, MC, AX, DC. English spoken (Paolo & Carla), direct-dial phone, satellite TV w/English channel, renovated 15th-century palazzo w/nicely furnished comfortable rms., public rms. w/original fresco ceilings, towel warmers, hair driers, pleasant ambiance, central heating, some rms. have air-conditioning, noisy location, although the rms. in the front have double-paned windows, the rms. in the back are much quieter & have a view of an enormous magnolia tree, #6, 11, 14 & 20 are the best rms., bar, elevator, 2 flrs., valet parking (45,000L per day). *10% rm. discount when you show owner/manager Paolo Lombardi or staff this book and pay in cash.*

Energetic Paolo will help you with all your questions. With the train tracks at your back, exit to the left near track #16, cross the street to McDonald's which is near the corner of Via Nazionale, walk up Via Nazionale about 5 blocks, turn right onto Via Guelfa for about 4 blocks, turn right onto Via Cavour. Buses #1, 6, 17, 7 & 20 go to Piazza San Marco from train station, walk down Via Cavour from San Marco square. (Closed last 2 wks. in Jan.)

CONCORDIA: Via Amorino 14. **Tel:** 055-213233. **Fax:** 055-213337. **Web site:** http://www.fol.it/concordia/
E-mail: concordia@fol.it (16 rms., all w/toilet & bath or shower.) 85,000-110,000L (44-56E) single; 125,000-165,000L (64-85E) double; 170,000-220,000L (87-113E) triple; 220,000-240,000L (113-123E) quad. Children under 5 free. Buffet breakfast (7:30-10:30am) is included in the rates & cannot be deducted but can be served in the room. Breakfast is served in the patio in warm weather. Visa, MC, AX, DC. English spoken (Fabrizio), direct-dial phone, satellite TV w/English channel, great charming modern hotel w/nicely furnished comfortable bright airy pretty rms., #5 (large rm. w/separate shower & toilet rm.), 2, 28 & 10 are the best rms., many rms. w/balconies, patio, noisy location, central heating, bar, no elevator, 3 flrs., parking (40,000L per day). Owned/managed by Fabrizio Romeo since '97. With the train tracks at your back, exit to the left near track #16, cross the street to McDonald's, cross the street to Piazza Unita Italiana, turn left onto Via San Antonio, turn right onto Via Amorino.

ERINA: Via Fiume 17, 3rd fl. **Tel:** 055-288294. **Fax:** 055-284343. (7 rms., 6 w/toilet & bath or shower.) 85,000-95,000L (44-50E) single; 170,000L (87E) double; 200,000L (103E) triple; 240,000L (123E) quad. Children under 8 free. Breakfast (8-10am) is included in the rates & can be served in the room but can be deducted to reduce room price. Visa, MC, AX. English spoken (Sergio) direct-dial phone, TV, old building w/simply furnished large rms., #4, 5 & 6 have balconies & bathrooms, #7 has a balcony but no bathroom, central heating, double-paned windows, elevator, 1 fl. *Free breakfast when you show owner/manager Sergio Calabrese or staff this book.* For directions, see Hotel Berkleys.

ENZA: Via San Zanobi 45. **Tel:** 055-490990/473672. **Fax:** 055-292192. (16 rms., 7 w/toilet & bath or shower.) 80,000-85,000L (41-44E) single; 100,000-135,000L (51-69E) double; 140,000-170,000L (72-87E) triple. No breakfast available. Cash only. English spoken (Eugenia & Julio), nicely furnished simple cozy rms., all the rms vary in size, #20, 21, 22, 23 (private bathroom in the hall), 24 (private bathroom in the hall), 25 & 26 (loft) all have bathrooms, rooms in the back are quiet, central heating, no elevator, 2 flrs. Tryccky, the Chihuahua dog is the cutest. With the train tracks at your back, exit to the left near track #16, cross the street to McDonald's which is near the corner of Via Nazionale, walk up Via Nazionale about 5 blocks, turn right onto Via Guelfa, turn left onto Via San Zanobi.

GLOBUS: Via S. Antonio 24. **Tel:** 055-211062. **Fax:** 055-2396225. **Web site:** http://www.venere.it/firenze/globus/ **E-mail:** hotel.globus@firenze.albergo.it (23 rms., 5 w/toilet & bath or shower.) 70,000-115,000L (36-60E) single; 95,000-155,000L (50-79E) double; 140,000-210,000L (72-108E) triple; 160,000-240,000L (82-123E) quad. Children under 6 free. Buffet breakfast (7:30-10am) at 9,500L pp is obligatory (except in winter) & can be served in the room (11,500L pp). Visa, MC, AX. English spoken (Serena & Michele), direct-dial phone, nice wonderful hotel w/simply furnished large bright rms., #304 (balcony), 209, 307 (no bathroom) & 309 (view & shower only) are the best rms., rooms facing the street have double-paned windows, central heating is restricted in the winter, fans, bar, no elevator, 4 flrs. *5% rm. discount when you show owners/managers Serena Forzieri, Michele Piccione or staff this book.* The hotel will be renovating in mid-1999 to add more bathrooms. From the station, head straight out to Piazza Unita Italiana, turn left onto Via San Antonio. (Closed 2 wks. in Dec.)

IL BARGELLINO: Via Guelfa 87. **Tel:** 055-2382658. **Fax:** 055-2382698. (10 rms., 5 w/toilet & bath or shower.) 75,000L (38E) single; 115,000-125,000L (60-64E) double. Call for triple & quad rates. Breakfast (8:30-9:30am) at 9,500L pp is not obligatory & can be served in the room. Breakfast is served on the terrace in warm weather. Visa, MC, AX. American English spoken (Carmel), quaint pleasant hotel w/old-fashioned furnished pretty rms., high ceilings, #7, 8, 9

& 10 are large rooms that open up onto a wonderful large garden terrace, central heating, no elevator, 2 flrs., garage parking (25,000L per day). Owned by Pino Gallo & managed by Carmel Coppola. Renovated in Dec. 1998 to add 2 more bathrooms. Carmel has a sister in Boston who has an **E-mail** address: J9copp@aol.com With the train tracks at your back, exit to the left near track #16, cross the street to McDonald's which is near the corner of Via Nazionale, walk up Via Nazionale about 5 blocks, turn right onto Via Guelfa.

JOHANNA: Via Bonifacio Lupi 14, 1st fl. **Tel:** 055-481896. **Fax:** 055-482721. (11 rms., 9 w/toilet & bath or shower.) 90,000L (46E) single; 135,000L (69E) double; 165,000L (85E) triple. Breakfast (anytime w/instant coffee) is included in the rates & cannot be deducted but you can bring it to your room. Cash only. English spoken (Stephanie), 19th-century palazzo hotel w/old-fashioned furnished comfortable nice-size pretty rms., #10, 5 & 6 have balconies, reception desk closes at 7pm, central heating, quiet residential location, elevator, 1 fl. Owned/managed by Evelyne Arriahi. With the train tracks at your back, exit to the left near track #16, cross the street to McDonald's which is near the corner of Via Nazionale, walk up Via Nazionale which becomes Via Santa Caterina d'Alessandria to Viale Spartaco Lavagnini, turn right from Viale Lavagnini to Via Bonifacio Lupi, take the stairs to the right after you enter the gate. 30-minute walk to Duomo & train station. Taxi 18,000L.

LORENA: Via Faenza 1.
Tel: 055-282785/282786. **Fax:** 055-288300.
Web site: http://www.florentia2000.com/att_commerciali/hotel_lorena/
E-mail: hotellorenaalbergo@tin.it (19 rms., 13 w/toilet & bath or shower.) 55,000-95,000L (28-50E) single; 85,000-175,000L (44-90E) double; 120,000-210,000L (62-108E) triple; 160,000-230,000L (82-118E) quad. Children under 10 free. Breakfast (6-9:30am) at 11,500L pp is not obligatory & can be served in the room. Visa, MC, AX, DC. English spoken (Roberto, Lorenzo, & Virgillo), direct-dial phone, TV, basic hotel w/simply furnished comfortable rms., #30, 20, 22 & 42 are the best rms. w/minibars, 9 rms. w/minibars, central heating, double-paned windows, noisy location, walk up one flight of stairs

to elevator, 5 flrs. *5% rm. discount when you show owner/manager Roberto & Lorenzo Galli or staff this book.* With the train tracks at your back, exit to the left near track #16, cross the street to McDonald's, cross the street to Piazza Unita Italiana, turn left from the piazza and walk up Via Sant' Antonio for 2 blocks, turn right onto Via Faenza.

MARINI: Via Faenza 56, 2nd fl. **Tel/Fax:** 055-284824. (12 rms., 6 w/toilet & bath or shower.) 70,000-120,000L (36-62E) single; 95,000-165,000L (50-85E) double. Breakfast (8-10am) at 11,500L pp is not obligatory & can be served in the room. Cash only. Limited English spoken (Musacchio), basic hotel w/simply furnished bright large airy rms., nice flrs., #7 (huge terrace & bathroom) & 13 are the best rms., #8 has a balcony & bathroom, central heating, no elevator, 3 flrs. (Closed sometimes in Feb. & Nov.) For directions, see Hotel Azzi.

MARY: Piazza Indipendenza 5, 3rd fl. **Tel/Fax:** 055-496310. (12 rms., 8 w/toilet & bath or shower.) 85,000-115,000L (44-60E) single; 95,000-155,000L (50-79E) double; 125,000-180,000L (64-92E) triple; 160,000-210,000L (82-108E) quad. Breakfast (8-9:30am) at 6,500L pp is not obligatory & can be served in the room (20%L extra pp). Visa, MC. English spoken (Beatrice), nice hotel w/simply furnished nice-size comfortable rms., many w/views of the Duomo & Belltower, #4, 1 & 9 are the best rms. w/bathrooms & views, #5 & 6 have bathrooms but no views, #11 view but no bathroom, central heating, double-paned windows, popular with students, quiet location, no elevator, 4 flrs., parking (35,000-45,000L per day). *10% rm. discount when you show owner/manager Iolanda Giangreco or staff this book.* With the train tracks at your back, exit to the left near track #16, cross the street to McDonald's which is near the corner of Via Nazionale, walk straight up Via Nazionale to Piazza Indipendenza.

MERLINI: Via Faenza 56, 3rd fl. **Tel:** 055-212848. **Fax:** 055-283939. (10 rms., 1 w/toilet & bath or shower.) 70,000-90,000L (36-46E) single (no toilets); 95,000-120,000L (50-62E) double; 120,000-145,000L (62-74E) triple; 145,000-155,000L (74-79E) quad. Breakfast (7:30-9:30am) at 9,500L pp is not obligatory & can be served in the room. Breakfast is served on the terrace in warm weather. Visa, MC. English spoken (Gabriela & Mara), basic charming hotel w/

old-fashioned simply furnished airy bright large rms., top fl. rms. have views of the hills surrounding Florence, glassed-in terrace w/ panoramic view, #8 has a bathroom, #2 has a shower only, #4 has a balcony but no bathroom, central heating, no elevator, 4 flrs. For directions, see Hotel Azzi. (Closed sometimes in Aug.)

MIA CARA: Via Faenza 58, 2nd fl. **Tel:** 055-216053. **Fax:** 055-2302601. (20 rms., 9 w/toilet & bath or shower.) 95,000-105,000L (50-54E) double; 128,000-140,000L (66-72E) triple. No breakfast is served. Cash only. English spoken (Angela), basic hotel w/simply furnished large airy rms., high ceilings, rooms vary quite a bit, #18, 8, 12, 16, 20, 14, 18, 26 & 32 have bathrooms, no elevator. Same family manages the hostel on the ground fl. For directions, see Hotel Azzi.

NAZIONALE: Via Nazionale 22, 2nd fl. **Tel:** 055-2382203. **Fax:** 055-2381735. (9 rms., 5 w/toilet & bath or shower.) 90,000L (46E) single; 120,000-145,000L (62-74E) double. Call for triple & quad rates. Breakfast (8-9:30am) is included in the rates & cannot be deducted but is served in the room. Visa, MC. English spoken, direct-dial phone, pleasant hotel w/simply furnished rms., #6 has a balcony & bathroom, front rooms have double-paned windows, rooms in the back are quiet, the rooms w/o bathrooms are huge, central heating, no elevator, 2 flrs. Owned/managed by Marie Claude. Sabrina Pagani, Marie Claude's daughter, has 6 rms. for rent but no private bathrooms. 95,000L double. **E-mail:** sabrpaga@tin.it For directions, see Hotel Ausonia.

PEZZATI I: Via San Zanobi 22, 2nd fl. **Tel:** 055-291660. **Fax:** 055-287145. (6 rms., all w/toilet & bath or shower.) 80,000L (41E) single; 110,000L (56E) double; 150,000L (77E) triple. No breakfast served. Visa, MC. English spoken (Daniela), charming hotel w/simply furnished bright airy nice-size rms., #1 (wonderful) & 5 are the best rms. & have minibars, #6 has a minibar, double-paned windows w/ mosquito screens which are definitely needed in the summer, central heating, fans, no elevator, 2 flrs. Owned/managed by Daniela Pezzati. For directions, see Hotel Enza. Daniela's family also manages Hotel Pezzati II across the Arno river. **PEZZATI II:** Via Borgo San Frediano 6, 50124. Call Pezzati I before calling. **Tel:** 055-290424. (5 large rms., all w/toilet, shower & minibars.) Same price & cash only.

FLORENCE

RABATTI: Via San Zanobi 48. **Tel:** 055-212393. (4 rms., 1 w/toilet & bath or shower.) 95,000L (50E) double; 125,000L (64E) triple. No breakfast served. Cash only. English spoken (Marcella), simple hotel w/plainly furnished rms., #2 is large w/bathroom, #3 is beautiful, central heating, double-paned windows. Charming Marcella turned her apt. into rooms for rent. There is only one public bathroom for 3 rms. *5% rm. discount when you show owner/manager Marcella Rabatti or staff this book in low season.* For directions, see Hotel Enza.

SERENA: Via Fiume 20, 1st fl. **Tel:** 055-213643. **Fax:** 055-280447. (7 rms., 3 w/toilet & bath or shower.) 135,000L (69E) double; 182,000L (93E) triple; 224,000L (115E) quad. Breakfast (7-9am) at 11,500L pp is not obligatory & can be served in the room. Visa, MC, AX, DC. Limited English spoken (Antonea), direct-dial phone, TV, simple hotel w/comfortable bright airy rms., stained-glass French doors, #5, 6 & 7 are large w/bathrooms, high ceilings, 4 rms. w/ terraces, central heating, elevator, 2 flrs. *10% rm. discount when you show owner/manager Giovanni Bigazzi or staff this book.* For directions, see Hotel Berkleys.

HOTELS OVER $100 A NIGHT FOR TWO
These hotels may have rooms under $100 a night for two because it is low season or the rooms do not have private bathrooms.

ACCADEMIA: Via Faenza 7. **Tel:** 055-293451. **Fax:** 055-219771. **Web site:** http://www.venere.it/firenze/accademia/ **E-mail:** hotaccad@tin.it (16 rms., 14 w/toilet & bath or shower.) 95,000-175,000L (50-90E) single; 115,000-220,000L (60-113E) double; 170,000-270,000L (87-138E) triple; 200,000-320,000L (103-164E) quad. Buffet breakfast (7:30-10am) is included in the rates & cannot be deducted but can be served in the room. Breakfast is served in the garden in warm weather. Visa, MC, AX. English spoken, direct-dial phone, satellite TV w/English channel, 18th-century palace w/simply furnished comfortable large rms., carved wooden ceilings, beautiful stained-glass door entrance, double-paned windows, central heating, 9 rms. w/air-conditioning, quiet location, bar, no elevator, 3 flrs. Owned/managed by Angelo Mari. With the train tracks at your back, exit to the left near track #16, cross the street to McDonald's, cross the street to Piazza Unita Italiana, turn left from the piazza and walk up Via Sant' Antonio for 2 blocks, turn right onto Via Faenza.

ANNABELLA: Via Fiume 17, 2nd fl. **Tel:** 055-281877. **Fax:** 055-2396814. **Web site:** http://www.dex-netcom/XD185/ **E-mail:** hab@mail2.dex-netcom (8 rms., all w/toilet & shower.) 115,000-205,000L (60-105E) double; 190,000-260,000L (97-133E) triple. Breakfast (8-10am) is included in the rates & can be served in the room (6,500 extra pp) but can be deducted in low season to reduce room price. Visa, MC, AX. English spoken (Victoria & Sirmone), direct-dial phone, TV, wonderful beautiful hotel w/nicely furnished bright airy large pretty rms., 5 rms. w/balconies, #6 is a magnificent huge rm. w/balcony, high ceilings, nice flrs., double-paned windows, central heating, bar, elevator, 1fl. Same family manages the Hotel Stella Mary in the same bldg. To avoid the crowd on Via Nazionale, with the train tracks at your back, exit to the left near track #16, continue past the taxi stand, cross the island, cross the street, turn left, make the 1st right onto Via Bernardo Cennini, 1st right to Via Fiume.

COLOMBA: Via Cavour 21, 1st fl. **Tel:** 055-289139/2654562. **Fax:** 055-284323. (14 rms., 10 w/toilet & bath or shower.) 95,000-115,000L (50-60E) single; 145,000-195,000L (74-100E) double; 200,000-250,000L (103-128E) triple; 250,000-300,000L (128-154E) quad. Breakfast (8-9:30am) is included in the rates & cannot be deducted but can be served in the room. Visa, MC, AX, DC. English spoken (Rosanna), direct-dial phone, recently renovated hotel w/nicely furnished comfortable bright airy rms., #6 large w/terrace, 1 rm. has handicapped access even though wheelchair doesn't fit into elevator, noisy location, central heating, fans, bar, elevator, 1 fl. *10% rm. discount when you show owners/managers Michelle & Rosanna Rossi or staff this book.* With the train tracks at your back, exit to the left near track #16, cross the street to McDonald's which is near the corner of Via Nazionale, walk up Via Nazionale about 5 blocks, turn right onto Via Guelfa for about 4 blocks, turn left onto Via Cavour. Buses #1, 6, 17, 7 & 20 go to Piazza San Marco from train station, walk down Via Cavour from San Marco square. (Closed Nov.-March.)

FLORENCE

DESIREE: Via Fiume 20, 2nd fl. **Tel:** 055-2382382. **Fax:** 055-291439. (26 rms., all w/toilet & bath or shower.) 165,000-195,000L (85-100E) double; 200,000-240,000L (103-123E) triple; 260,000L (133E) quad. Buffet breakfast (7:30-9am) is included in the rates but can be deducted to reduce room price. Visa, MC, DC. English spoken (Costa), direct-dial phone, TV w/English channel, wonderful hotel w/nicely furnished comfortable pretty rms., high ceilings, arched stained-glass windows, #15 is the best rm., #21 wonderful w/balcony, 6 rms. w/balconies, central heating, 7 rms. w/air-conditioning, elevator, 3 flrs. Same family manages the beautiful Hotel Cellini in the same bldg.: #202 is the best rm. w/balcony & view. *10% rm. discount when you show owner/manager Ferdinando Cellini or staff this book.* For directions, see Hotel Annabella. (Closed 10 days in Aug.)

KURSAAL: Via Nazionale 24, 2nd fl. **Tel:** 055-496324. **Fax:** 055-474014. **Web site:** http://www.firenze.net/kursonia/
E-mail: kursonia@firenze.net (9 rms., 5 w/toilet & bath or shower.) 115,000-150,000L (57-77E) single; 165,000-215,000L (84-110E) double; 210,000-260,000L (108-134E) triple; 255,000-305,000L (130-157E) quad. Children under 4 free. Buffet breakfast (7:30-10am) is included in the rates & can be served in the room (6,500 extra pp) but can be deducted in low season to reduce room price. Visa, MC. English spoken (Paola & Celeste), direct-dial phone, 5 rms. have satellite TV w/English channel, nice hotel w/simply furnished nice-size rms, #27 has a balcony, #27 & 29 are the best rms., central heating, rooms facing the street have double-paned windows although the rooms in the back are very quiet, bar, laundry services available, elevator, 3 flrs. They offer half- and full-board rates with a restaurant near the hotel. *5% rm. discount in high season & 15% rm. discount in low season when you show owner/manager Paola Angelini or staff this book.* You can receive free E-mail messages at the hotel. Sending costs 5,500L per page. Managed by the same owners as the hotel Ausonia e Rimini. (The hotel Kursaal is the expensive side of the hotel Ausonia e Rimini.) With the train tracks at your back, exit to the left near track #16, cross the street to McDonald's which is near the corner of Via Nazionale.

MARIO'S: Via Faenza 89. **Tel:** 055-216801.
Fax: 055-212039. **Web site:**http://www.webitaly.com/hotel.marios/

E-mail: hotel.marios@webitaly.com (16 rms., 15 w/toilet & bath or shower.) 115,000-225,000L (60-115E) single; 175,000-275,000L (90-141E) double; 240,000-370,000L (123-190E) triple; 290,000-420,000L (149-215E) quad. Children under 3 free. Buffet breakfast (7:15-9:30am) is included in the rates & cannot be deducted. Visa, MC, AX, DC. English spoken (Cristina), direct-dial phone, satellite TV w/English channel, cozy old Florentine hotel w/old-fashioned furnished rms., beamed ceilings, some rms. w/stained-glass windows, #6, 16 & 4 are the best rms., hair driers, central heating, air-conditioned, double-paned windows, bar, no elevator. Owned/managed by Mario Noce. With the train tracks at your back, exit to the left near track #16, continue past the taxi stand, cross the island, cross the street, turn left, make the 1st right onto Via Bernardo Cennini, 2nd right to Via Faenza.

MONICA: Via Faenza 66, 1st fl. **Tel:** 055-283804. **Fax:** 055-281706. (15 rms., 10 w/toilet & bath or shower.) 75,000-115,000L (38-60E) single; 115,000-195,000L (60-100E) double; 140,000-250,000L (72-128E) triple; 180,000-270,000L (92-138E) quad. Children under 4 free. Buffet breakfast (8-9:30am) is included in the rates but can be deducted to reduce room price. Breakfast can be served in the room at no extra cost and on the terrace in warm weather. Visa, MC, AX, DC. English spoken (Rhuna & Barbara, sisters), direct-dial phone, TV, basic hotel w/simply furnished airy nice-size rms., #18 (terrace), 19, 20 & 27 are the best rms., #24 has a terrace but no bathroom, some rms. are dark, outdoor terrace, central heating, air-conditioned, double-paned windows but the rms. in the back are quieter, bar, elevator, 2 flrs. *10% rm. discount when you show owners/managers Rhuna or Barbara Cecchini or staff this book.* For directions, see Hotel Mario's.

NUOVA ITALIA: Via Faenza 26. **Tel:** 055-268430/287508. **Fax:** 055-210941. (20 rms., all w/toilet & bath or shower.) 113,000-150,000L (58-77E) single; 150,000-218,000L (77-112E) double; 225,000-258,000L (115-132E) triple; 240,000-300,000L (123-154E) quad. Breakfast (7:30-10:30am) is included in the rates & cannot be deducted but can be served in the room. Visa, MC, AX. English spoken (Luciano, Eileen & Daniela), direct-dial phone, 17th-century renovated bldg. w/simply furnished comfortable bright rms., #2, 4,

7, 27 & 28 are the best rms., air-conditioned, some also have fans, most rms. have triple-paned windows but request a room on the inside for assurance, mosquito window screens, central heating, bar, no elevator, 3 flrs. Hotel will get all new furniture in '99. *8% rm. discount when you show owners/managers Luciano & Eileen Viti (Canadian) or staff this book and pay in cash.* Wonderful owners who give lots of helpful information. With the train tracks at your back, exit to the left near track #16, cross the street to McDonald's which is near the corner of Via Nazionale, walk up Via Nazionale, turn right onto Via Faenza.

PORTA FAENZA: Via Faenza 77. **Tel:** 055-217975. **Fax:** 055-210101. **Web site:** http://www.emmeti.it/hfaenza.html/
E-mail: hfaenza@mbox.itnet (25 rms., all w/toilet & bath or shower.) 195,000-315,000L (100-162E) single; 215,000-355,000L (110-182E) double; 320,000-460,000L (164-236E) triple; 420,000-620,000L (215-318E) quad. Buffet breakfast (8-10am) is included in the rates & cannot be deducted but can be served in the room (6,500L extra pp). Visa, MC, AX, DC. This higher price 3-star hotel was formerly known as Tony's Apollo Inn. I had to include it because they agreed to give my readers a room discount. English spoken, direct-dial phone, satellite TV w/English channel, beautiful 18th-century renovated bldg. w/elegantly furnished comfortable bright rms., mixture of modern & old Italian architecture, lobby is a work of art, wood-beamed ceilings, stone arches, indoor well, nice flrs., #108, 208 & 303 are the best rms., 2 rms. have handicapped access, double-paned windows, central heating, air-conditioned, bar, elevator, 4 flrs., parking (30,000L per day). *10% rm. discount when you show owners/managers Antonio & Rose Lelli (Canadian) or staff this book.* For directions, see Hotel Mario's.

SEMPIONE: Via Nazionale 15.
Tel: 055-212462/283012. **Fax:** 055-212463.
Web site: http://www.firenzealbergo.it/home/hotelsempione/
E-mail: hotel.sempione@firenzealbergo.it (27 rms., all w/toilet & bath or shower.) 145,000-205,000L (75-105E) single; 205,000-305,000L (105-157E) double; 295,000-375,000L (151-193E) triple. Breakfast (8-10am) is included in the rates & cannot be deducted but can be served in the room. Breakfast is served on the terrace in warm

weather. Visa, MC, AX, DC. English spoken (Ilaria & Neri), direct-dial phone, TV, newly renovated modern hotel w/nicely furnished comfortable rms., they renovated themselves into a 3-star hotel, #19 has a balcony, #44 has view of the Duomo but is noisy, 2 rms. have handicapped access, hair driers, minibars (1999), laundry services, central heating, air-conditioned, double-paned windows, bar, elevator, 5 flrs., parking (45,000-55,000L per day). *5% rm. discount when you show owner/manager Guia Nutini or staff this book.* For directions, see Hotel Kursaal. (Closed Dec.)

STELLA MARY: Via Fiume 17, 2nd fl.
Tel: 055-281877/215694. **Fax:** 055-264206.
Web site: http://www.dex-netcom/XD185/
E-mail: hsm@mail2.dex-netcom (7 rms., 5 w/toilet & bath or shower.) 105,000-195,000L (54-100E) double; 180,000-250,000L (92-128E) triple. Breakfast (8-10am) is included in the rates & can be served in the room (6,500 extra pp) but can be deducted in low season to reduce room price. Visa, MC, AX. English spoken (Victoria & Sirmone), direct-dial phone, TV, wonderful simple hotel w/nicely furnished bright airy large rms., #26 has a balcony, double-paned windows, central heating, bar, elevator, 1fl. They may renovate in '99 to include 2 more bathrooms. Same family manages the beautiful Hotel Annabella in the same bldg. For directions, see Hotel Annabella.

Hotels west of Santa Maria Novella train station
A good area if you are using Florence as a base and need to be close to the train station. Nice during the day, a perfect area for shopping and sightseeing but the station area does attract lots of hookers at night. The nights are quite noisy because of traffic.

ELITE: Via Scala 12, 2nd fl. **Tel/Fax:** 055-215395. (8 rms., 5 w/toilet & bath or shower.) 95,000-115,000L (50-60E) single; 115,000-145,000L (60-74E) double; 180,000-200,000L (92-103E) triple; 200,000-220,000 (103-113E) quad. Breakfast (8-9:30am) at 11,500L pp is not obligatory & can be served in the room. Cash only. English spoken (Nadia & Vittorio), direct-dial phone, beautiful 19th-century bldg. w/nicely furnished comfortable bright airy nice-size pretty rooms, #6 (view) & 8 (large w/no view & no a/c) are the best rms. w/

bathrooms, double-paned windows, central heating, 4 rms. w/air-conditioning, fans, quiet location, no elevator, 2 flrs. Owned/managed by Quinto Maccarini. With the train tracks at your back, exit to the right near track #5, turn right onto Via Santa Caterina from the corner of Piazza Stazione, turn left onto Via Scala.

ESPERANZA: Via Inferno 3. **Tel:** 055-213773. **Fax:** 055-218364. (11 rms., all w/toilet & bath or shower.) 85,000-105,000L (44-54E) single; 125,000-155,000L (64-79E) double; 150,000-200,000L (77-103E) triple; 180,000-220,000 (92-113E) quad. Breakfast (7:30-10:30am) at 6,500-11,500L pp is not obligatory. Visa, MC. English spoken (Claudio), nice charming hotel w/simply furnished comfortable rms., 2 rms. w/balconies, #11 is wonderful w/large balcony, central heating, wonderful quiet location, bar, no elevator, 3 flrs., parking (45,000L per day). *10% rm. discount when you show owner/manager Claudio Castellani or staff this book.* Located one street over from an elegant shopping area. Low-keyed Claudio is wonderful & very accommodating. I stayed here and loved the area & this simple hotel. With the train tracks at your back, exit to the left near track #16, cross the street to McDonald's, cross the street to Piazza Unita Italiana, continue onto Via Panzani, turn right onto Via Rondinelli, follow it as it becomes Via Tornabuoni, turn right onto Via Vigna Nuova, take 1st left to Via Inferno.

FERRETTI: Via Belle Donne 17. **Tel:** 055-2381328. **Fax:** 055-219288. **Web site:** http://www.emmeti.it/Hferretti/
E-mail: pensioneferretti@pronetit (16 rms., 8 w/toilet & bath or shower.) 86,000-105,000L (44-54E) single; 125,000-145,000L (64-74E) double; 166,000-186,000L (85-95E) triple; 185,000-205,000 (95-105E) quad. Breakfast (7:30-10am) is included in the rates & cannot be deducted but can be served in the room (4,500L extra pp). Visa, MC, AX, DC. English spoken (Luciano and Susan, who is South African), direct-dial phone, basic odd-shaped hotel w/simply furnished rms., lots of character, #11 (shower only) & 21 (no bathroom) are the best rms., #1 & 3 have bathrooms but no views, fan, central heating, noisy location, no elevator, 3 flrs. *Owner/Manager Luciano Michel will extend a 10% discount to seniors over 60.* With the train tracks at your back, exit to the left near track #16, cross the street to McDonald's, cross the street to Piazza Unita Italiana, con-

tinue onto Via Panzani, turn right onto Via Rondinelli, turn right onto Via Trebbio which intersects w/Via Belle Donne.

FIRENZE: Piazzale Donati (Via Corso) 4. **Tel:** 055-214203/268301. **Fax:** 055-212370. (62 rms., all w/toilet & bath or shower.) 105,000L (54E) single; 145,000L (74E) double; 200,000L (105E) triple; 245,000L (126E) quad. Breakfast (8-10:30am) is included in the rates & cannot be deducted. Cash only. English spoken (Rosanna & Alex), direct-dial phone, TV, newly renovated American-style no-atmosphere hotel combined w/an older wing, the rooms in the new wing are nicely furnished tiled bright rms. & modern bathrooms., #503 is one of the best rms. w/a view of the Duomo, 3 rms. have handicapped access, hair driers, central heating, quiet location, elevator, 2 flrs. The hotel is not family-owned and it shows. This is a nice hotel but there is nothing warm about it or the people who manage it . With the train tracks at your back, exit to the left near track #16, cross the street to McDonald's, cross the street to Piazza Unita Italiana, continue onto Via Panzani, turn right onto Via Rondinelli, follow it as it becomes Via Tornabuoni, turn left at Piazza Trinita onto Via Porta, which becomes Loggia Rossa, then Via Condotta, turn left onto Via Cerchi, turn right onto Via Corso, Piazzale Donati is located on the right side of Via Corso. Bus #14 or 23 from the train station. Stop: Proconsolo.

GIACOBAZZI: Piazza Santa Maria Novella 24, 4th fl. **Tel:** 055-294679. **Fax:** 055-2654310. (7 rms., 5 w/toilet & bath or shower.) 105,000L (54E) single (no toilets); 160,000-170,000L (82-87E) double. Call for triple rates. Breakfast (7:30-930am) is included in the rates but can be deducted to reduce room price. Visa, MC. No English spoken, direct-dial phone, TV, basic hotel w/simply furnished rms., attracts lots of Italians, central heating, no elevator, 1 fl. (Closed Aug.) With the train tracks at your back, exit to the right near track #5, turn right onto Via Santa Caterina from the corner of Piazza Stazione, turn left onto Via Scala which runs into Piazza Santa Maria Novella.

IL PERSEO: Via Cerretani 1, 4th fl. **Tel:** 055-212504. **Fax:** 055-288377. (19 rms., 7 w/toilet & bath or shower.) 90,000-105,000L (46-54E) single; 130,000-150,000L (67-77E) double; 175,000-195,000L (90-100E) triple; 195,000-225,000L (100-115E) quad. Breakfast (7-10am) is included in the rates & cannot be deducted.

Visa, MC, AX. (extra charge for using credit cards). English spoken (Susan & Louise), direct-dial phone, wonderful old hotel w/nicely furnished bright airy large rms., lots of character & personality, most w/great views of Florence rooftops, belltower and the Duomo, #7, 8, 9 & 10 open up to one garden terrace, #30 has a terrace & bathroom, #36 has a wonderful view & bathroom, #32 has a bathroom, ceiling fans, double-paned windows, central heating, bar, elevator, 2 flrs. Lots of artwork on the walls. Susan who is from New Zealand is an artist. Owned/managed by Susan, Louise & Giacinto Bianchi. With the train tracks at your back, exit to the left near track #16, cross the street to McDonald's, cross the street to Piazza Unita Italiana, continue onto Via Panzani which becomes Via Cerretani.

MONTREAL: Via Scala 43. **Tel:** 055-2382331.
Fax: 055-287491. **E-mail:** hotelmontreal@dada.it (14 rms., 6 w/ toilet & bath or shower.) 90,000L (46E) single; 113,000L (58E) double; 150,000L (77E) triple; 180,000L (92E) quad. No breakfast is served. Cash only. English spoken (Sylvia), direct-dial phone, nice hotel w/simply furnished comfortable pretty rms., #13 w/balcony is the best rm., central heating, double-paned windows, noisy location, no elevator. *5% rm. discount when you show owner/manager Roberto Boccacelli or staff this book.* For directions, see Hotel Elite.

SOLE: Via Sole 8, 3rd fl. **Tel/Fax:** 055-2396094. (8 rms., 2 w/toilet & bath or shower.) 80,000L (41E) single (no toilets); 120,000L (62E) double; 143,000L (73E) triple. No breakfast is served. Cash only. No English spoken, cozy hotel w/simply furnished rms., 1:00am curfew, no elevator, 3 flrs. Anna is a charming owner. In 1999, the hotel will be completely renovated to include direct-dial phone, TV, bathrooms and new furniture in all the rooms. With the train tracks at your back, exit to the right near track #5, turn right onto Via Santa Caterina from the corner of Piazza Stazione, turn left onto Via Scala which becomes Via Sole.

TOSCANA: Via Sole 8, 1st fl. **Tel/Fax:** 055-213156. **E-mail:** h.toscana@data.it (13 rms., all w/toilet & bath or shower.) 80,000-95,000L (41-50E) single; 110,000-165,000L (56-85E) double; 130,000-190,000L (67-97E) triple; 150,000-220,000L (77-113E) quad. Breakfast (8am) at 6,500L pp is not obligatory & can be served in the room (4,500L extra pp). Visa, MC, AX, DC. English spoken, direct-dial phone, satellite TV (1999), nice basic hotel w/simply furnished nice-size rms., double-paned windows, central heating, bar (1999), elevator, 3 flrs. *10% rm. discount when you show owners/ managers Gianpiero & Giancinto Calabro or staff this book.* The 3rd brother lives in Boston. Giancinto has a charming personality. For directions, see Hotel Sole.

TOURIST HOUSE: Via Scala 1. **Tel/Fax:** 055-268675. **Tel:** 055-2678198. (11 rms., all w/toilet & bath or shower.) 85,000-105,000L (44-54E) single; 115,000-140,000L (60-72E) double. Call for triple rates. Breakfast (8-10am) at 9,500L pp is not obligatory & can be served in the room. Visa, MC, AX, DC. Limited English spoken (Emanuela), direct-dial phone, TV, wonderful new hotel w/simply furnished large wood-beamed high ceilings, nice flrs., 1 rm. w/balcony, central heating, ceiling fans, bar, no elevator, 1 fl. *Free breakfast when you show owner/manager Emanuela Albano or staff this book.* This hotel just opened up in Sept. '99. Emanuela also manages Hotel Giappone which is not reviewed in this book. For directions, see Hotel Aprile. Located in front of the Piazza Santa Maria Novella.

VISCONTI: Piazza Ottaviani 1. **Tel/Fax:** 055-213877. (10 rms., 2 w/toilet & bath or shower.) 65,000-77,000L (33-40E) single; 85,000-114,000L (44-59E) double; 110,000-146,000L (56-75E) triple; 120,000-168,000 (62-86E) quad. Children under 10 free. Buffet breakfast (6-11am) is included in the rates & can be served in the room but can be deducted to reduce room price. Breakfast is served on the roof garden in warm weather. Cash only. English spoken (Paolieri), elegant mansion w/comfortable rms., #1 has a balcony & perfect for a family, #10 is nice, 4 rms. have handicapped access, roof garden, central heating, double-paned windows, bar, 5 steps up to elevator, 1 fl., parking. Owned/managed and newly designed by architect Gaetano Manara. With the train tracks at your back, exit to the right near track #5, turn right onto Via Santa Caterina from the corner of Piazza Stazione, turn left onto Via Scala, continue past Piazza Santa Maria Novella, turn right onto Via Fossi which runs through Piazza Ottaviani.

HOTELS OVER $100 A NIGHT FOR TWO

These hotels may have rooms under $100 a night for two because it is low season or the rooms do not have private bathrooms.

APRILE: Via Scala 6. **Tel:** 055-216237/289147. **Fax:** 055-280947. (28 rms., 20 w/toilet & bath or shower.) 135,000-205,000L (69-105E) single; 185,000-275,000L (95-141E) double. Breakfast (7:30-10:30am) is included in the rates & cannot be deducted. Breakfast is served in the garden in warm weather. Visa, MC, AX, DC. English spoken (Antonio), direct-dial phone, TV w/English channel, 15th-century charming palazzo hotel w/old-fashioned furnished comfortable rms., original frescoes on the ceilings, rms. vary greatly in size & decor, #29 is beautiful w/view, the quiet rms. at the back overlook the shady garden, front rooms have double-paned windows, 20 rms. w/air-conditioning & hair driers, minibars, central heating, bar, elevator, 3 flrs., garage parking (30,000-50,000L per day). Every weekday morning a professor gives a 9:30-10:30 free English lecture on history & art of Florence in a beautiful frescoed-ceiling room with Sophia, the black mascot cat, nearby. With the train tracks at your back, exit to the right near track #5, turn right onto Via Santa Caterina from the corner of Piazza Stazione, turn left onto Via Scala.

IL PORCELLINO: Piazza Mercato Nuovo 4. **Tel:** 055-282686. **Fax:** 055-218572. **Tel:** 055-2678198. (6 rms., all w/toilet & bath or shower.) 105,000-135,000L (54-69E) single; 155,000-195,000L (79-100E) double. Breakfast (8-10:30am) is included in the rates & can be served in the room but can be deducted to reduce the room price. Visa, MC, AX, DC. English spoken (Pamela), direct-dial phone, TV, wonderful new hotel w/nicely furnished rms., some overlook the square, nice flrs., central heating, ceiling fans, no elevator, 2 flrs. (Closed sometimes in Aug.)

UNIVERSO: Piazza Santa Maria Novella 20. **Tel:** 055-281951. **Fax:** 055-292335. (43 rms., 31 w/toilet & bath or shower.) 85,000-145,000L (44-74E) single; 135,000-195,000L (69-100E) double; 182,000-260,000L (93-133E) triple; 320,000L (164E) quad. Breakfast (7:30-10am) is included in the rates & cannot be deducted. Visa, MC, AX, DC. English spoken (Antonio), direct-dial phone, 31 rms.

w/TVs, basic hotel w/simply furnished nice-size rms., some rms. are dark, 1 rm. w/balcony & view, front rooms have double-paned windows, elevator, 5 flrs. This hotel is not family-owned.With the train tracks at your back, exit to the right near track #5, turn right onto Via Santa Caterina from the corner of Piazza Stazione, turn left onto Via Scala which runs into Piazza Santa Maria Novella.

VIGNE (Le): Piazza Santa Maria Novella 24, 2nd fl. **Tel:** 055-294449. **Fax:** 2302263. (25 rms., 2 suites, 15 w/toilet & bath or shower.) 105,000-130,000L (54-67E) single; 135,000-205,000L (69-105E) double; 275,000L (141E) triple; 340,000L (174E) quad (suite). Breakfast (7:30-10am) is included in the rates. Visa, MC, AX, DC. English spoken, direct-dial phone, nice hotel w/nicely furnished large rms., high ceilings, rms. on the top floor are the best rms., #110 has a view & bathtub, 6 rms. w/bathtubs, 6 rms. w/air-conditioning, front rms. have double-paned windows, some original frescoes still visible, rooms on the top flrs. great views of the square, no elevator, 2 flrs. New management as of Dec. '98. This hotel is not family-owned. For directions, see Hotel Universo.

Hotels near Piazza Duomo (the Cathedral)
Great location but it is the most expensive part of Florence. It is about a 10-15-minute walk from the train station to this historic center of Florence. From here you can walk to everything. Located here are the magnificent Duomo, Piazza Repubblica, the Jewish Ghetto and Via Tornabuoni (the Fifth Ave. of Florence). Remember the church rings its bells constantly so be prepared for early morning ringing.

BRUNORI: Via Proconsolo 5, 2nd fl. **Tel:** 055-289648. (9 rms., 1 w/toilet & bath or shower.) 103,000-127,000L (53-65E) double; 138,000-172,000L (71-88E) triple. Call for quad rates. Breakfast (8-9am) at 10,500L pp is not obligatory & is served in the room. Cash only. English spoken (Leonardo & Giovanni), basic hotel w/simply furnished large rms., high ceilings, #4 has bathroom & balcony, #12 & 15 have balconies, noisy location, some rms. w/double-paned windows, central heating, no elevator, 2 flrs. Hotel offers lots of helpful information about Florence and tours. Leonardo and Francesca, his Boston wife, enjoy working with tourists. With the train tracks at your back, exit to the left near track #16, cross the street to McDonald's, cross the street to Piazza Unita Italiana, continue onto Via Panzani which becomes Via Cerretani, follow it around the Duomo to the right, it then becomes Via Proconsolo. (Closed for 1 month between Jan. & Feb.)

CRISTINA: Via Condotta 4, 1st fl. **Tel/Fax:** 055-214484. (9 rms., 5 w/toilet & bath or shower.) 55,000-85,000L (28-44E) single; 75,000-125,000L (38-64E) double; 100,000-160,000L (51-82E) triple; 120,000-200,000L (62-103E) quad. Children under 5 free. Breakfast (8:30-10:30am) at 9,500L pp is not obligatory & can be served in the room. Visa, MC, DC. English spoken (Lori), basic hotel w/simply furnished rms., #7 & 5 are the best rms., some rms. have double-paned windows, central heating, no elevator. *10% rm. discount when you show owner/manager Giulia Ghimi or staff this book from Nov.10-Dec. 26 & Jan. 10-March 10.* With the train tracks at your back, exit to the left near track #16, cross the street to McDonald's, cross the street to Piazza Unita Italiana, continue onto Via Panzani, turn right onto Via Rondinelli, follow it as it becomes Via Tornabuoni, turn left at Piazza Trinita onto Via Porta, which becomes Loggia Rossa, then Via Condotta.

DEI MORI: Via Danta Alighieri 2, 1st fl. **Tel/Fax:** 055-211438. **Web site:** http://www.bnb.it/deimori/ **E-mail:** deimori@bnb.it (6 rms., 3 w/toilet & bath or shower.) 105,000-145,000L (54-74E) single; 145,000-175,000L (74-90E) double. Breakfast (8-10am) which offers homemade fruit cakes is included in the rates & cannot be deducted but can be served in the room. Visa, MC. English spoken (Dan & Franco), wonderful charming quaint hotel w/no-smoking beautifully furnished comfortable pretty rms., you can only smoke on his balcony, wonderful atmosphere, access to his refrigerator & kitchen (just clean up after yourself), #3, 6, & 7 have the bathrooms, double-paned windows, central heating, air-conditioned, quiet location, no elevator, 2 flr. E-mail computer service available. Try to reserve ahead for these rooms that are in high demand. *10% rm. discount when you show owners/managers Dan & Franco this book & pay in cash.* A wonderful Australian couple turned me on to this fabulous hotel. With the train tracks at your back, exit to the left near track #16, cross the street to McDonald's, cross the street to Piazza Unita Italiana, continue onto Via Panzani, turn right onto Via Rondinelli, follow it as it becomes Via Tornabuoni, turn left at Piazza Trinita onto Via Porta, which becomes Loggia Rossa, then Via Condotta, turn left onto Via Magazzini which intersects Via Danta Alighieri.

MARIA LUISA DE MEDICI: Via Corso 1, 3rd fl. **Tel/Fax:** 055-280048. (9 rms., 2 w/toilet & bath or shower.) 116,000-144,000L (59-74E) double. Call for triple & quad rates. Buffet breakfast (7-10am) is included in the rates & cannot be deducted but is served in the room. Cash only. English spoken (Evelyn), faded 17th-century palazzo w/large unusually eclectic furnished comfortable large rms., homey atmosphere, high ceilings, #5 & 6 are the best rms., quiet location, central heating, no elevator, 3 flrs. Owned/managed by Evelyn who is from Wales. None of the rooms have views but walking through the lobby of her hotel is like walking through a museum. She has a fabulous collection of 17th-century artwork. With the train tracks at your back, exit to the left near track #16, cross the street to McDonald's, cross the street to Piazza Unita Italiana, continue onto Via Panzani which becomes Via Cerretani.

MAXIM: Via Medici 4/Via Calzaiuoli 11, 3rd fl.
Tel: 055-217474. **Fax:** 055-283729.
Web site: http://www.firenzealbergo.it/home/hotelmaxim/
E-mail: hotmaxim@tin.it (22 rms., all w/toilet & bath or shower.) 135,000L (69E) single; 155,000L (79E) double; 190,000L (97E) triple; 230,000L (118E) quad. Children under 3 free. Breakfast (8-10am) is included in the rates & cannot be deducted. Visa, MC, AX. Limited English spoken (Paolo & Andrea), basic hotel w/old-fashioned simply furnished bright rms., some rooms have double-paned windows, ask for courtyard rooms, central heating, laundry services available, elevator at another entrance at Via Calzaiuoli 11. Owned/managed by Paolo Maioli. With the train tracks at your back, exit to the left near track #16, cross the street to McDonald's, cross the street to Piazza Unita Italiana, continue onto Via Panzani, turn right onto Via Rondinelli, follow it as it becomes Via Tornabuoni, turn left at Via Corsi which becomes Via Campi then Via Tosinghi, turn right on either Via Medici or Via Calzaiuoli.

SAN GIOVANNI: Via Cerretani 2. **Tel:** 055-288385. **Tel/Fax:** 055-213580. (9 rms., 2 w/toilet & bath or shower.) 100,000-125,000L (51-64E) double; 130,000-150,000L (67-79E) triple; 150,000-160,000L (77-82E) quad. Children under 5 free. Breakfast (8:15-11am) at 9,500L pp is not obligatory & is served in the room. Visa, MC, AX, DC. English spoken (Olivia), old faded palazzo hotel w/ large simply furnished bright airy rms., lots of character & history, #2, 4 (frescoes), 5 (frescoes & view) & 9 (bathroom) are the best rms., #8 large rm. w/bathroom, #6 (large & view), panoramic view of the Duomo, high ceilings, fans, lots of American visitors, elevator, 1 fl. Owned/managed by Umberto Zanobetti. For directions, see Hotel Maria Luisa Medici. (Closed Dec.)

HOTELS OVER $100 A NIGHT FOR TWO
BELLETTINI: Via Conti 7. **Tel:** 055-213561. **Fax:** 055-283551. **Web site:** http://www.firenze.net/hotelbellettini/ **E-mail:** hotel.bellettini@dada.it (27 rms., 23 w/toilet & bath or shower.) 130,000-155,000L (67-79E) single; 175,000-205,000L (90-105E) double; 275,000L (141E) triple; 340,000L (174E) quad. Children under 10 free. Buffet breakfast which offers homemade fruit cakes (7:30-10am) is included in the rates & cannot be deducted but can be served in the room (4,500L extra pp). Visa, MC, AX, DC. English spoken (Claudio), direct-dial phone, 11 rms. w/TVs, 15th-century wonderful charming palazzo w/nicely furnished nice-size airy bright pretty rms., modern bathrooms, hotel has stained-glass windows, lots of character & history, painted ceilings, top-floor rooms, #44 (balcony) & 45 (view of Duomo & wonderful sunrise) are the best rms., #28 is large w/a view, #24 is considered the worst w/a private bathroom in the hall but it is nice, double-paned windows, central heating, air-conditioned, bar, elevator, 2 flrs. *Depending on the season you can get a 5-10% rm. discount when you show owner/ manager Cini Delli or staff this book.* With the train tracks at your back, exit to the left near track #16, cross the street to McDonald's, cross the street to Piazza Unita Italiana, continue onto Via Panzani which becomes Via Cerretani, turn left onto Via Conti.

CENTRALE: Via Conti 3, 2nd fl. **Tel:** 055-215761. **Fax:** 055-215216. (18 rms., 12 w/toilet & bath or shower.) 176,000-195,000L

(90-100E) double. Call for triple rates. Buffet breakfast (8-10am) is included in the rates & cannot be deducted but can be served in the room (extra cost pp). Visa, MC, AX, DC. English spoken (Franco), direct-dial phone, TV, 14th-century charming palazzo w/nicely furnished comfortable large bright pretty rms., old-world ambiance, #3 is the best rm., 1 rm. has handicapped access, some rms. w/views of Medici chapels, central heating, bar, elevator, 2 flrs. Same owners also manage Hotel Liana not reviewed in this book. *5% rm. discount when you show Franco or staff this book.* For directions, see Hotel Bellettini.

Hotels near Piazza San Marco
A nice long walk from the train station. From here you are within a 15-minute walk to most sites. It is right around the corner from the Accademia where you can view Michelangelo's *David.*

GINORI: Via Ginori 24. **Tel:** 055-218615/210454. **Tel/Fax:** 055-211392. (7 rms., all w/toilet & bath or shower.) 135,000-175,000L (69-90E) double; 200,000-236,000L (103-121E) triple; 220,000-270,000L (113-138E) quad. Children under 4 free. Breakfast (8-10am) is included in the rates but can be deducted to reduce room price. Buffet breakfast can be served in the room at extra cost of 6,500L pp. Visa, MC, AX. English spoken (Simon & Daniela), direct-dial phone, TV w/English channel, wonderful hotel w/comfortable nicely furnished bright modern airy pretty rms., #28 & 32 are the best rms., double-paned windows, central heating, air-conditioned, bar, no elevator, 3 flrs. Popular with students. *5% rm. discount when you show owner/manager Daniela Nerozzi or staff this book.* With the train tracks at your back, exit to the left near track #16, cross the street to McDonald's which is near the corner of Via Nazionale, walk up Via Nazionale about 5 blocks, turn right onto Via Guelfa, turn right onto Via Ginori. Bus #17. Stop: Via Cavour.

SAMPAOLI: Via San Gallo 14. **Tel:** 055-284834. **Tel/Fax:** 055-282448. (12 rms., 6 w/toilet & bath or shower.) 75,000-115,000L (38-60E) single; 95,000-135,000L (50-69E) double; 110,000-140,000L (56-72E) triple; 140,000-180,000L (72-92E) quad. Children under 4 free. No breakfast served. Cash only. English spoken

(Floriana), direct-dial phone, nice hotel w/simply furnished bright airy rms., lots of Italian ambiance, #7 has a terrace, refrigerators on each fl., this hotel has 5 public bathrooms for the 6 rooms that don't have private bathrooms, double-paned windows, central heating, no elevator, 2 flrs. Owned/managed by Santa Canestrini. With the train tracks at your back, exit to the left near track #16, cross the street to McDonald's which is near the corner of Via Nazionale, walk up Via Nazionale about 5 blocks, turn right onto Via Guelfa for about 3 blocks, turn left onto Via San Gallo.

SAN MARCO: Via Cavour 50, 3rd fl. **Tel:** 055-281851. **Tel/Fax:** 055-284235. (14 rms., 12 w/toilet & bath or shower.) 95,000-115,000L (50-60E) single; 125,000-165,000L (64-85E) double; 220,000L (113E) triple; 280,000L (144E) quad. Breakfast (8-9am) is included in the rates & cannot be deducted. Visa, MC. English spoken (Alessia), nice hotel w/simply furnished bright airy rms., #9 is a huge w/terrace, #3 is perfect for a family, #2 is cute, central heating, noisy location, no elevator, 3 flrs. Note: If you are paying for your room by credit card, make sure Alessia is around because her parents don't know how to use the machine. *10% rm. discount when you show Alessia or her family this book from Nov.-April excluding holidays.* With the train tracks at your back, exit to the left near track #16, cross the street to McDonald's which is near the corner of Via Nazionale, walk up Via Nazionale about 5 blocks, turn right onto Via Guelfa for about 4 blocks, turn left onto Via Cavour. Buses #1, 6, 17, 7 & 20 go to Piazza San Marco from train station, walk down Via Cavour from San Marco square. Located around the corner from the Accademia museum.

TINA: Via San Gallo 31. **Tel:** 055-483519. **Fax:** 055-483593. (16 rms., 2 w/toilet & bath or shower.) 110,000-125,000L (56-64E) double; 130,000L (67E) triple (no toilets); 145,000L (74E) quad (no toilets). No breakfast is served. Cash only. English spoken (Lorenzo & Piero), 50% rms. w/direct-dial phone, high ceilings, simple hotel w/modern furnished rms.& homey atmosphere, #29 & 28 have bathrooms, front rooms have double-paned windows, central heating, no elevator, 1 fl. Owned/managed by Lorenzo Aiello. For directions, see Hotel Sampaoli.

HOTEL OVER $100 A NIGHT FOR TWO

CENTRO: Via Ginori 17. **Tel:** 055-2302901/2302902. **Fax:** 055-212706. **Web site:** http://www.travelita.com/hotelcentro/ **E-mail:** centro@pronet.it (16 rms., 14 w/toilet & bath or shower.) 145,000L (74E) single; 205,000L (105E) double. Call for triple & quad rates. Buffet breakfast (7:30-11am) is included in the rates & can be served in the room (11,500 extra pp) but can be deducted to reduce room price. Visa, MC, AX. English spoken (Rudina), direct-dial phone, satellite TV w/English channel, renovated palazzo contemporary hotel w/large modern rms. & new bathrooms, 1 rm. w/ balcony, fans, rooms in front have double-paned windows, central heating, bar, no elevator except from the 2nd fl to the 3rd fl., 3 flrs. They are planning to renovate in '99 to have elevator go to the ground fl. Owned/managed by Andrea Vendali. Located close to Mercato San Lorenzo. With the train tracks at your back, exit to the left near track #16, cross the street to McDonald's which is near the corner of Via Nazionale, walk up Via Nazionale about 5 blocks, turn right onto Via Guelfa, turn right onto Via Ginori. Bus #17. Stop: Via Cavour.

Hotels near the Arno river or Ponte Vecchio

A good 30-minute walk from the train station. Great location; from here you can walk to everything, including historic Florence and Pitti Palace.

BRETAGNA: Lungarno Corsini 6. **Tel:** 055-289618. **Fax:** 055-289619. **Web site:** dbweb.agora.stm.it/market/bretagna/ **E-mail:** hotelpens.bretagna@agora.stm.it (18 rms., 8 w/toilet & bath or shower.) 95,000-115,000L (50-60E) single; 115,000-180,000L (60-92E) double; 150,000-240,000L (77-123E) triple; 180,000-260,000L (92-133E) quad. Breakfast (8am) is included in the rates & cannot be deducted. Visa, MC, AX, DC. English spoken (Antonio & Maura), direct-dial phone, satellite TV, faded old-world 15th-century palazzo hotel w/simple old-fashioned furnished rms., lots of art on the walls, great view of the Arno river from the balcony of the sitting rm., high ceilings, #21 & 29 are the best rms. but #34 has a view of the river, #30 is a great family rm., bar, elevator to hotel, 3 flrs. E-mail computer services available. *5% rm. discount when you show owner/manager Antonio Castaldini or staff this book.* Located on the right bank of the Arno river near the corner of Ponte San Trinita and Corsini. It is a 20-minute walk on a cobbled street from the train station. With the train tracks at your back, exit to the left near track #16, cross the street to McDonald's, cross the street to Piazza Unita Italiana, continue onto Via Panzani, turn right onto Via Rondinelli, follow it as it becomes Via Tornabuoni, walk to the water, turn right onto Lungarno Corsini. Taxi 18,000L.

HOTEL OVER $100 A NIGHT FOR TWO
ALESSANDRA: Borgo S.S. Apostoli 17, 2nd fl. **Tel:** 055-283438/ 217830. **Fax:** 055-210619.
E-mail: htlalessandra@mclink.it (25 rms., 16 w/toilet & bath or shower.) 115,000-175,000L (59-89E) single; 175,000-235,000L (90-121E) double; 230,000-305,000L (118-157E) triple; 275,000-345,000L (141-177E) quad. Children under 3 free. Breakfast (7:30-9:30am) is included in the rates & cannot be deducted but can be served in the room. Visa, MC, AX. English spoken (Andrea & Anna), direct-dial phone, 15 rms. w/TVs, 16th-century palazzo w/a mixture of beautifully furnished large rms., lots of character, modern bright bathrooms, lots of character & wood-beamed high ceilings, #7 & 16 are the best rms., #11 is magnificent, central heating, 15 rms. w/air-conditioning (cost extra), walk 1 flight up to elevator, 3 flrs. Owned/managed by Arnaldo & Andrea Gennarini. With the train tracks at your back, exit to the left near track #16, cross the street to McDonald's, cross the street to Piazza Unita Italiana, continue onto Via Panzani, turn right onto Via Rondinelli, follow it as it becomes Via Tornabuoni, turn left as you go through Piazza San Trinita onto Borgo S.S. Apostoli.Taxi 18,000L. (Closed Dec. 9-27.)

Hotels in Oltrarno (south of the Arno river)
Across the river between the Pitti Palace and the Ponte Vecchio. A great local neighborhood with not a lot of budget choices.

HOTEL OVER $100 A NIGHT FOR TWO
These hotels may have rooms under $100 a night for two because it is low season or the rooms do not have private bathrooms.

SCALETTA (La): Via Guicciardini 13, 2nd fl. **Tel:** 055-283028/ 214255. **Fax:** 055-289562.
Web site: http://www.italyhotel.com/firenze/lascaletta/
E-mail: lascaletta.htl@dada.it (13 rms., 11 w/toilet & bath or shower.) 75,000-155,000L (38-79E) single; 155,000-220,000L (79-113E) double; 170,000-250,000L (87-128E) triple. Call for quad rates. Buffet breakfast (8-9:30am) is included in the rates & cannot be deducted but can be served in the room (8,500L extra pp). Visa, MC. English spoken (Manfredo), satellite TV on request (6,500 extra per day), direct-dial phone, wonderful elegant historical palazzo w/old-fashioned furnished comfortable rms., some have marble fireplaces, rooms on the 2nd flr. are larger, have better views & high ceilings, #21 has a view of the rooftops, front rooms have double-paned windows, two rooftop terraces w/great panoramic views where you can enjoy a drink but no food, hair driers, central heating, bar, elevator, 3 flrs. Check to see if the charming Manfredo is cooking one of his fabulous delicious dinners (approx. 30,000L pp). Located a block south, off the river between Piazza de Pitti and the Ponte Vecchio near the American Express office. With the train tracks at your back, exit to the left near track #16, cross the street to McDonald's, cross the street to Piazza Unita Italiana, continue onto Via Panzani, turn right onto Via Rondinelli, follow it as it becomes Via Tornabuoni, walk to the water, turn left onto Lungarno Acciaioli to Ponte Vecchio, cross over the bridge onto Via Guicciardini.Taxi 18,000L.

SORELLE BANDINI: Piazza Santo Spirito 9, 2nd fl. **Tel:** 055-215308. **Fax:** 055-282761. (13 rms., 5 w/toilet & bath or shower.) 150,000-195,000L (77-100E) double; 200,000-250,000L (103-128E) triple; 240,000-295,000L (123-151E) quad. Singles are available low season. Breakfast is included in the rates. Cash only. English spoken (Mimmo), faded 15th-century palazzo hotel w/old-world-type furnished musty rms., romantic ambiance but hotel could use more elbow grease on some of the furniture, great view from balcony, rooms vary quite a lot, some are large bright & have marble fireplaces, high ceilings, others are dark, quiet location, elevator. Hotel attracts art students. With the train tracks at your back, exit to the left near track #16, cross the street to McDonald's, cross the street to Piazza Unita Italiana, continue onto Via Panzani, turn right onto Via Rondinelli, follow it as it becomes Via Tornabuoni, walk to the water over Ponte San Trinita, continue straight on Via Maggio, turn right onto Via Mazzetta into Piazza Santo Spirito.

Still unable to find a room? Try Informazioni Turistiche Alberghiere (ITA) hotel association booth next to the *farmacia* opposite track #16 inside the SMN train station, between platform 9 and 10. They charge a commission. Hrs.: Daily 9am-9pm.

Complaints: For any disputes over prices, tourists may present a documented complaint to the Tourist Council Department for Province, Via Cavour 37. **Tel:** 055-27601.

MONEY
Most of the banks give great rates but check commission rates. Hrs.: Mon.-Fri. 8:20am-1:20pm & 2:45pm-3:45pm. Some banks are open on Saturdays. Check out the exchange rates at the post office. Central Post Office: Via Pellicceria 3. **Tel:** 055-211127. Hrs.: Mon.-Fri.: 8:15am-6pm. Located off the southwest corner of Piazza Repubblica. Walk up the stairs to the 2nd fl.

LAUNDROMATS (Lavanderia)
Daily: 8am-10pm. 13,000L for 14 lbs. of wash, dry and soap. Self-service.

Near the train station
Wash & Go: Via Guelfa 55R.
Wash & Dry: Via Scala 52/54R.
Wash & Go: Via Scala 30R.
Tintoria La Serena: Via Scala 30R.
Onda Blu: Via Guelfa 22aR/55R.
Wash & Dry Lavarapido: Via Nazionale 129R.
Lavanderia Superlava Splended: Via Sole 29/R. Hrs.: Mon.-Fri.: 8:30am-7:30pm.

Wash & Dry: Via Servi 105R. Located north of the Duomo.
Wash & Dry Lavarapido: Via Serragli 87R. Located in the Oltrarno district.

FLORENCE

Wash & Dry Lavarapido: Viale Morgagni 21R.
Wash & Dry Lavarapido: Via G.P. Orsini 39R.

RESTAURANTS

Please check page 20 for my criteria for selecting restaurants.

BENVENUTO (Da): Via Mosca 16R. **Tel:** 055-214833. Mon.-Sat. Hrs.: Lunch 12pm-2:30pm; dinner 7pm-10:30pm. Closed Sun. A full dinner complete with a liter of house wine and dessert will cost about 80,000L for two people. Visa, MC, AX. Wonderful little Florentine favorite that serves great food. The minute you arrive in Florence make reservations at this family-style three-room casual trattoria. This place is booked weeks in advance. The *risotto nero* is to die for. Owner/waiter Giuseppe who speaks English will take care of you. *Show Giuseppe this book and he will give you a complimentary after-dinner drink.* From the Duomo walk down Via Calzaioli to Piazza Signoria, walk through the square, turn left on Via Ninna near Palazzo Vecchio, which becomes Via Neri. Located on the corner of Via Neri & Via Mosca.

BUZZINO: Via Leoni 8R. **Tel:** 055-2398013. Tues.-Sun. Hrs.: Lunch 12pm-3pm; dinner 7pm-10:30pm. Closed Mon. Visa, MC, AX. About 35,000L pp including a 10% gratuity which is added to your check. A cozy 14-table restaurant that has been managed by the same family for 21 years and serves delicious food & homemade desserts. If you can't decide which dessert, ask for a combination. *Show owner/ waiter Giuseppe Angeli or son/waiter Giovanni this book and they will give you a complimentary vin santo & biscuits.* Giuseppe speaks English. From the Duomo walk down Via Calzaioli to Piazza Signoria, walk through the square, turn left on Via Ninna near Palazzo Vecchio, turn left on Via Leoni.

MILAN (Milano)
Lombardy, zip code 20121
Area code 39, city code 02

Orientation: Milan makes a great base for doing day trips to Lake Como but it is not the best city for low-cost hotels. It is more a convention city than a tourist city so many of the hotels are booked most of the time for some kind of event or convention. That is the reason I included some hotels that are priced higher than $99 a night for two. **Milan Stazione Central** is the main train terminal located in **Piazza Duca d'Aosta**. It is 3 miles northeast of the **Duomo** (historic center of Milan) where most of the attractions are located. To get to the Duomo from this area, exit the station opposite the large information office, turn left onto **Piazza Luigi Savoia**, make a right onto **Via Pergolesi** which goes through **Piazza Caiazza**, continue on Via Pergolesi, right onto **Corso Buenos Aires**, walk down Corso Buenos Aires which becomes **Corso Venezia**, then **Corso Vittorio Emanuele II** all the way to the Duomo. You can also catch bus #60 to the Duomo.

You have two choices when it comes to the hotels in Milan. If you are looking for the typical charming Italian hotel with old-fashioned elegance and character, then go right to the hotels listed near the Duomo. However, you will pay more because they are conveniently located near the Duomo or the historic area. Most of the affordable hotels in the city are usually renovated hotels with simply furnished rooms, no ambiance and at least a 15-minute walk to the Duomo.

Milan's Tourist Information Centers (APT)
Web sites for Milan: http://www.rcs.it/nmailano and http://www.hellomilano.it/ **1.)** Main APT office, Piazza Duomo, "Palazzo di Turismo," Via Marconi 1 **Tel:** 02-72524300. **Fax:** 02-72524350. Located to the right as you face the church. Hrs.: Mon.-Fri. 8:30am-7pm, Sat. & Sun. 9am-1pm. & 2-5pm. Longer hrs. in season. **2.)** Branch office: Stazione Central **Tel:** 02-72524360. Hrs.: Mon.-Sat. 9am-6pm, Sun. 9am-12pm. & 1:30-6pm. Located on the top level facing away from the tracks.

TRANSPORTATION TO AND FROM AIRPORT

Malpensa Airport to Central Train Station/Bus Terminal:
Web site: http://www.seaaeroportimilano.it/ Airpullman airport shuttle buses leave every half hour in the morning until 12noon and every hour until late evening. 6:30am-9pm. Cost is 15,000L pp. The trip takes about an hour to Milan's Stazione Central. Bus tickets can be purchased at the shuttle bus ticket office at the airport. When you exit through the doors from customs, walk straight, then go to your right and walk to the ticket office where you buy your shuttle bus tickets to the Central station. If you don't have lire or euros, walk from the ticket window straight down to the Banco Milano where they have excellent exchange rates and charge a 5,000L commission charge. When you get your shuttle ticket walk outside to the shuttle stop. Make sure you get in the right line that says "Centrale Station" which is literally in front of the taxi line. **Central Train Station/ Bus Terminal to Malpensa Airport:** STAM airport shuttle buses leave from the east side of the station to Malpensa Airport. A shuttle bus also runs between Malpensa airport and Piazza Castello (**Metro:** Cairioli), near the Duomo. Buy your ticket before you board the bus unless the ticket office is closed. **Taxi:** Malpensa airport to center is approximately 130,000L. **Linate Airport:** STAM airport shuttle buses depart from the east side of Central Train station to bus terminal Piazza Luigi Savoia every 20 min. to 1/2 hr. from 7am-9pm, and until 11:30pm from Linate airport to the train station. The trip takes about 20 min. to Milan's Stazione Central. 5,000L pp. Malpensa Express train **Web site:** http://www.malpensaexpress.com/

CIT Railway Office

You can buy train tickets at the CIT office in Galleria Vittorio Emanuele. **Tel:** 02-86370228. Hrs.: Mon.-Sat. 9am-7pm. If you plan to do a lot of traveling by train in Italy, purchase the invaluable *InTreno Tutt'Italia* which is the Ferrovie's official train timetable. Available at most newsstands at the train stations. Worth every penny of the 8,000L if you don't want to wait in those long train information lines.

Low season June-Aug.; high season March-May, Sept. & Oct.

Hotels Near the Duomo
Great location. Taxis run about 25,000L from train station to these

hotels. These hotels are in high demand so I suggest you reserve a room in advance.

ANTICA LOCANDA MERCANTI: Via San Tomaso 6, 2nd fl. Milano. **Tel.** 02-8054080. **Fax:** 02-8054090. **E-mail:** locanda@iol.it (16 rms., all w/toilet & bath or shower.) 185,000-315,000L (95-162E) single/double; 270,000-320,000L (138-164E) triple. Small buffet breakfast (7:30-10am) at 13,500L pp including freshly squeezed o.j. is not obligatory & is served in the room. Visa, MC, AX. English spoken (Bruce or Greta), direct-dial phone, TV upon request, antique 19th-century charming hotel w/wonderfully furnished comfortable small rms. & small bathrooms, #11, 12, 13 & 14 are the most expensive rms. w/large terraces, air-conditioning & minibars, double-paned windows, central heating, elevator. All the rooms have names so the Baronessa & Agnese are the best rooms but range from 240,000-270,000L for two. For lower-price rooms, ask for the Dei Belgioso or others like it which cost about 200,000L for two. The newly re-opened renovated hotel (1997) is not family-owned but is managed by Ms. Ora Paola, Bruce (husband) & Alex (son). Fresh flowers are put into each room every day. Take Malpensa airport bus to Piazza Cairoli. I know this hotel is a little above the price points I cover but many people wrote me about this place. I decided to include it because it was such a wonderful friendly hotel and they wanted very much to be in the book. You will enjoy spending your money on your room if you are looking for a true Italian experience. **Metro:** Carioli. From metro stop, exit onto Via Dante, walk down Via Dante, make a left onto San Tomaso, don't look for an outside sign on the 2nd block-there isn't any. Just look for the large green doors on the left. Walk up the stairs to the elevator.

LONDON: Via Rovello 3.
Tel. 02-72020166. **Tel/Fax:** 02-8057037.
Web site: http://www.traveleurope.com/hotellondon.htm/ **E-mail:** hotel.london@traveleurope.it (29 rms., 25 w/toilet & bath or shower.) 135,000-155,000L (69-79E) single; 195,000-235,000L (100-121E) double; 220,000-280,000L (113-144E) triple. Breakfast (7:30-10:30am) at 13,500L pp is not obligatory & can be served in the room (16,500L pp). Visa, MC. English spoken, direct-dial phone, satellite TV w/English channel, overpriced charming hotel w/nice-

size bright nicely furnished comfortable modern rms., #8 & 28 (2 balconies) are the best rms., 6 rms. w/balconies, central heating, air-conditioned, quiet location, bar, elevator, 4 flrs. *Free breakfast when you show owner/manager Francesco Gambino or staff this book.* **Metro:** Cairoli. From metro stop, exit onto Via Dante, walk down Via Dante, make a left on San Tomaso, left onto Via Rovello. 10-minute walk from the Duomo. (Closed Aug. & Dec. 23-Jan. 3.)

SPERONARI: Via Speronari 4. Tel. 02-86461125. **Fax:** 02-72003178. (32 rms., 19 w/toilet & bath or shower.) 85,000-105,000L (44-54E) single; 125,000-165,000L (64-85E) double; 150,000-220,000L (77-113E) triple; 270,000L (138E) quad. Breakfast (8am-12pm) at 8,500L pp is not obligatory. Visa, MC. Limited English spoken, direct-dial phone, TV, newly renovated hotel w/simply furnished bright comfortable nice-size rms. & nice bathrooms, 9 rms. w/balconies & 1 w/terrace, #30 (terrace) & 35 are the best rms., #14 is small but has balcony & large bathroom, #15, 16 & 18 have balconies, tiled flrs., central heating, ceiling fans, no elevator, 5 flrs. Great location one block from the Duomo. *Discount on room when you show owner/manager Paolo Isoni or staff this book.* **Metro:** Duomo. With your back to the Duomo, walk straight ahead, look for the Auto-Grill restaurant on Via Torino, walk down Via Torino, Via Speronari is the 1st left. The Isoni family will offer you a free cappuccino upon your arrival.

Hotels in between the train station and the Duomo
The accommodations in this area are better priced than those near the Duomo but are a 20-minute walk to the sights. I don't list any hotels that are in the neighborhood of the Milan Central train station which can be seedy and colorful at night even though it is still reasonably safe. All the hotels listed in this section are at least a 15-minute or more walk from the train station so I suggest you taxi (12,000L) from the station to the hotels.

ARNO: Via Lazzaretto 17, 4th fl. **Tel:** 02-6705509/6706373. (9 rms., 3 w/toilet & bath or shower.) 85,000L (44E) single (no toilets); 113,000-135,000L (58-69E) double. Call for triple & quad rates. Breakfast (8:30-9:30am) at 11,500L pp is not obligatory & can be served in the room. Visa, MC, AX, DC. English spoken, direct-dial phone, basic hotel w/nice-size simply furnished bright airy rms., double-paned windows (street side only), central heating, bar, elevator, 1 fl. Hotel is on the same floor as Hotel Eva which run by the same manager. *10% rm. discount when you show owner Giovanni Cammarano, manager Lami or staff this book.* **Metro:** Porto Venezia. From metro stop, walk down Viale Vittorio Veneto for about 4 blocks, make a right on Via Lazzaretto. When you walk through the door, make a quick right to the elevator.

AURORA: Corso Buenos Aires 18, 1st fl. **Tel:** 02-2047960. **Fax:** 02-2049285. (16 rms., 14 w/toilet & bath or shower.) 75,000-100,000L (38-51E) single; 125,000-145,000L (64-74E) double; 160,000-190,000L (82-97E) triple. Call for quad rates. Breakfast (8-10am) at 6,500L pp is not obligatory & can be served in the room. Visa, MC, AX, DC. English spoken (Donato Casello), direct-dial phone, TV, nice hotel w/simply furnished modern large comfortable airy bright rms., #14, 10 & 11 are the best rms., double-paned windows, some rms. w/balconies, 1 rm. has a minibar, 1 rm. has handicapped access, noisy location, elevator, 1 fl., parking (25,000L per day). *5% rm. discount when you show owner/manager Donato or staff this book.* My husband and I stayed here on one of our trips. Donato is very helpful and speaks great English. He can probably answer all your questions. You will be pleasantly surprised with the rooms once you get past the basic outside appearance of the building. Walk through the open courtyard to the elevator. To walk from the train station, turn left from Piazza Duca d'Aosta, in front of the train station, onto Via Vitruvi which intersects Corso Buenos Aires (15-minute walk). Great neighborhood. Corso Buenos Aires is a major blvd. with lots of activity. Donato's son Gerry co-manages the Hotel Promessi Sposi. **Metro:** Porta Venezia. From metro stop, walk up Corso Buenos Aires with the even numbers going up.

CASA MIA: Viale Vittorio Veneto 30, 1st fl. **Tel:** 02-6575249/6552228. **Fax:** 02-6552228. (15 rms., all w/toilet & bath or shower.) 115,000-155,000L (60-79E) single; 155,000-165,000L (79-85E) double; 220,000L (113E) triple. Buffet breakfast is included in the rates & can be served in the room but can be deducted in low season to reduce room price. Visa, MC. English spoken (Fausto), direct-dial phone, TV, cozy newly renovated hotel w/plainly furnished comfortable rms., double-paned windows, bar, no elevator, 1 fl. Owned/managed by Fausto Loguercio. **Metro:** Repubblici. Viale Vittorio Veneto runs between the metro stations Repubblici and Porto Venezia. The hotel is across the street from a park. This is a great hotel with good prices next to a metro stop that is fine during the day, but the neighborhood atmosphere next to metro Repubblici gradually changes very late at night to attract drug dealers and hookers.

EVA: Via Lazzaretto 17, 4th fl. **Tel:** 02-6706093/6705907. (10 rms., 2 w/toilet & bath or shower.) 85,000L (44E) single (no toilets); 113,000-135,000L (58-69E) double. Call for triple & quad rates. Breakfast (8:30-9:30am) at 11,500L pp is not obligatory & can be served in the room. Visa, MC, AX, DC. English spoken, direct-dial phone, basic hotel w/nice-size simply furnished bright airy large rms., double-paned windows (street side only), central heating, bar, elevator, 1 fl. Hotel is on the same floor as Hotel Eva run by the same manager. *10% rm. discount when you show owner/manager Lami Marinbua or staff this book.* **Metro:** Porto Venezia. For directions, see Hotel Arno.

KENNEDY: Via Tunisia 6, 6th fl. **Tel:** 02-29400934. **Fax:** 02-29401253. (12 rms., 2 w/toilet & bath or shower.) 85,000L (44E) single (no toilets); 95,000-135,000L (50-69E) double; 160,000L (82E) triple; 180,000L (92E) quad. Breakfast (8-9am) at 9,500L pp is not obligatory & can be served in the room. Visa, MC, AX, DC. Limited English spoken (Rafaello), direct-dial phone, homey hotel w/simply furnished rms., #21 & 13 are the best rms. because they both have private baths & balconies, #14 also has a balcony and by Jan. '99 will have a private bath as well as #16 & 18, central heating, bar, tiny elevator. *Discount on room when you show owners/managers Rafaello & Ivana or staff this book.* Located in the same bldg. as Hotel San Tomaso. To walk from the train station, walk straight through Piazza Duca d'Aosta, in front of the train station, walk down Via Pisani for about 5 blocks, make a left onto Via Tunisia. **Metro:** Porto Venezia. From the metro stop, walk up Buenos Aires (odd numbers going up), turn left onto Via Tunisia.

PROMESSI SPOSI: Piazzale Oberdan 12 **Tel**. 02-29513661. **Fax:** 02-29404182. **Web site:** http://www.milanoin.it/ **E-mail:**

Prosposi@tin.it (33 rms., all w/toilet & bath or shower.) 95,000-115,000L (50-60E) single; 155,000-185,000L (79-95E) double; 200,000-220,000L (103-113E) triple. Call for quad rates. Buffet breakfast (7-10:30am) at 11,500L pp is not obligatory & can be served in the room. Visa, MC, AX, DC. English spoken (Gerry), direct-dial phone, satellite TV w/English channel, newly remodeled hotel w/ plainly furnished modern comfortable rms., #104 (balcony), 222 & 332 (corner rm.) are the best rms., 10 rms. w/balconies, rms. in front are sunny and noisy, rms. in back are quiet and darker, hair drier, double-paned windows, central heating, air-conditioned, bar, garden, elevator, 3 flrs. *5% rm. discount when you show owners/managers Donato & Gerry Castella or staff this book.* **Metro:** Porta Venezia. Located right on the square off Corso Buenos Aires in front of the metro stop. Gerry's father Donato manages the Hotel Aurora.

SAN TOMMASO: Via Tunisia 6, 3rd fl. **Tel/Fax:** 02-29514747. **Web site:** http://web.tin.it/hotelsantomaso/ **E-mail:** hotelsantomaso@tin.it (12 rms., 1 w/toilet & bath or shower.) 85,000L (44E) single (no toilets); 110,000-135,000L (56-69E) double; 140,000L (72E) triple; 180,000L (92E) quad. Breakfast (8-10am) at 9,500L pp is not obligatory & can be served in the room. English spoken (Christina & Francesco), direct-dial phone, TV, basic hotel w/simply furnished nice comfortable rms., tiled flrs., 6 rms. w/showers, 4 rms. w/terraces, #106 (only room w/private bath), #104 (shower & terrace) & 112 (shower & huge terrace) are the best rms., central heating, bar, tiny elevator, 1 fl. Computer e-mail service available for 7,500L per hr. *5% rm. discount when you show owner/manager Francesco or staff this book.* Located in the same bldg. as Hotel Kennedy. For directions, see Hotel Kennedy. **Metro:** Porto Venezia.

SERENA: Via Boscovich 59. **Tel:** 02-29404483. **Fax:** 02-29404958. **Web site:** http://web.tin.it/hotelserena/ **E-mail:** hotelserena@tin.it (39 rms., all w/toilet & bath or shower.) 115,000L (60E) single; 175,000L (90E) double; 220,000L (113E) triple; 270,000L (138E) quad. Buffet breakfast (7-10am) is included in the rates & cannot be deducted. Visa, MC, AX, DC. Limited English spoken (Isabel), direct-dial phone, TV, basic friendly hotel w/simply furnished airy rms., front rms. are brighter than the quiet dark rms. in the back, 19 rms.

w/balconies, #7, 23 & 34 (balcony) are the best rms., central heating, bar, no elevator, 4 flrs. *10% rm. discount when you show owner/ manager Enrico Nicodemo or staff this book.* **Metro:** Lima. Located one block off Corso Buenos Aires.

SIENA: Via Lazzaretto 6. **Tel/Fax:** 02-29516108. **Tel/Fax:** 02-29514615. (15 rms., all w/toilet & bath or shower.) 85,000-115,000L (44E) single; 115,000-155,000L (60-79E) double; 170,000-220,000L (87-113E) triple. Breakfast (7am-12pm) is included in the rates & can be served in the room. Visa, MC, AX, DC. No English spoken, direct-dial phone, TV, basic hotel w/simply furnished small dark rms. & tiled flrs., 1 rm. w/balcony, #24 is the best rm., central heating, double-paned windows, bar, no elevator, 1 flr., parking (40,000L per day). *10% rm. discount when you show owner/manager Giuseppe Loguercio, Arcanuelo or staff this book.* **Metro:** Porto Venezia. From metro stop, walk down Viale Vittorio Veneto for about 4 blocks, make a right on Via Lazzaretto. Hotel is on the corner of Via Castaldi and Via Lazzaretto.

Hotels away from the tourist area
These hotels are not convenient to either the train station or the Duomo. They are located in a safe, residential neighborhood and you will have to taxi (18,000L) or metro to the Duomo unless you don't mind a 40-minute walk
.

CA' GRANDE: Via Porpora 87. **Tel:** 02-26145295/26144001. (20 rms., 12 w/toilet & bath or shower.) 75,000-95,000L (38-50E) single; 105,000-125,000L (54-64E) double; 150,000L (77E) triple. Breakfast (7:30-10:30am) is included in the rates & can be served in the room but can be deducted to reduce room price. English spoken (Fadil & Iole who are wonderful young owners), direct-dial phone, TV, nice hotel w/simply furnished rms. & modern bathrooms, 3 rms. w/ balconies, #27 & 36 are the best rms., rms. on the inside are quieter than the street side, central heating, double-paned windows, elevator, 3 flrs. *Discount when you show owners/managers Fadil & Iole Sullini or staff this book.* **Metro:** Loreto. Tram #33-Direction Lambrate, near the McDonald's at the train station gets you closer to this hotel than the metro. Ask for stop Porpora-Ampere. (Closed 2 wks. mid-Aug.)

PACE (La): Via Catalani 69. **Tel/Fax:** 02-2619700. (20 rms., all w/ toilet & bath or shower.) 105,000L (54E) single; 125,000-165,000L (64-85E) double; 150,000-200,000L (77-103E) triple. Breakfast (7-10am) at 11,500L pp is not obligatory & can be served in the room (4,500L extra pp). MC, Visa, AX, DC. English spoken (Giuseppe & Loreno Vassalli), direct-dial phone, TV, attractive hotel w/modern comfortable rms. & modern bathrooms, small garden terrace, 5 rms. w/balconies, #1 (balcony), 2 (balcony), 5 & 6 are the best rms., central heating, bar, elevator, 6 flrs., parking (15,000 lire per day). Owned/ managed by Biagio Vassalli. **Metro:** Loreto. Tram #33-Direction Lambrate, near the McDonald's at the train station gets you closer to this hotel than the metro. Ask for stop Porpara-Ampere. Walk down Porpora with the numbers going down, turn right onto Via Catalani.

PAGANINI: Via Paganini 6. **Tel:** 02-2047443. (8 rms., 1 w/toilet & bath or shower.) 85,000L (44E) single (no toilets); 95,000-115,000L (50-60E) double; 140,000-170,000L (72-87E) triple; 150,000-180,000L (77-92E) quad. No breakfast is served. MC, Visa, AX, DC. English spoken (Charly Boy), direct-dial phone, TV, old-fashioned charming hotel w/large simply furnished rms. & high ceilings, best rooms are in the back overlooking a private garden, 3 rms. w/ balconies, #1 has the bathroom but it faces the street on the 1st fl., central heating, double-paned windows, quiet location, bar, no elevator, 2 flrs. Newly owned/managed by Caroni Mira. Charly Boy still owns a restaurant in NYC. **Metro:** Loreto.

SAN FRANCISCO: Viale Lombardia 55. **Tel:** 02-2361009. **Fax:** 02-26680377. (31 rms., all w/toilet & bath or shower.) 95,000-115,000L (50-60E) single; 155,000-175,000L (79-90E) double; 190,000-220,000L (97-113E) triple. Breakfast (7-10am) is included in the rates & cannot be deducted but can be served in the room (11,500L extra pp). MC, Visa, AX, DC. English spoken (Pino), direct-dial phone, TV w/English channel, modern hotel w/simply furnished comfortable dark rms., #24 (balcony) & 62 are the best rms., 5 rms. w/balconies & 6 rms. w/terraces, double-paned windows, central heating, 4 rms. w/air-conditioning, garden, bar, elevator, 4 flrs. *5% rm. discount when you show owners/managers Franco & Pino Volante, Cicco or staff this book.* Located in the University area.

Metro: Loreto or Piola. Tram #33-Direction Lambrate, near the McDonald's at the train station gets you closer to this hotel than the metro. Ask for stop Porpara-Ampere. Walk down Porpora with the numbers going down, turn left onto Viale Lombardia. Owner Pino is the brother of Gianni who owns Hotel San Marco.

SAN MARCO: Via Nicola Piccinni 25.
Tel: 02-29516414/2049536. **Fax:** 02-29513243. (11 rms., 7 w/toilet & bath or shower.) 95,000-105,000L (50-54E) single; 105,000-135,000L (54-69E) double; 160,000L (82E) triple; 200,000L (103E) quad. Breakfast (7-10:30am) at 10,500L pp is not obligatory & is served in the room. Visa, MC, AX, DC. English spoken (Gianni), direct-dial phone, TV, great hotel w/nicely furnished comfortable large rms., lots of American students, 4 rms. w/balconies, #1 & 2 (balcony) are the best rms., noisy location, central heating, double-paned windows, bar, no elevator, 2 flrs. *5% rm. discount when you show owner/manager Gianni, Cicco or staff this book.* Located in a safe part of town, although late at night you may see some prostitutes from your window. (I stayed here on one of my trips-nothing to worry about.) I suggest you take a taxi to this hotel. To walk from the train station, exit the station opposite the large information office, turn left onto Piazza Luigi Savoia, make a right onto Via Pergolesi which goes through Piazza Caiazza, continue on Via Pergolesi passing Corso Buenos Aires, it then becomes Via Piccinni. Hotel is located on the left side of the street. **Metro:** Loreto. Buses travel back and forth from the station to the hotel along Via Pergolesi/Via Piccinni. Owner Gianni is the brother of Pino who owns Hotel San Francisco.

Hotels to the far right of the Duomo
These hotels are not convenient to either the train station or the Duomo. This area is considered a working-class neighborhood. It is about a 20-minute walk to the Duomo. Taxi 18,000-23,000L.

AMERICA: Corsco XXII (Ventidue) Marzo 32, 4th fl. **Tel.** 02-7381865. **Fax:** 02-7381490. (10 rms., 2 w/toilet & bath or shower.) 70,000L (36E) single (no toilets); 95,000-115,000L (50-60E) double; 130,000-170,000L (67-87E) triple. No breakfast is served. Visa, MC, AX, DC. English spoken (Angelo), direct-dial phone, TV, basic hotel w/simply furnished rms., #6 & 3 (balcony) are the best rms. be-cause they have the bathrooms, #10, a single, has a terrace, #1, 2 & 4 have balconies but no bathrooms, central heating, elevator, 1 fl. Owned/managed by Angelo Telesca. The hotel is located in the same bldg. that has a discotheque on the street level, but according to Angelo, you can't hear the loud music. It is in a very popular shop-ping area filled with lots of pedestrians. Catch Tram #92 or 90 from the train station. Both trams stop at Ventidue Marzo.

BRASIL: Via Gustavo Modena 20, 4th fl. **Tel/Fax:** 02-7492482. **Web site:** http://www.city2000com/TL/hotel.brasil.html/ (12 rms., 4 w/toilet & bath or shower.) 75,000-105,000L (38-54E) single; 95,000-125,000L (50-64E) double; 120,000-155,000L (62-79E) triple; 145,000-180,000L (74-92E) quad. Breakfast (8-11am) at 9,500L pp is not obligatory & can be served in the room. Visa, MC, AX, DC. English spoken (Valfriano), direct-dial phone, TV, 18th-century charm-ing Italian hotel w/old-fashioned furnished large rms. & high ceil-ings, tiled flrs., #5 & 6 are the best rms. & have bathrooms, #18 & 3 also have bathrooms, 6 rms. w/balconies, central heating, elevator, 1 fl. Owned/managed by a wonderful woman named Luisa Ramella. Don't let the outside appearance of the bldg. discourage you. Catch bus #60 from square in front the train station, ask for bus stop Gustavo Modena. **Metro:** Palestro. From the metro stop, take Via Serbelloni, quick left onto Via Cappuccini, continue straight as it becomes Via Bellotti, walk through Piazza Bandiera, as it becomes Via Gustavo Modena. About a 15-minute walk from the metro stop.

CANADA: Via Santa Sofia 16. **Tel.** 02-58304844. **Fax:** 02-58300282. **Web site:** http://web.tin.it/hotel/canada/ **E-mail:** canadah@tin.it (35 rms., all w/toilet & bath or shower.) 105,000-215,000L (54-110E) single; 195,000-395,000L (100-203E) double; 270,000-400,000L (138-205E) triple; 420,000L (215E) quad. Breakfast (7-10:30am) is included in the rates & cannot be deducted but can be served in the room (6,500L extra pp).Visa, MC, AX, DC. English spoken (Simonetta), direct-dial phone, satellite TV w/English channel, mod-ern hotel w/comfortable nicely furnished rms. & modern bathrooms, #605, 505, 405 & 105 are huge rooms w/sitting area, 1 rm. has handi-capped access, lots of closet space, minibars, double-paned windows, central heating, air-conditioned, bar, quiet location, elevator, 8 flrs., parking (40,000L per day). Owned/managed by Iano Bricoli. Catch bus #4, 24 or 15. Ask bus driver for bus stop Santa Sofia.

CINQUE GIORNATE: Piazza Cinque Giornate 6. **Tel.** 02-5463433/ 55194862. **Fax:** 02-5513611. (23 rms., 10 w/toilet & bath or shower.) 125,000L (64E) single; 175,000L (90E) double; 260,000L (133E) triple; 300,000L (154E) quad. Breakfast (7-10am) is included in the rates & can be served in the room (16,500L extra pp) but can be deducted to reduce room price. Visa, MC, AX, DC. English spoken (Franco & Laures), direct-dial phone, TV, basic hotel w/simply furnished dark rms., #36 & 45 are the best rms., central heating, no elevator, 2 flrs. Owned/managed by Franco & Laures Valenti. Rosario will take care of you if they are not around. Located in a very popular shopping area filled with lots of pedestrians.

Still having problems finding a low-cost hotel? Contact Dr. Ibrahim Gouda. **Tel:** 0347/2454036 or 0336/367377. He can find you affordable plush lodging at 3-star hotels for 2-star prices. The problem is the hotels are not centrally located so you'll be forced to catch a metro or a taxi to and from your hotel. One of his Viagi Wastell offices is located in the Central train station. English spoken.

MONEY
Banco Milano: Malpensa Airport bank. 8am-8pm. Located just past customs. There are weekend exchange offices at airport.

Banca Comunicazioni: Hrs.: Mon.-Sat. 8:35am-12:30pm & 2:05-7pm. Located at Central train station. Check the commission fee.

Central Post Office: Via Cordusio 4. Located near the Duomo off Piazza Cordusio (not the bldg. marked "Poste"). **Tel:** 02-8692069. Hrs.: Mon.-Fri. 8:30am-7pm. Window #11. **Metro:** Cordusio.

LAUNDROMATS (Lavanderia)
Daily: 8am-10pm. 13,000L for 14 lbs. of wash, dry and soap. **Onda Blu:** Via Scarlatti 19.
Lavanderia Automatica: Corso Porta Vittoria 51.
Minola: Via San Vito 5.

RESTAURANTS

Please check page 20 for my criteria for selecting restaurants. The Milanese love good food and they frequently dine out. For this reason, it is always better to reserve a table well in advance. I am sure there are plenty of good restaurants near the Duomo but I wanted to find some that were a slight distance away.

AZZURO GRILL: Via San Gregorio 11. **Tel/Fax:** 02-29406115. Hrs.: noon-3pm & 7pm-12midnight. Closed Sat. afternoon & Sun. Visa, MC, AX. Since 1988, this wonderful family-owned restaurant is managed by Matteo, the father, Tina, the mother, Fabrizio, the son & Franco, the son/waiter who speaks good English. Large simple restaurant w/wonderful fresh fish, delicious pizzas and homemade pastas. A restaurant filled with Italians. A full dinner complete with a liter of house wine and dessert will cost about 100,000L for two people. The father walks the floor with a watchful eye making sure everyone is satisfied. The only problem I had with the restaurant was the bright lights. *Show Franco or the family the book and they will give you a complimentary Vinassa or limoncello.* Don't forget to bring your *Eating and Drinking in Italy* menu reader. **Metro:** Lima. Walk down Corso Buenos Aires about two blocks, turn right onto Via San Gregorio.

SABATINI: Via Boscovich 54. **Tel:** 02-29402814. **Fax:** 02-72022857. Hrs.: noon-2:30pm & 7-11:15pm. Closed Sun. Open every day in Dec. Visa, MC, AX, DC. Family-owned restaurant for 35 years. Managed by David who speaks limited English. Great food. The only problems I had with the restaurant were the bright lights and the cigarette smoke. A full dinner complete with a liter of house wine and dessert will cost about 100,000L for two people. *Show David the book and he will give you a complimentary limoncello.* **Metro:** Lima. Walk down Corso Buenos Aires about two blocks, turn right onto Via Boscovich.

TEMPERANZA (Abele): Via Temperanza 5. **Tel:** 022613855. **Web site:** http://www.venturnet.com/abele/ Hrs.: 8pm-12am. Closed Mon. Dinner only. Visa, MC. DC. Reservations are necessary. A typical, old-style small Italian trattoria with a simple, good-tasting menu that changes every evening. 27 checkered-clothed tables with a warm and relaxing atmosphere that fills up with Italians by 9:00pm. Owned by Roberto & Billy since 1981. Billie speaks English. Don't expect any pasta at this restaurant. The true specialty of Temperanza is the *risotto*. The classic *nero di seppia* (black squid ink) is wonderful. The desserts are wonderful. A full dinner complete with a bottle of house wine (no liters available) will cost about 100,000L for two people. If you don't drink the whole bottle of wine, they only charge you half the cost. The waiters are students, actors & friends. *Show Roberto or Billie this book and they will give you a complimentary after-dinner drink.* The only problem I had with the restaurant was not being able to read the handwritten menu and the Turkish hole-in-the-floor bathroom. Don't forget to bring your *Eating and Drinking in Italy* menu reader. This restaurant is not conveniently located to anything including the hotels. It is better to take a taxi (20,000L) to and from this restaurant though I took the metro to and from the restaurant and never felt threatened. **Metro:** Pasteur. Look for the exit sign Via Transiti/Via Monzi. Exit the train station, turn right onto Via Transiti, past the Goldmark store, turn right onto Via Temperanza.

NAPLES (Napoli)
Area code 39, city code 081, zip code 80142

Orientation: Naples is Italy's third-largest city and a very congested one. After many requests from my readers, I have decided against my better judgment to include this city. The mayor has made a serious commitment to clean up Naples and close off many streets to create pedestrian zones where people can stroll. But remember, this is a port city. Don't go down alleys alone and always stay alert to your surroundings. When making hotel reservations always make sure you have a firm price. My husband and I usually prefer to stay in Sorrento which is one hour away by the local train.

The main heart of Naples stretches from **Naples Stazione Centrale** at the immense **Piazza Garibaldi** in the east to **Naples Stazione Mergellina** in the west. From Piazza Garibaldi, the wide, commercial **Corso Umberto I** heads southwest to the docks, ending just before them in the downtown area of **Piazza Bovio**. From here **Via Agostino Depretis** branches to the left to the huge **Piazza Municipio** and nearby **Piazza Plebiscito**. To the north is the historical center of Old Naples and to the south is the port. Farther west, along the coast past Piazza Plebiscito are the more attractive and fashionable areas of **Santa Lucia** and **Chiaia** and the upscale area of the waterfront district, **Mergellina**. Naples has two train stations: 1.) Naples Stazione Centrale, the main station facing Piazza Garibaldi, located northeast of Old Naples and the port. It is also where you can catch the *Ferrovia Circumvesuviana* commuter trains to Sorrento, Herculaneum and Pompeii; 2.) Naples Stazione Mergellina, **Corso Vittorio Emanuele 4** across town, where it is a direct ten-minute subway ride to Naples Centrale. If you arrive here at night catch a taxi to your hotel. Make sure you agree on a price to your hotel before you get into the cab. Many drivers are not honest or pretend their meters are not working. I definitely suggest you have a map of Naples so you'll know where the taxi is taking you and you can avoid getting ripped off.

Naples Tourist Information Centers
1.) Piazza Martiri 58, scala B. **Tel:** 081-405311. **Fax:** 081-401961. Hrs.: Mon.-Fri. 9am-2pm. **2.)** Stazione Centrale, opposite track #16.

Tel: 081-268779. Hrs.: Mon.-Sat. 9am-7pm; Sun. 9am-1pm. **3.)**
Stazione Mergellina. **Tel:** 081-7612102. Hours listed above are not
etched in stone.

Hotels near the train station
The area is unattractive and reasonably safe but be very careful late
at night. Although it is home to many brothel-type hotels, there are
plenty of policemen around to discourage any problems that may
occur. The farther away you stay from the train station area, the more
acceptable and expensive the hotels become.

CASANOVA: Corso Garibaldi 333/Via Venezia 2. **Tel:** 081-268287.
Fax: 081-269792. (18 rms., 13 w/toilet & bath or shower.) 53,000-
60,000L (27-31E) single; 90,000-100,000L (46-51E) double; 104,000-
140,000L (53-72E) triple; 128,000-152,000L (66-78E) quad. Breakfast (7-10am) at 11,500L pp is not obligatory & can be served in the
room (extra cost). Breakfast is served on the terrace in warm weather.
Visa, MC, AX, DC. English spoken (Giuseppe), direct-dial phone,
10 rms. w/minibars & satellite TV w/English channel, wonderful
charming hotel w/simply furnished nice-size rms., #14 & 16 are the
best rms., rooftop terrace w/bar service in the summer, ivy-covered
front, central heating, quiet location, bar, no elevator, 2 flrs. Hotel
started renovating in Nov. '98. *10% rm. discount when you show
owner/manager Vittorio Arzillo or staff this book.* I prefer the more
attractive entrance on Via Venezia. From the train station, walk bearing to your right through Piazza Garibaldi, take the 3rd right onto Via
Milano, turn left onto Via Venezia, walk to the end of the street.

CAVOUR: Piazza Garibaldi 37. **Tel:** 081-283122. **Fax:** 081-287488.
Web site: http://www.cavour.com/ **E-mail:** info@cavour.com (92
rms., 89 w/toilet & bath or shower.) 125,000-155,000L (64-79E)
single; 165,000-195,000L (85-100E) double; 200,000-260,000L (103-
133E) triple; 220,000-300,000L (113-154E) quad. Buffet breakfast
(7-10am) is included in the rates. Visa, MC, AX, DC. English spoken (Enzo & Paolo), direct-dial phone, satellite TV w/English channel, fabulous historic charming hotel w/elegantly furnished comfortable rms., lovely atmosphere, #610 & 609 w/terraces are the best
rms., #601, 602, 607 & 608 have terraces, #84 is jr. suite, 50 rms. w/

balconies, needs new carpeting, central heating, 50% rms. are air-conditioned & have minibars, noisy location, bar, 4-star restaurant, elevator, parking (28,000L per day). *Show managers Michele Catuogno or Peppino this book and they will give you a special price on lunch or dinner in their 4-star restaurant.* They offer half- (35,000L pp) and full-board (70,000L pp) rates. From the train station, walk straight through Piazza Garibaldi, bear right.

EDEN: Corso Novara 9. **Tel:** 081-285344. **Tel/Fax:** 081-285690. (44 rms., all w/toilet & bath or shower.) 67,000L (34E) single; 81,000L (42E) double; 110,000L (56E) triple; 124,000L (64E) quad. No breakfast is served. Cash only rates. Visa, MC, AX. English spoken (Nick), direct-dial phone, basic hotel w/simply furnished rms, many are on the dark side, 21 rms. w/balconies, central heating, double-paned windows, noisy location, bar, elevator. *The rates for the rooms quoted above are only if you show owner/manager Enzo Lopomo, Nick or staff this book and pay cash.* From the train station, turn right onto Corso Novara, walk under an elevated road to hotel. If you call from the station, they'll come help with your bags.

GINERVA: Via Genova 116. **Tel/Fax:** 081-283210. **Tel/Fax:** 081-5541757. **E-mail:** hginevra@tin.it (15 rms., 6 w/toilet & bath or shower.) 55,000L (28E) single; 80,000-93,000L (41-48E) double; 118,000-137,000L (61-70E) triple; 140,000L (72E) quad (no shower). Breakfast (anytime) at 7,500L pp is not obligatory & can be served in the room. Visa, MC, AX, DC. English spoken (Lello), direct-dial phone, TV, wonderful charming hotel w/simply furnished bright pretty nice-size airy rms., cheerful ambiance, #18, 19, 20, 22, 23 & 24 have bathrooms, 3 rms. w/balconies, nice flrs., rms. in the back are quiet, laundry facilities, no elevator, 2 flrs. Sometimes in the evenings they have sing-alongs w/guitar. *10% rm. discount when you show owner/ manager Anna Manzo or staff this book and pay in cash.* The entire family tries hard to make your stay enjoyable. From the train station, turn right onto Corso Novara, walk under an elevated road for two blocks, turn right onto Via Genova.

GALLO: Via Silvio Spaventa 11. **Tel:** 081-200512/286009. **Fax:** 081-201849. (16 rms., all w/toilet & bath or shower.) 90,000L (46E) single; 155,000L (79E) double; 200,000L (103E) triple; 220,000L

(113E) quad. Breakfast (8-10am) at 6,500L pp is obligatory & can be served in the room (2,500L extra pp). Visa, MC, AX. English spoken (Salvio), direct-dial phone, TV, nice modern hotel w/nicely furnished comfortable rms., 5 rms. w/balconies, one rm. has a private bathroom in the hall, central heating, air-conditioned, bar, restaurant, elevator, 3 flrs. Located to the left of the train station, just off Piazza Garibaldi.

IDEAL: Piazza Garibaldi 99. **Tel:** 081-269237.
Fax: 081-285942. **Web site:** http://www.export.it/ideal/
(41 rms., 39 w/toilet & bath or shower.) 80,000L (41E) single; 130,000L (67E) double; 165,000L (85E) triple. Call for quad rates. Breakfast (7-9:30am) is included in the rates & cannot be deducted but can be served in the room. Visa, MC, AX, DC. English spoken (Max), direct-dial phone, TV, newly renovated hotel w/nicely furnished nice-size rms., some of the rms. are quite pretty, nice flrs., 10 rms. w/ balconies, some of them overlook the square, #6 is the best rm., central heating, double-paned windows, noisy location, no elevator, 2 flrs. From the train station, walk to the left of the square to the hotel.

NUOVO REBECCHINO: Corso Garibaldi 356.
Tel: 081-5535327. **Fax:** 081-268026.
Web site: http://www.napleshotels.na.it/nuovorebecchino/
(58 rms., all w/toilet & bath or shower.) 150,000-175,000L (77-90E) single; 210,000-245,000L (108-126E) double; 260,000-300,000L (133-154E) quad. Buffet breakfast (7-10am) is included in the rates & cannot be deducted but can be served in the room. Visa, MC, AX, DC. English spoken (Valeria & Pasquale), direct-dial phone, TV, modern hotel w/nicely furnished comfortable nice-size pretty rms., best rms. are on the 4th fl., some rms. w/double-paned windows, #418 has a balcony, central heating, air-conditioned, minibars, bar, elevator, 5 flrs. Owned/managed by Ciro Gentile. From the train station, walk straight through Piazza Garibaldi, turn right onto Corso Garibaldi.

PALACE: Piazza Garibaldi 9. **Tel:** 081-267044. **Fax:** 081-264306.
(100 rms., all w/toilet & bath or shower.) 135,000L (69E) single; 195,000L (100E) double; 240,000L (123E) triple; 280,000L (144E) quad. Buffet breakfast (7-10am) is included in the rates & cannot be

deducted but can be served in the room. Visa, MC, AX, DC. English spoken (Marco), direct-dial phone, TV, wonderful charming modern hotel w/nicely furnished comfortable large rms., 50 rms. w/balconies & 3 rms. w/terraces, #601, 602 & 603 are beautiful w/terraces, hair driers, double-paned windows, central heating, 50% rms. w/air-conditioning (33,000L extra per day), restaurant, bar, noisy location, 2 elevators, 6 flrs., parking (23,000L per day). They offer half- and full-board rates. This hotel is not family-owned. From the train station, walk straight ahead through Piazza Garibaldi to the hotel.

PRATI: Via Cesare Rosaroll 4. **Tel:** 081-268898/282882. **Fax:** 081-5541802. (43 rms., all w/toilet & bath or shower.) 115,000-155,000L (60-79E) single; 175,000-195,000L (90-100E) double; 220,000L (113E) triple; 260,000L (133E) quad. Buffet breakfast (7-10am) at 16,500L pp is not obligatory & can be served in the room. Visa, MC, AX, DC. English spoken, wonderful charming hotel w/nicely furnished large pretty rms., direct-dial phone, 21 rms. w/TVs, #9 & 10 w/terraces & views are the best rms. on the top flrs., nice flrs., #108 (front) & 109 (back) have terraces, 23 rms. w/balconies, some rms. w/air-conditioning, rms. in the back are quiet, bar, top fl. restaurant w/outside terrace, elevator, 4 flrs. Owned/managed by Maria Derogatis. From the train station, walk straight through Piazza Garibaldi, turn right onto Corso Garibaldi, bear left through Piazza Umberto which will lead you to Via Cesare Rosaroll.

SAN PIETRO: Via San Pietro ad Aram 18. **Tel:** 081-5535914. **Fax:** 081-286040. (50 rms., 18 w/toilet & bath or shower.) 70,000-100,000L (36-51E) single; 100,000-150,000L (51-77E) double; 130,000-195,000L (67-100E) triple. Breakfast (7:30-10am) at 11,500L pp is not obligatory & can be served in the room. English spoken (Enzo), direct-dial phone, TV, modern hotel w/simply furnished comfortable rms., 10 rms. w/balconies, bar, elevators, 6 flrs., nearby parking (25,000L per day). There is usually a flea market on Sun. in front of the hotel. From the train station, walk straight ahead through Piazza Garibaldi, bear left to Corso Umberto, turn right onto Via S. Candida, which intersects Via San Pietro ad Aram.

Hotels in the historical quarter
DUOMO: Via Duomo 228. **Tel/Fax:** 081-265988. (9 rms., all w/

toilet & bath or shower.) 65,000-75,000L (33-38E) single; 115,000L (60E) double; 150,000L (77E) triple; 160,000L (82E) quad. Children under 6 free. No breakfast is served. Cash only. English spoken (Salvatore, Luigi & Enrico), direct-dial phone, TV, charming hotel w/simply furnished comfortable airy large rms., double-paned windows, central heating, nice flrs., ceiling fans, no elevator, 1 fl. *5% rm. discount when you show owner/manager Enrico Lacentra or staff this book.* Don't be put off by the entrance. From the train station, walk straight ahead through Piazza Garibaldi, bear left to Corso Umberto, walk up Corso Umberto (10 min.) to Piazza Nicola Amore, turn right onto Via Duomo (20-min walk). Or catch any of the buses to Piazza Nicola Amore, walk up Via Duomo (away from the water and up). Bus #42 does go past the hotel on Via Duomo but I don't know the stop.

ORCHIDEA (Le): Corso Umberto 7/Piazza Bovio, 5th fl. **Tel/Fax:** 081-5510721. (7 rms., all w/toilet & bath or shower.) 105,000L (54E) single; 145,000L (74E) double; 190,000L (97E) triple; 220,000L (113E) quad. Breakfast (7-10am) at 6,500L pp is not obligatory & can be served in the room. Cash only. English spoken, nice charming hotel w/simply furnished nice-size airy pretty rms., high ceilings, nice flrs., #42-46 & 48 have balconies & views of the square, noisy location, elevator. The police station is located around the corner from the hotel. From the train station, walk straight ahead through Piazza Garibaldi, bear left to Corso Umberto, walk up Corso Umberto (20 min.) to Piazza Bovio. Or catch any of the buses to Piazza Bovio.

SANSEVERO: Via S. Maria Costantinopoli 101, 2nd fl. **Tel:** 081-210907. **Tel/Fax:** 081-211698. (17 rms., 11 w/toilet & bath or shower.) 55,000-95,000L (28-50E) single; 95,000-165,000L (50-85E) double; 130,000-200,000L (67-103E) triple; 200,000-230,000L (103-118E) quad. Children under 10 free. Breakfast (7-11am) is included in the rates & can be served in the room but can be deducted to reduce room price. Visa, MC. English spoken (Giuseppe), direct-dial phone, charming renovated old palace w/simply furnished large pretty rms., 2 rms. w/balconies, #201 & 202 are the best rms., central heating, elevator, 2 flrs. *Free breakfast when you show owner/ manager Armida Auriemma or staff this book.* Take Bus #42 to the National museum, cross the street and take Via S. Maria

Costantinopoli in front of the museum straight down to the hotel. I didn't get a chance to revisit this hotel on this trip.

Hotels near the waterfront
This is a beautiful safe area near the ports of Naples but a lot more money. Stay here if you plan to use ferries for your day trips to Capri, Ischia or Sorrento. Great area for strolling.

FONTANE DEL MARE: Via Niccolo Tommaseo 14, 4th fl. **Tel:** 081-7643811. **Fax:** 081-7643470. (20 rms., 7 w/toilet & bath or shower.) 90,000-105,000L (46-54E) single (no toilets & no views); 105,000-135,000L (54-69E) double. Call for triple rates. Breakfast (8-11:30am) at 13,500L pp is not obligatory & can be served in the room (3,500L extra pp). Visa, MC, AX, DC. English spoken (Claudio), 19th-century charming hotel w/simply furnished nice-size bright airy rms., #25 has a view & bathroom, #3, 4, 5 & 6 have wonderful views but no bathrooms, #9 & 20 have bathrooms & partial views, #11, 21, 23 & 24 have bathrooms but no views, all the rms. have balconies, elevator, 4 flrs. You need 200L coins to feed/use the elevator. This hotel is not family-owned but managed by Claudio. From train station, catch tram #1 to last stop before Piazza Vittoria or call hotel for bus directions. Via Niccolo Tommaseo intersects Via Caracciolo at the waterfront.

REX: Via Palepoli 12. **Tel:** 081-7649389. **Fax:** 081-7649227. (40 rms., all w/toilet & bath or shower.) 145,000L (74E) single; 195,000L (100E) double; 215,000L (110E) triple; 240,000L (123E) quad. Breakfast (7:30-10:30am) is included in the rates & cannot be deducted but can be served in the room. Visa, MC, AX, DC. English spoken, charming art-nouveau basic hotel w/nicely furnished comfortable nice-size airy rms., some rms. are dark, 20 rms. w/balconies, double-paned windows, central heating, air-conditioned, quiet location, bar, no elevator, 2 flrs., parking (35,000L per day). This hotel occupies part of the Palazzo Coppedé. From train station, catch R2. Stop: Teatro San Carlo, or call hotel for bus directions. Via Palepoli intersects Via Sauro at the waterfront.

ORVIETO
Umbria, zip code 05018
Area code 39, city code 0763

Orientation: Orvieto sits magnificently on volcanic stone. From the train station (Orvieto Scalo), it is 1 1/2 miles up a winding steep road to the **Piazza Duomo** (center of town). Take the funicular (every 15min.) to **Piazza Cahen** which acts only as a transportation hub at the entrance to the hilltop town. From Piazza Cahen, catch the orange shuttle bus to Piazza Duomo. Buy your funicular/orange shuttle bus ticket (1,600L) at the train station tobacco shop. Save yourself some time and buy round-trip tickets. After you buy your tickets, exit the train station and walk across the street to the funicular. You won't have to wait in line to buy a ticket inside because you already have one. When you get off the funicular at Piazza Cahen (top of the hill), walk immediately to the waiting orange shuttle bus. The bus will drop you off in front of the tourist office in the Piazza Duomo. The **Duomo** is the most spectacular Duomo in all of Italy. My husband and I decided to walk to the Duomo from Piazza Cahen. To do this, walk straight down **Corso Cavour**, make a left onto Via Duomo which takes you to the Piazza Duomo (15-min. walk).

Orvieto Tourist Information Center
1.) Piazza Duomo 24. **Tel:** 0763-341772/341911.
Fax: 0763-344433. **Web sites:** http://www.orvienet.it
or http://www.argoweb.it/orvietano/ **E-mail:** infoargo@argoweb.it or compass@orvienet.it Hrs.: Mon.-Fri. 8:15am-1:50pm & 4-7pm; Sat. 10am-1pm & 4-7pm; Sun. & holidays 10am-12pm & 4-6pm. Located on the cathedral square. Longer hours in-season. The orange shuttle bus from Piazza Cahen drops you in front of the tourist office.

Hotels within the center
CORSO: Corso Cavour 343. **Tel/Fax:** 0763-342020. (16 rms., all w/toilet & bath or shower.) 85,000-115,000L (44-60E) single; 115,000-155,000L (60-79E) double; 170,000-200,000L (87-103E) triple; 190,000-220,000L (97-113E) quad. Buffet breakfast (7-10:30am) at 11,500L pp is not obligatory & can be served in the room. Breakfast is served on the terrace in warm weather. Visa, MC.

English spoken (Carla), direct-dial phone, satellite TV w/English channel, wonderful charming renovated hotel w/modern comfortable bright airy rms. & new bathrooms, #9 is wonderful w/loft bedroom, terrace & view, #16, 6, 8 & 23 (wood-beamed ceiling) have balconies & views, nice flrs., 5 rms. w/minibars, 1 rm. has handicapped access, double-paned windows, central heating, terrace, elevator, 3 flrs., parking (25,000L per day). *Free breakfast when you show owner/manager Carla Caponeri or staff this book.* From Piazza Cahen where the funicular drops you off, walk down Corso Cavour (10 minutes).

POSTA: Via Luca Signorelli 18. **Tel:** 0763-41909. (20 rms., 8 w/toilet & bath or shower.) 65,000-85,000L (33-44E) single; 90,000-110,000L (46-56E) double. Call for triple rates. No breakfast is served. Cash only. No English spoken, direct-dial phone, old medieval hotel w/old-fashioned furnished comfortable large simple rms., #8 is nice but w/o bathroom, high ceilings, #10, 13, 20-22, 24, 33 & 53 have bathrooms, check your bed before committing, garden, bar, no elevator, 3 flrs. Facing the tourist office in Piazza Duomo, walk to your right down Via Duomo, turn left onto Via Luca Signorelli. (Closed Jan. or Feb.)

VIRGILIO: Piazza Duomo 5/6. **Tel:** 0763-341882. **Fax:** 0763-343797. (13 rms., all w/toilet & bath or shower.) 95,000-135,000L (50-69E) single; 115,000-180,000L (60-92E) double. Call for triple & quad rates. Breakfast (7-9am) at 16,500L pp is not obligatory & can be served in the room. Visa, MC. English spoken, direct-dial phone, wonderful charming renovated palazzo hotel w/modern bright comfortable bright airy small rms., #15 (bathtub), 16, 18, 24-26 have wonderful views, #18, 26, 15, 24 are the best rms., 1 rm. has handicapped access, central heating, bar, elevator, parking (15,000L per day). Owned/managed by Vladmiro Belcapo. Located on the square facing the cathedral. (Closed Jan.-mid-Feb.)

Hotel near the train station
Boring neighborhood but convenient to the funicular & train station.

PICCHIO: Via G. Salvatori 17. **Tel:** 0763-301144. **Tel/Fax:** 0763-301846. (16 rms., 12 w/toilet & bath or shower.) 70,000L (36E) single;

ORVIETO

90,000L (46E) double; 115,000L (60E) triple; 125,000L (64E) quad. Breakfast (7-11am) is not obligatory. English spoken (Marco & Alessandra), direct-dial phone, satellite TV w/English channel, nice modern hotel w/simply furnished comfortable nice-size airy rms., #5A has a balcony, 4 rms. w/balconies, some rms. w/views of the fortress, bar, parking (20,000L per day). Owned/managed by Marco who also owns Hotel Alessandra. Exit the train station, turn left, go through the gas station, cross the street and walk up Via Pesa which becomes Via G. Salvatori.

PADUA (Padova)
Veneto, zip code 35123
Area code 39, city code 049

Orientation: Most people stay in Padua simply because they can't find a room in Venice. Padua has a lot of its own charm and is much cheaper than its neighbors. It is Italy's most ancient city and has the 2nd oldest university in Italy. Padua is full with students during the school term but empty of them on weekends and summer. It is only a half-hour away from Venice by train. The train station is located in **Piazza Stazione**, at the northern edge of town, just outside the 16th-century walls. It is about a 10-minute walk from the station to the center. Walk through the piazza directly in front of the station to **Corso Popolo**, which becomes **Corso Garibaldi**, then becomes **Via Cavour**, then **Via VIII Febbraio** where you can make a right turn into **Piazza Erbe** and **Piazza Signori** (the center of town). To get to the south edge of the center **Basilica Sant'Antonio** and **Prato Valle** (stay away at night), continue walking on Via VIII Febbraio as it becomes **Via Roma** then **Via Umberto I**.

Padua's Tourist Information Center
Web site: http://www.padovanet.it/turcul/apt/apt.html/
E-mail: apt@padovanet.it **1.)** Stazione Ferrovie (train station) 35123. **Tel:** 049-8752077. Hrs.: Mon.-Sat. 9:15am-5:30pm & Sun. 9am-12pm. Later hrs. in-season. **2.)** Museo Civico, on Piazza Eremitani. **Tel:** 049-8750655. **Fax:** 049-650794. Hrs.: Tues.-Sun. 10am-12:30pm & 1:30-4:30pm.

Hotels
AL FAGIANO: Via Locatelli 45. **Tel/Fax:** 049-8753396. (29 rms., all w/toilet & bath or shower.) 105,000L (54E) single; 145,000L (74E) double; 160,000L (82E) triple; 170,000L (87E) quad. Breakfast (7-11am) at 11,500L pp is not obligatory & can be served in the room (4,500L extra pp). Visa, MC, AX, DC. English spoken (Andre & Armato), direct-dial phone, TV, newly renovated wonderful hotel w/nicely furnished bright comfortable nice-size pretty rms., #56, 57 & 58 are the best rms. w/arched wood-beamed ceilings, 2 rms. have handicapped access, towel warmers, hair driers, nice flrs., central

heating, air-conditioned, bar, elevator, 4 flrs., parking (20,000L per day). *Free breakfast when you show owners/managers Anita & Rossella or staff this book.* Bus #8, 3 or 12. From Prato Valle, turn right on Via Belludi, turn left onto Via Locatelli. Located close to Piazza Santo.

AL SANTO: Via Santo 147. **Tel/Fax:** 049-8752131. (16 rms., 11 w/ toilet & bath or shower.) 55,000L (28E) single; 90,000L (46E) double; 120,000L (62E) triple; 145,000L (74E) quad. Breakfast (8-10am) at 8,500L pp is not obligatory. Cash only. English spoken, direct-dial phone, basic hotel w/simply furnished nice-size rms., #18 & 28 are the best rms., bar, restaurant, no elevator, 3 flrs. They offer half- (100,000L pp) and full-board (120,000L pp) rates. Manager is in the bar next door. Good location but noisy. Bus #8, 11 or 18. Stop: Sant' Antonio. Via Santo runs off Piazza Santo.

BUENOS AIRES: Via Luca Belludi 37.
Tel: 049-665633/651844. **Fax:** 049-658685. (17 rms., 12 w/toilet & bath or shower.) 90,000-115,000L (46-60E) single; 95,000-155,000L (50-79E) double; 130,000-185,000L (67-95E) triple; 150,000-210,000L (77-108E) quad. Breakfast (7-10am) at 11,500L pp is not obligatory & can be served in the room (6,500L extra pp). Visa, MC, AX, DC. English spoken (Franco), direct-dial phone, TV, 18th-century grand old hotel w/nicely furnished comfortable rms., rooms vary in size from huge to small, high ceilings, #107 (balcony) & 218 (huge & view) are the best rms., central heating, air-conditioned, bar, no elevator, 3 flrs., parking (20,000L per day). In 1999, they will replace the carpeting & doors of the rooms. The hotel is not family-owned. Bus #3, 8, 12 or 18. Stop: Sant' Antonio. From Prato Valle, turn right on Via Belludi. Located between the Prato Valle and Piazza Santo.

LEON BIANCO: Piazzetta Pedrocchi 12.
Tel: 049-8750814/657225. **Fax:** 049-8756184.
E-mail: leonbianco@writeme.com (22 rms., all w/toilet & bath or shower.) 145,000L (74E) single; 177,000L (91E) double; 215,000L (110E) triple; 248,000L (127E) quad. Buffet breakfast (7:30-10:30am) at 16,500L pp is not obligatory & can be served in the room (2,500L

extra pp). Breakfast is served on the roof terrace overlooking the town in warm weather. Visa, MC, AX, DC. English spoken, direct-dial phone, TV, 18th-century modern palazzo w/contemporary furnished (combination of antique & modern) comfortable rms., #35 & 25 are the best rms., #45 has a bathtub & view of the square, central heating, air-conditioned, minibars, roof garden w/panoramic view of Padua, elevator, 4 flrs., parking (30,000L per day). Owned/managed by Paolo Morosi. Great location. From the train station, walk through the piazza directly in front of the station to Corso Popolo which becomes Corso Garibaldi, then becomes Via Cavour, continue straight to Piazza Cavour, turn right into Piazzetta Pedrocchi. 10-minute walk.

RIVIERA: Via Rudena 12. **Tel:** 049-665413. (10 rms., 3 w/toilet & bath or shower.) 57,000-79,000L (29-41E) single; 72,000-95,000L (37-50E) double; 130,000L (67E) triple. Breakfast (7-9am) at 7,500L pp is not obligatory. Cash only. Limited English spoken (Mirco), direct-dial phone, basic hotel w/simply furnished nice-size rms., #15 & 10 w/bathrooms are the best rms., #14 also has a bathroom, central heating, bar, no elevator, 3 flrs., street parking. Owned/managed by Mirco Sanguin. From Prato Valle, turn right on Via Belludi, left onto Riviera Businello, right on Via Rudena. Bus #8, 3, 18 or 24. Stop: Sant' Antonio. (Closed 1 week in Aug.)

MIGNON: Via Luca Belludi 22. Avoid the extremely rude staff. They refused to show me any of the rooms.

MONEY
Banca Antoniana: Piazza Frutte 39/Via VIII Febbraio 5. **Tel:** 049-839111. Hrs.: Mon.-Fri. 8:30am-1:20pm & 2:35-3:35pm. Good rates.

PERUGIA
Umbria, zip code 06123
Area code 39, city code 075

Orientation: Perugia, a city made for walking, is mainly known for its infamous university and as home to Biuttoni and Perugina chocolate. It makes a perfect base to explore Umbria's small towns like Assisi, Spoleto & Spello. **Stazione Fontivegge**, Perugia's main train station, is inconveniently located in **Piazza Vittorio Veneto** (suburbs), a challenging 5km downhill below the town, outside the center. The old city revolves around **Corso Vannucci**, which is lined with historical cafes, bars and stores and is the center's medieval main avenue. Corso Vannucci runs south-north with **Piazza Repubblica** and **Piazza Italia** (historical center) at the southern end and **Piazza IV Novembre** enclosed by the **Duomo** on the northern end. Behind the Duomo lies the university area. It is too far and too steep to walk from the train station to the center. Catch buses #6, 7, 9,11 or 15 in front of the train station to the right at the orange sign. Just look for the buses with the destination *"Piazza Italia"* on the front (20-minute ride). Purchase your bus ticket (1,400L) at the *La Repubblica* newsstand before you leave the train station. For your convenience, buy enough bus tickets to get you to & from the station.

Perugia Tourist Information Center
Piazza IV Novembre 3. **Tel:** 075-5723327/5736458. **Fax:** 075-5739386. Hrs.: Mon.-Sat. 8:30am-1:30pm and 3:30-6:30pm, Sun. 9am-1pm. Located in Palazzo Priori, in the back of the Duomo at the end of Corso Vannucci, the historic center's main avenue.

Hotels
ANNA: Via Priori 48. **Tel/Fax:** 075-5736304. **Web site:** http://www.freetown.com/ParadiseValley/GreenHaven/2127/
E-mail: annahotel@hotmail.com (13 rms., 9 w/toilet & bath or shower.) 70,000L (36E) single; 91,000L (47E) double; 125,000L (64E) triple; 148,000L (76E) quad. Children under 4 free. No breakfast is served. Cash only. English spoken (Catia), direct-dial phone, TV (6,500L extra per day), wonderful 17th-century hotel w/old-fashioned furnished rms., lots of character, high ceilings, #4 (jr. suite, interior terrace & view), 5 (large w/view) & 3 (large w/interior ter-

race & view) are the best rms., #6 & 10 share a bathroom, #9 & 8 are large w/high ceiling, chandelier & bathroom, some rms. have double-paned windows, central heating, no elevator, 3 flrs., parking (10,000L per day). *5% rm. discount when you show owner/manager Emma Citti or staff this book.* Emma's son & daughter each own a separate hotel. The family organizes Italian language, culture and cooking courses. From Piazza Italia, walk straight down Corso Vannucci to Piazza Repubblica, turn left on Via Priori (behind the Palazzo Priori) & walk 2 1/2 blocks down the steep street to the hotel.

ALLA RESIDENZA DOMUS MINERVAE:
Viale Pompeo Pellini 19. **Tel/Fax:** 075-5732238.
Web site: http://www.edisons.it/homepages/domusminervae/
E-mail: domusminervae@edisons.it (6 rms., 4 w/toilet & bath or shower.) 60,000-70,000L (31-36E) single; 85,000-91,000L (44-47E) double; 116,000-125,000L (59-64E) triple. Children under 4 free. Breakfast (8-10:30am) at 8,500L pp is not obligatory & can be served in the room. Cash only. English spoken (Catia), TV (6,500L extra per day), wonderful charming hotel w/old-fashioned furnished nice-size rms., #4 & 3 w/balconies, views & bathrooms are the best rms., #2 w/view & bathroom, #1 w/bathroom, #5 w/balcony & no bath-room, central heating, garden, no elevator, 2 flrs., parking (10,000L per day). *5% rm. discount when you show owner/manager Catia Mugnani or staff this book.* Catia, daughter of the owner of Hotel Anna, also has a 2-bedroom fully equipped apt. for rent available on a weekly basis. The family organizes Italian language, culture and cooking courses. Catia's brother Giacomo with his American wife Michela also manage Hotel Europa in the same bldg. Bus #6 or 7. Stop: Piccina Pellini, on the corner of where the hotel is located, just in front of an escalator (*scalia mobile*) that links Viale Pompeo Pellini to the historic center.

EDEN: Via Cesare Caporali 9. **Tel:** 075-5728102. **Fax:** 075-5720342. (15 rms., all w/toilet & bath or shower.) 75,000L (38E) single; 105,000L (54E) double; 140,000L (72E) triple; 170,000L (87E) quad. Visa, MC, AX, DC. Breakfast (8-10am) at 9,500L pp is not obliga-tory & can be served in the room (11,500L extra pp). Limited En-glish spoken, direct-dial phone, TV, wonderful charming modern hotel w/nicely furnished comfortable rms., rooms vary in size & decor, some w/wooden flrs. & high wood-beamed ceilings, nice atmosphere, #201 w/huge terrace/garden is the best rm. for 4 people, #309 for 3 people, #25 & 24 have view of the hills, 1 rm. has handicapped access, great location, central heating, elevator, 4 flrs. From Piazza Italia, look for Banco Italia, walk to the right of the bank down the steps, turn left on Via Luigi Bonazzi, turn right around the corner to Via Cesare Caporali. (Closed 20 days from Dec.-Jan.)

ETRURIA: Via Bella Luna 21. **Tel:** 075-5723730. (8 rms., 5 w/ toilet & bath or shower.) 60,000L (31E) single (no toilets); 99,000L (51E) double. Cash only. English spoken (Louisa & Maria), 13th-century wonderful medieval hotel w/antique furnished comfortable rms., #5 & 7 w/views & bathrooms are the best rms., #6 w/view but no bathroom, #8 w/bathroom but no view, central heating, no elevator, 1 fl. Owned/managed by Louisa & Antonetta, who are extremely interesting women. Kimbo is the hotel's small black poodle mascot. From Piazza Italia, walk straight down Corso Vannucci to Piazza Repubblica, turn left on Via Bella Luna (the 1st arched portal next to the pharmacy), walk down the steep steps to the hotel.

EUROPA: Viale Pompeo Pellini 19. **Tel:** 075-5726883.**Fax:** 075-5736304. (13 rms., 9 w/toilet & bath or shower.) 60,000-70,000L (31-36E) single; 85,000-91,000L (44-47E) double; 116,000-125,000L (59-64E) triple. Children under 4 free. Breakfast (8-10am) at 8,500L pp is not obligatory. Cash only. American English spoken (Michela), direct-dial phone, TV (6,500L extra per day), charming hotel w/old-fashioned furnished nice-size rms., #23 & 3 w/balconies, views & bathrooms are the best rms., #25 w/balcony & bathroom, 1 rm. has handicapped access, central heating, no elevator, 2 flrs., parking (10,000L per day). *5% rm. discount when you show owners/managers Giacomo & Michela Mugnani or staff this book.* The family organizes Italian language, culture and cooking courses. Bus #6 or 7. Stop: Piccina Pellini. For directions, see Hotel Alla Residenza Domus Minervae.

FORTUNA PERUGIA: Via Luigi Bonazzi 19.
Tel: 075-5722845. **Fax:** 075-5735040. (34 rms., 33 w/toilet & bath or shower.) 130,000-165,000L (67-85E) single; 175,000-200,000L (90-103E) double; 240,000-270,000L (123-138E) triple; 340,000-355,000L (174-182E) quad. Children under 12 free. Buffet breakfast (7:30-

10:30am) is included in the rates but can be deducted to reduce room price. Breakfast can be served in the room at extra cost of 7,500L pp and is served on the terrace in warm weather. Visa, MC, AX, DC. English spoken (Valeria), direct-dial phone, satellite TV w/English channel (mid-1999), wonderful beautiful provincial hotel w/contemporary furnished comfortable rms., lots of ambiance, #502 romantic rm. w/terrace & view, 309 w/frescoed ceiling & 2 baths & 504 are the best rms., #501 w/view, 6 rms. w/terraces, some rms. w/views of the valley or the center, central heating, air-conditioned (mid-1999), minibars, beautiful veranda terrace w/fabulous panoramic view, bar, elevator, 6 flrs. They offer half- (29,000L extra pp) and full-board (78,000L extra pp) rates. Valeria Rencaroni bought the hotel in July '98. *10% rm. discount when you show owner/manager Valeria or staff this book.* From Piazza Italia, look for Banco Italia, walk to the right of the bank down the steps to Via Luigi Bonazzi, hotel is on the right.

PICCOLO: Via Luigi Bonazzi 25. **Tel:** 075-5722987. (10 rms., 8 w/toilet & bath or shower.) 70,000-90,000L (36-46E) double; 95,000-130,000L (50-67E) triple; 120,000-150,000L (62-77E) quad. No breakfast is served. Cash only. English spoken (Alessandro & Francesca), basic hotel w/simply furnished rms., #6 & 7 w/balconies are the best rms., central heating, double-paned windows, no elevator, 2 flrs. *5% rm. discount when you show owner/manager Alessandro Meacci or staff this book.* For directions, see Hotel Fortuna Perugia. (Closed Dec. 25-Jan. 2.)

PRIORI: Via Priori/Vermiglioli 3.
Tel: 075-5723378/5723378. **Fax:** 075-5723213.
Web site: http://www.assind.perugia.it/hotel/priori/
E-mail: priori@assind.perugia.it (64 rms., all w/toilet & bath or shower.) 85,000-105,000L (44-54E) single; 95,000-145,000L (50-74E) double; 140,000-190,000L (72-97E) triple;
160,000-220,000L (82-113E) quad. Buffet breakfast w/bacon & scrambled eggs (7:15-10am) is included in the rates & cannot be deducted but can be served in the room (3,500L extra pp). Breakfast is served in the garden in warm weather. Visa, MC, AX, DC. English spoken (Raffaele, Marzia & Franziska), direct-dial phone, satellite TV w/CNN (extra charge), elegant 18th-century hotel w/modern furnished & antique furnished comfortable large bright airy rms., old & new

hotel in one bldg., 3 rms. w/balconies & 7 rms. w/terraces, many rms. w/views of the valley, fabulous terrace w/panoramic view, double-paned windows, central heating, 10 rms. w/air-conditioning (extra charge), bar, no elevator, 4 flrs., garage parking (20,000-30,000L per day). Owned/managed by Raffaele Stoppini. Raffaele still uses his faithful antique cash register to total up your bill. His two friendly boxers stand guard behind the reception desk. For directions, see Hotel Anna.

UMBRIA: Via Boncambi 37. **Tel/Fax:** 075-5721203. (17 rms., all w/toilet & bath or shower.) 70,000-85,000L (36-44E) single; 85,000-110,000L (44-56E) double; 120,000-140,000L (62-72E) triple; 150,000-160,000L (77-82E) quad. Breakfast (7:30am-12pm) at 9,500L pp is not obligatory & can be served in the room. Visa, MC. Limited English spoken (Miri), direct-dial phone, 50% rms. w/TVs, basic hotel w/simply furnished comfortable nice-size rms. & new bathrooms, #32 has a balcony, central heating, bar, no elevator, 2 flrs. Owned/managed by Miri Lavasani. Hotel will have email address in '99. From Piazza Italia, walk straight down Corso Vannucci to Piazza Repubblica, turn left on Via Boncambi (the 3rd arched portal next to the pharmacy), walk down the steep steps, follow the curved street to the left to the hotel.

I didn't get a chance to see the following 2 hotels:
Morlacchi: Via Tiberi 2, 16 rms. **Tel:** 075-5720319. **Fax:** 075-5735084. 10 w/toilet & bath or shower. 105,000L double.

Primavera Mini: Via Vincioli 8. **Tel:** 075-5721657. **Fax:** 075-5727681. 105,000L double. 8 rms., all w/toilet & bath or shower. 105,000L double.

Aurora: Viale Indipendenza 21. They refused to show me the rooms.

LAUNDROMAT (Lavanderia)
Lava e Lava: Via Annibale Vecchi 5. Hrs.: Daily: 8am-10pm. (Get there before 9pm.) 14,000L for wash & dry. Extra for detergent. Another location at Corso Bersaglieri 2. Same hrs.
Ondablu: Via Bersaglieri 2/4. Hrs.: Daily: 9am-10pm. (Get there before 9pm.) 14,000L for wash & dry. Located on the corner of Via Pinturicchio.

POSITANO
Amalfi Coast, zip code 84017
Area code 39, city code 089

Orientation: The most picturesque of all the villages on the coast. This village was made for walking. Make sure your shoes have a good grip. The town is built on a steep cliffside and is divided in two sections by the cliff which has the **Torre Trasita** tower. **Spiaggia Grande** is the more expensive and the larger beach area and **Spiaggia Fornillo** is the smaller and less expensive beach area. There are only two SITA scheduled bus stops in Positano: *"Sponda"* & *"Chiesa."* As you leave Sorrento, "Chiesa" is Positano's main bus stop at the **Bar Internazionale** which is located at the top of the village on the main road. The "Sponda" bus stop is on the same side as Amalfi; from here it is a 15-minute walk down **Via Cristoforo Colombo** to the beach. To walk from Positano's "Chiesa" bus stop on the main road to the beach is about a 45-minute walk down the very steep one-way **Via G. Marconi** to the one-way **Viale Pasitea** near the water, and even steeper and longer if you decide to climb back up to it. Local orange buses make a circle from the main road and go down Via Marconi to Viale Pasitea, then the bus climbs back up Viale Pasitea where the name changes to Via Colombo as it continues to climb back up to the main road.

Positano Tourist Information Center
Via Saracino 4. **Tel:** 089-875067. **Tel/Fax:** 089-875760. Hrs.: Mon.-Fri. 8:30am-2pm; Sat. 8am-12pm. Hours are not etched in stone. With your back to the Duomo, look straight down to the red bldg.

Hotels close to bus stop "Sponda"
These hotels are a 15-minute steep hike down to the center.

BOUGAINVILLE: Via Cristoforo Colombo 25.
Tel: 089-875047. **Fax:** 089-811150.
Web site: http://www.argosid.it/aziende/bougan/index.sht/
E-mail: bougan@positano.argosid.it (14 rms., all w/toilet & bath or shower.) 95,000-105,000L (50-54E) single; 135,000-150,000L (69-77E) double; 180,000L (92E) triple. Breakfast (8-10:30am) at 11,500L

pp is not obligatory and is served on the terrace in warm weather. Visa, MC, AX, DC. English spoken (Carlo), direct-dial phone, wonderful charming hotel w/comfortable rms., 7 rms. w/balconies & views, #32, 34, 26, 24 & 20 have balconies w/wonderful views, #10 large terrace (share w/others) w/view, double-paned windows, nice flrs., central heating, noisy location, computer service available, no elevator, 1 fl. *5% rm. discount when you show owner/manager Carlo Cuomo or staff this book. Carlo will extend a free breakfast to seniors over 60.* Ask SITA bus driver for Sponda bus stop. Walk down Via Cristoforo Colombo to hotel. (Closed Nov.-Feb.)

CALIFORNIA: Via Cristoforo Colombo 141. **Tel/Fax:** 089-875382. (15 rms., all w/toilet & bath or shower.) 175,000L (90E) single; 185,000L (95E) double. Call for triple & quad rates. Breakfast (7:30am) at 11,500L pp is not obligatory & can be served in the room (4,500L extra pp). Visa, MC, AX, DC. American English spoken (Antonio, Frank & Maria), direct-dial phone, wonderful charming 18th-century renovated palazzo hotel w/antiquish furnished comfortable large rms., #61 (balcony & view), 62 (balcony & view) & 58 (2 balconies) are fabulous, best views are on the 3rd fl., 12 rms. w/ balconies, nice flrs., central heating, bar, garden, no elevator, 3 flrs., free parking. Great location. Owned/managed by Fratelli Cinque. The whole family is warm and energetic. For directions, see Hotel Bougainville. (Closed Nov. 15-March.)

TAVOLOZZA: Via Colombo 10. **Tel/Fax:** 089-875040. (8 rms., all w/toilet & bath or shower.) 145,000L (74E) double; 165,000-265,000L (85-136E) small apt; 320,000-370,000L (164-190E) large apt. Breakfast (8am-12noon) at 13,500L pp is not obligatory & is served in the room. Cash only. English spoken (Anna), direct-dial phone, wonderful charming hotel w/renovated airy bright rms., all the rms. vary in decor & color, #6, 5, 4 (the best view) & 1 w/balconies & views, #5 has a private bathroom in the hall, several fully equipped apts. w/views available for 3-7 people, no elevator. For directions, see Hotel Bougainville. (Closed Nov.-Feb.)

Hotels in the middle of the hills
These hotels are a 25-minute steep hike down to the center.

POSITANO

CELESTE: Via Fornillo 10. **Tel/Fax:** 089-875363. (4 rms., 3 w/ toilet & bath or shower.) 70,000-80,000L (36-41E) single; 125,000-145,000L (64-74E) double; 185,000-215,000L (95-110E) triple; 240,000-280,000L (123-144E) quad. Breakfast (8-10am, homemade jam) at 6,500L pp is not obligatory & can be served in the room. Breakfast is served on the terrace in warm weather. Cash only. English spoken (Marco), 17th-century quaint hotel w/simply furnished small rms., #1, 3 & 4 w/balconies, sea views & bathrooms are the best rms., #5 has a private bathroom in the hall, double-paned windows, no elevator, 1 fl., parking (25,000-35,000L per day). *5% rm. discount when you show owners/managers Celeste Desiderio, Marco Rispoli or staff this book.* Marco is very helpful. Marco's mother Celeste makes wonderful homemade *limoncello* and if she is not busy will make dinner. Catch the local orange bus. Stop: Grotto Fornillo. Via Fornillo is to the right off Viale Pasitea. As you exit the bus, with the sacred miniature churches carved in the hill to your back, look to your right for the sign/arrow "Alberto Victorio" which is on Via Fornillo. Turn right on Via Fornillo to your hotel.

GUADAGNO: Via Fornillo 22. **Tel:** 089-875042. **Fax:** 089-811407. (15 rms., all w/toilet & bath or shower.) 125,000-135,000L (64-69E) double. Call for triple rates. Breakfast (8-10am) is included in the rates & can be served in the room but can be deducted to reduce the room price. Breakfast is served on the terrace in warm weather. Visa, MC, AX, DC. English spoken (Guadagno), charming new hotel w/ simply furnished nice-size bright airy rms., all rooms w/balconies & 10 w/sea views, #4, 5 & 6 have the best views, #2 is wonderful, nice flrs., minibars, terrace, vegetable garden, bar, no elevator, 3 flrs. They offer half-board rates which may be required in summer. Guadagno's sister Teresa does the cooking. You eat what the family eats. For directions, see Hotel Celeste.

MARIA LUISA: Via Fornillo 40. **Tel/Fax:** 089-875023. (10 rms., all w/toilet & bath or shower.) 60,000-65,000L (31-33E) single; 105,000L (54E) double; 140,000L (72E) triple; 170,000L (87E) quad. Breakfast (8-10am) at 11,500L pp is not obligatory. Cash only. English spoken (Carlo), peaceful hotel w/large bright rms, #6 (wonderful), 5 (wonderful), 4 & 3 have balconies & sea views, #7 & 9 view of Positano but no balconies, spectacular panoramic view from terrace, access to refrigerator, nearby restaurant, no elevator, 3 flrs. Owned/managed by Giovanni & Carlo Milo. For directions, see Hotel Celeste. (Closed Dec. & Jan.)

SANTA CATERINA: Viale Pasitea 113. **Tel:** 089-811513. **Fax:** 089-875019 (12 rms., all w/toilet & bath or shower.) 95,000-135,000L (50-69E) single; 135,000-165,000L (69-85E) double; 200,000-220,000L (103-113E) triple. Breakfast (9-11am) at 11,500-16,500L pp is not obligatory. Visa, MC, AX, DC. English spoken (Francesca), wonderful charming hotel w/simply furnished nice-size airy rms., #5 w/private balcony & magnificent view, #1-5 share a large terrace w/magnificent view, most of the rooms have a wonderful view, lower priced rooms are w/o views, all rms. have bathtubs, spectacular panoramic view from terrace, bar, restaurant, no elevator, 3 flrs. Catch the local orange bus. Stop: Viale Pasitea. (Closed Jan. 6-March 6.)

Hotel near the main road
VILLA VERDE: Viale Pasitea 338. **Tel/Fax:** 089-875506. (12 rms., all w/toilet & bath or shower.) 130,000L (67E) double; 175,000L (90E) triple. Call for quad rates. Breakfast (8-10:30am) is included in the rates but can be deducted to reduce room price. Breakfast is served on the terrace in warm weather. Cash only. English spoken (Isabella), nice hotel w/simply furnished nice-size pretty rms., nice flrs., all rms. w/balconies, #5 & 3 are the best rms., garden, spectacular panoramic view from terrace, no elevator, 3 flrs., free parking. From Positano's main bus stop at the Bar Internazionale, walk (10 minutes) down Viale Pasitea. This hotel is a 40-minute steep hike down to the center. (Closed Nov. 20-Feb.)

When I was in Rome, Alex from Hotel Coronet told me about his friend Pietro Pane. Pietro is a 50-year-old fisherman who rents rooms in his home at a reasonable price. Rates include breakfast & dinner which is served at a specific time and you must be punctual. Via Canovaccio 5. **Tel:** 089-875360.

LAUNDROMATS (Lavanderia)
Citta Rum: Via Colombo 175. **Tel:** 089-811144. Daily: 8:30am-1pm. & 3:15-8:30pm. Closed Sun. in low season. Wash/dry 9,000L per piece.
Arcobaleno: Via G. Marconi 332. **Tel:** 089-811552.

RIVA DEL GARDA
Lake Garda. zip code 38066
Area code 39, city code 0464

Orientation: Riva del Garda is located on the northernmost tip of Lake Garda. A resort with a magnificent lakefront promenade where the Alpine cliffs meet the water, narrow winding cobblestone streets, medieval towers, renaissance churches and palm-tree-lined piazzas. If you enjoy walking trails, Riva del Garda has plenty of mountain trails. This is a wonderful, quaint memorable village. The heart of the town, the lakeside **Piazza 3 Novembre**, is surrounded by medieval palazzi. **Viale Roverto** is the main highway that goes through the town. If you arrive by boat, the port is right in the middle of the center. There is no bus station in Riva del Garda. You can get bus information from the various travel offices or look at the display signs posted at the bus stops along Viale Roverto.

Transportation: An easy way to get to Riva del Garda from the northern side of Italy using mass transportation is to catch a train to the town of Roverto. You can either wait in front of the Roverto train station for the bus to Riva del Garda or walk (10 min.) from the train station straight down the main street to the bus station on your left. Buses will take you on a 45-min. ride to Riva del Garda. From the southern side of Italy, catch a train to Desanzano. Don't look for a bus station at the Desanzano train station-there isn't any. Walk across the street to Bar Olympia, where there should be some bus drivers hanging out. Ask them for the departure times to Riva del Garda. Then go back to the train station and buy your bus ticket inside at the bar. It is a 2-hr. bus ride to Riva. Bus info tel: 045-8004129. Or you can walk (15 minutes) or taxi to Desanzano's port to catch a 3-hr. catamaran or a 6-hr. ferry boat ride to Riva del Garda. You can also catch a 2-hr. ferry boat ride from Sirmone to Riva del Garda. Navigazione Lago di Garda tel: 167-551801.

Riva del Garda's Tourist Information Center
Giardini Porta Orientale 8. **Tel:** 0464-554444.
Fax: 0464-520308. **Web site:** http://www.garda.com/
E-mail: aptgarda@anthesi.com Hrs.: Mon.-Fri. 9am-12pm. & 3-

5:30pm. Closed Sun. Open later hrs. & Sat. in season. Located near the water's edge behind a small children's playground on Via Liberazione.

Hotels in the center
ANCORA: Via Montanara 2. **Tel**: 0464-522131. **Tel/Fax:** 0464-550050. **Web site:** http://www.rivadelgarda.com/ancora/
E-mail: hotelancora@rivadelgarda.com (14 rms., all w/toilet & bath or shower.) 135,000-155,000L (69-79E) double; 210,000-220,000L (108-113E) triple. Buffet breakfast (7:30-10:30am) at 16,500L pp is not obligatory. Visa, MC, AX, DC. Limited English spoken (Loredana), direct-dial phone, TV, wonderful charming quaint hotel w/beautifully furnished comfortable nice-size rms., most rms. are either decorated in pink or white trimmings, #11 (balcony), 10 (balcony) & 4 are the best rms., #210 is also wonderful, 1 rm. has handicapped access, double-paned windows, central heating, bar, restaurant w/terrace, elevator, 4 flrs. They offer half-board rates. Friendly & accommodating staff. If you eat in the restaurant ask for Dimitri, the waiter who speaks American English. The hotel is not family-owned. Located on the pedestrian walkway, 150m from the lake. (Closed Feb.)

GIGLIO: Via Disciplini 23. **Tel**: 0464-552674. **Fax:** 0464-521069. (13 rms., all w/toilet & bath or shower.) 75,000L (38E) single; 135,000L (69E) double; 180,000L (92E) triple. Breakfast (8-10am) is included in the rates & can be served in the room (11,500 extra pp) but can be deducted to reduce room price. Visa, MC, AX, DC. Limited English spoken (Leda), direct-dial phone, TV, wonderful charming hotel w/comfortable nice-size bright rms., tiled flrs., 1 rm. has handicapped access, #101, 201 & 301 are the best rms., double-paned windows, central heating, bar, restaurant, elevator, 4 flrs. They offer half- (95,000L pp) and full-board (110,000L pp) rates. Owned/managed by Franco & Leda Lazzarotto. Franco & Leda do all the cooking for their restaurant.

PORTICI: Piazza III Novembre 19. **Tel**: 0464-555400. **Fax:** 0464-555453. (45 rms., all w/toilet & bath or shower.) 83,000-100,000L (43-51E) single; 73,000-90,000L (37-46E) double. Buffet breakfast (8-10am) is included in the rates & cannot be deducted. Visa, MC.

English spoken, direct-dial phone, satellite TV, charming modern hotel w/nicely furnished comfortable rms., #202 & 203 both w/balconies are the best rms. which face the square, 20 rms. have handicapped access, central heating, bar, restaurant, elevator, 5 flrs. They offer half- (85,000-105,000L pp) and full-board (105,000-128,000L pp) rates. Owned/managed by Giuliano Bertoldi. Located close to the dock, a few minutes from the water. (Closed Oct.-April.)

VITTORIA: Via Dante 39/Via Disciplini 18. **Tel:** 0464-554398. **Fax:** 0464-559567. (16 rms., all w/toilet & bath or shower.) 60,000L (31E) single; 95,000L (50E) double; 130,000L (67E) triple. Breakfast (8-10am) at 6,500L pp is not obligatory. Visa, MC. English spoken (Poco), quaint hotel w/simply furnished rms., central heating, bar, restaurant, no elevator, 3 flrs. They offer half- (70,000L pp) and full-board (100,000L pp) rates. Owned/managed by Maria Teresa Grottolo. (Closed Dec.-Feb.)

Hotels not far from center
These hotels are located near the first bus stop coming in from Roverto and the 2nd coming in from Desanzano.To get to these hotels on Viale Roverto by bus, just tell the bus driver you want Viale Roverto which is a stop in front of a supermarket. It is a 15-minute walk from the center of the village to these hotels. Taxi 12,000L. If you arrive in Riva del Garda and can't get a room, just walk down to Viale Roverto, with the numbers going up past hotel Rialto and start looking. Plenty of hotels line the streets.

BELLARIVA: Viale Roverto 58. **Tel:** 0464-553620. **Fax:** 0464-556633. **Web site:** http://www.rivadelgarda.com/bellariva/
E-mail: bellariva@rivadelgarda.com (30 rms., all w/toilet & bath or shower.) 115,000-135,000L (60-69E) single; 179,000-215,000L (92-110E) double. Call for triple & quad rates. Breakfast (7-10am) is included in the rates & can be served in the room but can be deducted to reduce room price. Visa, MC, AX, DC. Limited English spoken, direct-dial phone, satellite TV w/English channel, recently renovated wonderful hotel w/nicely furnished comfortable modern rms. & beautiful bathrooms, #210, 209 & 204 are the best rms., 20 rms. w/balconies, 20 rms. w/views, marble staircase but could use some new carpeting in the hallway, tranquil location, hair driers, beautiful garden,

central heating, air-conditioned, bar, restaurant/terrace facing the water, no elevator, 2 flrs., free parking. They offer half- and full-board rates. 5-minute walk to the water and a 20-minute walk to the center. (Closed Nov.-March.)

LUISE: Viale Roverto 9. **Tel:** 0464-552796. **Fax:** 0464-554250. **Web site:** http://www.rivadelgarda.com/luise/ **E-mail:** luise@rivadelgarda.com (69 rms., all w/toilet & bath or shower.) 180,000-255,000L (92-131E) double; 250,000-344,000L (128-176E) triple; 309,000-428,000L (158-219E) quad. Children under 8 free except in July & Aug. Buffet breakfast (7-10:30am) is included in the rates & cannot be deducted. Breakfast can be served in the room at extra cost of 11,500 pp. Visa, MC, AX, DC. English spoken, direct-dial phone, satellite TV w/English channel, modern large grand hotel w/comfortable rms., 19 rms. w/balconies, 10 rms. have handicapped access, minibars, hair driers, double-paned windows, central heating, air-conditioned, mountain bikes available, pool, tennis, pingpong, garden w/sunbeds, children's play area, bar, restaurant, elevator, free parking. The hotel divides its rooms into 3 types/prices: Orchidea, the most expensive, Gardenia, in the middle and Margherita, the cheapest. There are only 10 Margherita rooms of which 5 have balconies. I liked the Margherita rooms because they have not been renovated so they are old-fashioned nicely furnished large rms. w/bathtubs. They offer half-board rates at 35,000L extra pp. *5% rm. discount when you show owner/manager Stella Bertolini, director Fausto Franzoi or staff this book.*

PERLA (La): Viale Roverto 67. **Tel:** 0464-552204. **Fax:** 0464-520088. (100 rms., all w/toilet & bath or shower.) 80,000-135,000L (41-69E) single; 125,000-235,000L (64-121E) double. Buffet breakfast (7-9am) at 19,500L pp is not obligatory. Breakfast is served in the garden/terrace in warm weather. Visa, MC, AX, DC. English spoken (Erica & Silvia), direct-dial phone, satellite TV w/English channel, hotel is combination of 3 bldgs. (old, #2 & new) w/modern comfortable rms. that vary quite a bit, 65 rms. w/balconies, 10 rms. have handicapped access, garden, terraces, double-paned windows, central heating, pool, bar, restaurant, elevators, free parking. Old bldg.: 3 flrs. w/nothing special except has a terrace; bldg. #2 stands by itself near the pool w/a wonderful roof terrace; all rms. have balconies but try to get #70 w/balcony & view of the mountains, or a rm. on the 4th fl. because they have better views than the rest of the rms.; new bldg. also w/a terrace is connected to the old bldg., has 7 suites: #75, 78, 81, 84, 85, 87 & 92 which are extra-large rms. w/minibars; you won't get the intimate feeling & special attention of a small hotel like the Rialto next door because of its size but it is still a good hotel. They offer half- (35,000L extra pp) and full-board (70,000L extra pp) rates. After March '99, the reception area will move to the new bldg. One day a week in warm weather, the hotel has a get-together with music and food for half-board rates. Owned/managed by Averardo Zambonini. They should have a Web site by March '99. (Closed Nov.-Dec. 26 & Jan. 02-March.)

RIALTO: Viale Roverto 63. **Tel**: 0464-553123/553125. **Fax:** 0464-554496. (16 rms., all w/toilet & bath or shower.) 65,000-75,000L (33-38E) single; 95,000-110,000L (50-56E) double; 132,000-155,000L (68-79E) triple; 158,000-183,000L (81-94E) quad. Breakfast (8:30-10am) at 16,500L pp is not obligatory. Breakfast is served outside in warm weather. Visa, MC, DC. English spoken (Franco), direct-dial phone, TV, charming wonderful hotel w/modern furnished comfortable rms. & modern bathrooms, #101 (terrace) 102 (terrace) & 203 (balcony) are the best rms., #205, 103 & 204 have balconies, 5 rms. w/minibars, hair driers, central heating, quiet location, bar, restaurant, no elevator, 3 flrs., free parking. *5% rm. discount when you show owners/managers Franco & Ornello Dibiase or staff this book.* My husband & I stayed here and loved it. They are a very accommodating family. Franco & his family work very hard to make your stay enjoyable. 5-minute walk to the lake. Franco's son Giovanni manages another family-owned restaurant in the center near the lake. Mr. Buzz Daldos from Colorado told me via fax how satisfied he was with this hotel and wanted to make sure it was in the book. (Closed Wed. & Mid-Nov.-Dec.)

RESTAURANT
Please check page 20 for my criteria for selecting restaurants.

RIALTO: Viale Roverto 63. **Tel**: 0464-553123/553125. **Fax:** 0464-554496. Hrs.: 12-3pm & 6-11pm. Closed Wed. from Oct.-Dec. & March.) Visa, MC, DC. This hotel/restaurant is not located inside the village, yet people walk from town to eat here. I had the delicious *bogli* w/pesto which is a homemade thicker version of spaghetti, grilled vegetables, chicken w/rice, 1/2 liter of wine and homemade dessert for 30,000L. If you don't want french fries with your course, ask for rice instead. Franco & his family will take good care of you. *Show Franco this book and he will give you a complimentary limoncello.*

MALCESINE
Lake Garda
Area code 39, city code 045

Orientation: This quaint little medieval town is very appealing. My husband and I visited it on a day trip from Riva del Garda. We found two wonderful charming hotels if you are interested in spending a night here.

Malcesine Tourist Information Center
Via Capitanato, 37018. **Tel:** 045-7400044. Hrs.: Daily 9am-1pm. & 3-6:30pm.

LUCIA: Via Navena, 37018. **Tel:** 045-7400066. **Fax:** 045-6570446. (36 rms., all w/toilet & bath or shower.) April-May 95,000L double; June & Sept. 105,000L double; July-Aug. 115,000L double. Breakfast is included in the rates. English spoken (Linda), comfortable rms. Owned/managed by Gino & Linda Lazzaro. They offer half-board rates. Located in the pedestrian area by old town. 150m from lake and 200m from cable car to Monte Baldo. Gino will pick you up in Verona if necessary. (Closed Nov.-mid-March.)

ALPINO: Via Navena, 37018. **Tel:** 045-7400066. **Fax:** 045-6570446. All rms. w/toilet & bath or shower. They offer half-board rates. Located close to the port and the tourist office.

RESTAURANT
Fast Food 2001: Via Casella 6, 37018. **Tel:** 045-7400211. Hrs.: daily 10am-10pm. Try this place for delicious fast food, 1/2 chicken, french fries & 1/4 liter of wine 18,000L pp. You can substitute fish (15,000L pp) for the chicken. Located next to the *lavanderi* (laundromat). Mayonnaise costs extra.

ROME (Roma)
Latium, zip code 00186
Area code 39, city code 06

Orientation: Rome is sectioned into nine neighborhoods. Most trains stop at **Termini,** Rome's main rail station. If you are not staying near the train station, I suggest you catch a metro, bus or taxi to your hotel. It is a long walk to the historic center of Rome. The Termini train station is located at **Via Cavour/Via Marsala** on **Piazza Cinquecento** on the eastern edge of the center. Immediately to the station's north is **Piazza Repubblica**, which is almost connected to the Piazza Cinquecento. From Piazza Repubblica starts the wide, busy artery **Via Nazionale** which connects Termini to **Piazza Venezia**, the center of the tourist activity. It is at Piazza Venezia you will see the wedding cake-like building known as the **Vittorio Emanuele** monument, located at the end of the **Via Corso**. With your back to the monument, the wide, popular shopping street **Corso Vittorio Emanuele II** will be on your left. In between Corso Vittorio and the river to its left is **Campo de' Fiori** and **Piazza Farnese**. Continuing to stand with your back to the monument, if you look straight ahead down to the end of Via Corso will be **Piazza Popolo**. If you walk down Via Corso about 1/3 of the way and turn left, you'll run into **Piazza Navona** and the **Pantheon** area; a right turn will take you to the **Trevi Fountain**. If you keep walking down Via Corso about 2/3 of the way, a right turn will take you into the trendy **Piazza Spagna** and the **Spanish steps**. Depending on where you are staying and how many bags you have, you can walk, catch a metro, bus or a taxi from the Termini train station to your hotel. I suggest if your hotel is not near the train station that you taxi to the hotel because the metro and buses are extremely crowded. Look under the individual hotels for more transportation details.

Finding a street address: Before you start venturing out looking for street addresses, please keep in mind that depending on what part of Rome you find yourself in, the address numbers on the buildings usually occur in two different patterns: 1.) The numbers will run consecutively, with odd numbers on one side of the street and even numbers on the other side. 2.) The numbers begin on one side of the street, run all the way down that side in sequence till the end, then on the other side they run all the way back. Example: Building #45 will be opposite building #492. Also, Rome has a lot of small, winding, zigzagging streets that change from block to block and have their own numbering system. Look at both sides of the street to determine what logic if any the Romans are using.

TRANSPORTATION TO AND FROM AIRPORT

Termini Train station: Catch the **Termini line**, an air-conditioned express train (every hr.) from Rome's Leonardo da Vinci (Fiumicino) airport for 30-min. ride (20,000L pp) to the Termini train station. Hrs.: 7:30am-9pm. Simply follow the signs to your left for Stazione FS/Railway Station also labeled *"Treno."* Right after you walk through customs, when you leave the arrivals building, you'll see the train station about 40 feet in front of you across the street and up the ramp. If you plan to take the train back to the airport, purchase all your tickets at the same time. It will save you a lot of time when you get ready to leave Rome. Also, pick up a train schedule when you purchase your train ticket. Trains run from Termini to the airport every half-hour from track #22. Hrs.: 6:50am-9:15pm. (Check the large boards with the current train schedules posted high on walls of either side of tracks for current train info.) **Tiburtina train station:** Catch the **Tiburtina-Orte-Farasabina line**, an air-conditioned metro train (every 20 min.) from the airport to Tiburtina train station (not Termini). The trip takes about 45 min. (8,000L pp) and makes about six stops before Tiburtina. Hrs.: 6am-10pm. You can catch a metro or a bus from Tiburtina train station to Termini. Then a bus, metro or a taxi from Termini to your hotel. Look under the individual hotels for more transportation details. **Taxi:** Airport to center (45 min.) is approximately 90,000L including luggage.
Airport Shuttle: airportshuttle@tiscalinet.it
Tel: 06-42014507. **Fax:** 06-42014511

Rome Tourist Information Centers
1.) Central office: Via Parigi 5-11.
Tel: 06-48899255/48899253/4883748. **Fax:** 06-4819316. Hrs.: Mon.-Fri. 8:15am-7:00pm, Sat 8:15am-1:15pm. This office is about a 10-min. walk from the front of the train station diagonally to the left, cross the huge Piazza Cinquecento ahead bearing left near Piazza

Repubblica's large fountain. Via Parigi begins on the other side of the church. **2.**) Termini (main train station) **Tel:** 06-4871270/4824078. Hrs.: 8:15am-7:15pm. It is the only one open on Sundays. The office will keep changing locations within the train station until "Giubileo 2000." **3.**) Leonardo da Vinci Airport, just outside customs to your left. One desk for Italy and one desk for Rome. **Tel:** 06-6011255. Hrs.: Mon.-Sat. 8:30am-7:00pm. **4.**) Italian Government Office (ENIT): Via Marghera 2. **Tel:** 06-4971282. Exit the train station to the right, walk one block up to Via Marghera. Mon.-Fri. 9am-1pm. **5.**) CIT World Travel Group - Piazza Repubblica 68.

Low season Jan.-Feb. & Nov.12-Dec.24; mid-season March, June-Aug.; high season April, May, Sept.-Nov. 11, Christmas & New Year's. Starting Dec. 1, 1999 through the entire year of 2000, Rome will be celebrating "Giubileo 2000," a celebration that takes place once every 25 years involving the Pope and pilgrims coming in from all over the world. Lots of events are planned for the year so rooms will be scarce. For more info contact their office at **Tel:** 06-681671. **Fax:** 06-6864673. **Web site:** http://www.romagiubileo.it/ **E-mail:** agenzia@romagiubileo.it **Additional Web sites:** http://www.roma2000.it/ *Rome 2000:* http://www.inforoma.it/holyyear.htm/ http://www.romeguide.it/FILES/giub_in.htm/ http://www.annosanto2000.com/ENGLISH/home.htm/

Rome hotels listed alphabetically

Neighborhood surrounding Stazione Termini

There are some great hotels located on both sides at good prices. Most of these hotels have been newly renovated into modern comfortable hotels. If you are looking for old world hotels with Italian flavor, then you need to stay near the historic center and be willing to pay more lire for less comfort. The south side area of Stazione Termini is experiencing a restoration comeback, but it is still filled with fumes and noise from heavy traffic of buses and cars. The north side has really been improved tremendously over the past couple of years. It is a true renaissance in the making. Although both sides of the station are relatively safe, I find the north/right side/track 1 (the Russian & Turkish embassies, government offices and many banks are located on the north side) to be more appealing than the south/left side/track 22. As I mentioned in the introduction of this book, I don't consider any city in Italy including Naples to be as dangerous as New York City (where I was born and raised) or Los Angeles (where I currently live). There are a lot of people constantly hanging out around the train station as well as plenty of police officers (including undercover police officers). I walked around the entire area late at night by myself and never felt threatened. Your biggest concern should be the pickpockets when you are in the Termini train station or on Via Giovanni Giolitti which parallels the station. But then, they are everywhere in Rome, especially at the Vatican and Spanish Steps. Also, pickpockets disguise themselves as nuns and priests around the Vatican. The only down side to staying near the train station is that you are forced to catch the metro, bus or taxi back to your hotel in the evenings after visiting all the sights and the wonderful, energetic historic center.

Hotels south of Stazione Termini
Left side exit (near track 22)

Please see Neighborhood surrounding Stazione Termini above.

ELIDE: Via Firenze 50, 1st fl. **Tel:** 06-4741367/4883977. **Fax:** 06-48904318. (12 rms., 7 w/toilet & bath or shower.) 95,000-125,000L (50-64E) single (no toilets); 105,000-165,000L (54-85E) double. Call for triple rates. Breakfast (7:30-10:30am) is included in the rates & can be served in the room (4,500 extra pp) but can be deducted to reduce room price. Visa, MC, AX, DC. Limited English spoken (Enzo

& Giuseppe), direct-dial phone, 18th-century basic hotel w/simply furnished rms., #18 (shower only), 16 & 15 have 18th-century ceilings, #18 & 24 are the best rms., 4 rms. have showers only, elevators, 2 flrs. **Metro:** Repubblica. From Termini train station, go diagonally left across Piazza Cinquecento (in front of station), turn left onto Via Viminale, take 2nd right to Via Firenze.

GIUGIU: Via Viminale 8, 2nd fl. **Tel:** 06-4827734. **Fax:** 06-8912616. (24 rms., 16 w/toilet & bath or shower.) 75,000L (38E) single; 115,000L (60E) double; 150,000L (77E) triple; 180,000L (92E) quad. Breakfast (8-9am) at 11,500L pp is not obligatory. Cash only. English spoken (Carmen), basic hotel w/simply furnished nice-size dark rms., high ceilings, midnight curfew, elevator, 1 flr. Owned/managed by Caterina Ferraro. There is absolutely nothing special or warm about this hotel. **Metro:** Termini. From Termini train station, go diagonally left across Piazza Cinquecento (in front of station), turn left onto Via Viminale.

• **NARDIZZI AMERICANA:** Via Firenze 38, 4th fl. **Tel:** 06-4880368. **Fax:** 06-4880035. (18 rms., all w/toilet & bath or shower.) 100,000-115,000L (51-60E) single; 110,000-165,000L (56-85E) double; 130,000-220,000L (67-113E) triple; 140,000-240,000L (72-123E) quad. Children under 5 free. Breakfast (7:30-9:30am) is included in the rates & cannot be deducted but can be served in the room. Breakfast is served on the terrace in warm weather. Visa, MC, AX, DC. English spoken (Nik), direct-dial phone, satellite TV w/English channel, beautiful charming 19th-century palace w/nicely furnished comfortable airy bright rms., #10 a corner room w/views is one of the best, #14 has a balcony, #11 & 9 have floor to ceiling windows, 7 rooms will have the best views, modern bathrooms, front rooms are noisy, double-paned windows, towel heaters, central heating, air-conditioned, bar, garden, new rooftop terrace w/spectacular panoramic view, elevator, 1 fl., parking (30,000L per day). This magnificent hotel is in the middle of renovations. I am really sorry I didn't get to see this hotel after its renovation. Nik walked me through the floors and I was amazed at what they are doing. Elegant Roman-style decor w/columns, beautiful floors that resemble Roman streets & halls that conveniently light up when you walk through them. The room numbers mentioned above might change after renovations are completed.

10% rm. discount when you show owner/manager Fabrizio Tarquini or staff this book. **Metro:** Repubblica. For directions, see Hotel Elide. Located near Via XX Settembre & the American Embassy.

RIENZO: Via Principe Amedeo 79a, 1st fl. **Tel:** 06-4467131/4466980. (13 rms., 6 w/toilet & bath or shower.) 90,000-100,000L (46-51E) single; 100,000-115,000L (51-60E) double; 150,000L (77E) triple. No breakfast is served. Visa, MC, AX. English spoken (Daniella), charming basic hotel w/simply furnished rms., #16, 14 (bathtub) & 18 w/bathrooms are the best rms., #12 w/balcony but no bathroom, the rms. on the 3rd fl. are w/o bathrooms, nice flrs., quiet location, central heating, elevator, 3 flrs. **Metro:** Termini. Exit the train station near track 22, turn left walk down Via Giovanni Giolitti, turn right onto Via Gioberti for 2 blocks, turn left onto Via Principe Amedeo.

SAN PAOLO: Via Panisperna 95. **Tel:** 06-4745213/4745217. **Fax:** 06-4745218. **E-mail:** hsanpaolo@tin.it (13 rms., 3 w/toilet & bath or shower.) 55,000-80,000L (28-41E) single; 75,000-140,000L (38-72E) double; 100,000-140,000L (51-72E) triple. Breakfast (7:30-9:30am) at 11,500L pp is not obligatory. Visa, MC, AX, DC. English spoken (Rami, Dani & Virgilio), basic hotel w/simply furnished rms., #4, 19 & 27 have bathrooms, #34 (family rm.) will have a bathroom in '99, #28-32 have wood-beamed ceilings, 1 rm. w/balcony, local artist hand-painted his version of frescoes on the walls of the rooms, double-paned windows, central heating, no elevator, 4 flrs. *5% rm. discount when you show owner/manager Rami Lawi or staff this book.* **Metro:** Termini. Turn left from Piazza Cinquecento (in front of station) onto Via Cavour past the Basilica, turn right on Via S. Maria Maggiore which becomes Via Panisperna.

SELENE: Via Viminale 8, 3rd fl. **Tel:** 06-4744781. **Fax:** 06-47821977 (27 rms., 24 w/toilet & bath or shower.) 95,000L (50E) single; 125,000L (64E) double; 180,000L (92E) triple. Visa, MC, AX, DC. English spoken (Gianni), direct-dial phone, satellite TV w/ English channel, basic hotel w/simply furnished dark rms., 12:30 am curfew, elevator, 2 flrs. Owned/managed by Gianni Fratini. There is absolutely nothing special or warm about this hotel. **Metro:** Termini. For directions, see Hotel Giugiu.

STELLA ELSA: Via Principe Amedeo 79a, 3rd fl. **Tel/Fax:** 06-4460634. (9 rms., 7 w/toilet & bath or shower.) 75,000-115,000L (38-60E) single; 85,000-155,000L (44-79E) double; 110,000-175,000L (56-90E) triple; 140,000-220,000L (72-113E) quad. Call for family room rates. Buffet breakfast (7:30-10am) at 11,500L pp is not obligatory & can be served in the room. Breakfast is served on the roof garden in warm weather. Visa, MC. English spoken (Marco & Maria), direct-dial phone, satellite TV w/English channel ('99), charming hotel w/nicely furnished rms., #2 (small), 3 & 6 have balconies, #4 is pretty, #8 is huge, all rms. face the inner courtyard and are therefore quiet, double-paned windows, central heating, air-conditioned (4 rms. in Jan. '99), relaxing rooftop terrace, elevator, 3 flrs. *10% rm. discount when you show owners/managers Marco, Maria or staff this book.* Marco & Maria are wonderful owners who will try hard to please you. Marco has rooms for 6 people in another bldg. He will be opening up an Internet café called "Hollywood Internet Café." Call/fax him for his E-mail address. **Metro:** Termini. For directions, see Hotel Rienzo. Take the stairs on the right side of the courtyard at 79a.

HOTELS OVER $100 A NIGHT FOR TWO
These hotels may have rooms under $100 a night for two because it is low season or the rooms do not have private bathrooms.

ADLER: Via Modena 5, 2nd fl. **Tel:** 06-484466. **Fax:** 06-4880940. (16 rms., 9 w/toilet & bath or shower.) 125,000-135,000L (64-69E) single; 155,000-195,000L (79-100E) double; 210,000-260,000L (108-133E) triple, 260,000-330,000 (133-169E) quad. Breakfast (7:30-9:30am) is included in the rates & cannot be deducted but can be served in the room. Visa, MC, AX, DC. English spoken (Giorgio), direct-dial phone, 14 rms. w/TVs & a/c (1999), basic charming hotel w/old-fashioned furnished large rms., terrace, central heating, elevator, 2 flrs. The hotel will do more renovations in Dec. '99. From Termini train station, go diagonally left across Piazza Cinquecento (in front of station) to Piazza Repubblica, walk to the left around Piazza Repubblica, turn right onto Via Torino, turn left onto Via Modena. **Metro:** Repubblica.

BEL SOGGIORNO: Via Torino 117, 5th fl. **Tel:** 06-4881701/ 4815724. **Fax:** 06-4815755. (17 rms., all w/toilet & bath or shower.) 135,000L (69E) single; 195,000L (100E) double; 260,000L (133E) triple; 280,000L (144E) quad. Children under 6 free. Buffet breakfast (7-10am) is included in the rates. Visa, MC, AX. English spoken (Laura), direct-dial phone, TV, wonderful charming hotel w/nicely furnished comfortable nice-size airy rms., lots of ambiance & warmth, #103-105 w/balconies are the best, the rooms on the 5th fl. are older, larger & have more character than the smaller modern basic rooms on the 6th fl., high ceilings, 2 rooftop terraces w/spectacular panoramic views, central heating, 3 rms. w/air-conditioning, elevator, 2 flrs. *10% rm. discount when you show owners/managers Laura Lazznimi, Milvia Delmonaco or staff this book.* Per Laura, please mention this discount when you reserve the room. From Termini train station, go diagonally left across Piazza Cinquecento (in front of station), turn left onto Via Viminale which intersects Via Torino. **Metro:** Repubblica.

CONTILIA: Via Principe Amedeo 81.
Tel: 06-4466942/4466887. **Fax:** 06-4466904. **Web site:** paginegialle.it/contilia/ **E-mail:** contilia@tin.it (37 rms., 35 w/toilet & shower.) 135,000L (69E) single; 195,000L (100E) double; 240,000L (123E) triple, 280,000 (144E) quad. Children under 14 free. Breakfast (8-10am) at 11,500L pp is not obligatory & can be served in the room at extra cost of 4,500L pp. Breakfast is served on the patio in warm weather. Visa, MC, AX, DC. English spoken (Stepania), direct-dial phone, TV w/English channel, wonderful modern stylish hotel w/nicely furnished comfortable large rms., nice flrs., 15 rms. w/balconies, #503 (balcony & bathtub) & 510 are the best rms., central heating, air-conditioned, hair driers, double-paned windows, bar, garden/patio, elevator, 3 flrs., parking (30,000L per day). *5% rm. discount when you show owner/manager Gennaro Simeone or staff this book.* They offer half- (35,000L extra pp) and full-board (65,000L extra pp) rates. **Metro:** Termini. Exit the train station near track 22, turn left, walk down Via Giovanni Giolitti, turn right onto Via Gioberti for 2 blocks, turn left onto Via Principe Amedeo.

CORTORILLO: Via Principe Amedeo 79a, 5th fl. **Tel:** 06-4466934. **Fax:** 06-4454769. (14 rms., all w/toilet & bath or shower.) 65,000-

115,000L (33-60E) single; 85,000-265,000L (44-136E) double; 110,000-290,000L (56-149E) triple; 120,000-320,000 (62-164E) quad. Buffet breakfast (8am-12pm) at 16,500L pp is not obligatory & can be served in the room at extra cost of 6,500L pp. Visa, MC, AX, DC. English spoken (Giovanna), direct-dial phone, satellite TV w/English channel, all the rms. w/minibars, 1 rm. w/balcony, 1 rm. has handicapped access, #104 & 106 are the best rms., double-paned windows, central heating, air-conditioned, bar, restaurant, 2 elevators, 5 flrs. *Free breakfast when you show owner/manager Elena Salemme or staff this book.* They offer half- and full-board rates. This hotel was in the middle of renovating so I wasn't able to see the finished product but it will be ready Feb. '99. **Metro:** Termini. For directions, see Hotel Contilia. Take the stairs on the right side of the courtyard at 79a.

FIORINI: Via Principe Amedeo 62, 5th fl. **Tel:** 06-4885065. **Fax:** 06-4882170. (17 rms., all w/toilet & shower.) 150,000-175,000L (77-90E) single; 205,000-215,000L (105-110E) double; 255,000-300,000L (131-154E) triple. Buffet (huge) breakfast (7:30-10am) is included in the rates & can be served in the room but can be deducted in low season to reduce room price. Visa, MC, AX, DC. English spoken (Simona), direct-dial phone, satellite TV w/English channel, this wonderful charming modern hotel is in the middle of renovations which should be completed by March '99, simple elegantly furnished airy comfortable nice-size rms., 2 rms. have handicapped access ('99), double-paned windows, hair driers, minibars ('99), central heating, air-conditioned ('99), bar, restaurant (nearby), elevator, 1 fl. They offer half-board rates. **Metro:** Termini. Exit the train station near track 22, turn left, walk down Via Giovanni Giolitti, turn right onto Via Gioberti for 2 blocks, turn right onto Via Principe Amedeo.

FLAVIA: Via Flavia 42, 2nd fl. **Tel:** 06-4883037. **Fax:** 06-4819129. **E-mail:** hotelflavia@iol.it (30 rms., all w/toilet & bath or shower.) 150,000L (77E) single; 195,000L (100E) double; 265,000L (136E) triple. Breakfast (7:30-9am) is included in the rates & cannot be deducted but can be served in the room. Cash only. English spoken (Fulvio), direct-dial phone, TV, basic hotel w/nicely furnished nice-size dark rms., no ambiance or warmth, rooms that face the front are noisy, minibars, some rms. w/air-conditioning (cost extra), elevator,

2 flrs. Via Flavia parallels Via XX Settembre. From Termini train station, go diagonally left across Piazza Cinquecento (in front of station) to Piazza Repubblica, walk to the right around Piazza Repubblica, walk down Via Vitt. Em. Orlando, turn right onto Via XX Settembre, turn left onto Via Aureliana, turn right onto Via Flavia. **Metro:** Repubblica.

IGEA: Via Principe Amedeo 97. **Tel:** 06-4466913. **Tel/Fax:** 06-4466911. **Web site:** http://www.venere.it/roma/igea/ **E-mail:** igea@venere.it (42 rms., all w/toilet & bath or shower.) 95,000-155,000L (50-79E) single; 145,000-215,000L (74-110E) double; 200,000-250,000L (103-128E) triple. Children under 7 free. Breakfast (8-10am) at 11,500L pp is not obligatory & can be served in the room. Visa, MC, AX. Limited English spoken (Mario), direct-dial phone, satellite TV w/English channel, modern hotel w/nicely furnished large comfortable rms., double-paned windows, central heating, air-conditioned, elevator, 7 flrs. *5% rm. discount when you show owner/manager Mario Mariani or staff this book.* **Metro:** Termini or Vittorio Emanuele. For directions, see Hotel Contilia.

KENNEDY: Via Filippo Turati 62. **Tel:** 06-4465373. **Fax:** 06-4465417. **Web site:** http://www.panservice.it/alfasoft/kenn.htm/ **E-mail:** hotelkennedy@micanet.it (51 rms., all w/toilet & bath or shower.) 75,000-144,000L (38-74E) single; 100,000-214,000L (51-110E) double; 140,000-269,000L (72-138E) triple; 180,000-380,000L (92-195E) quad. Buffet breakfast (8-9:30am) is included in the rates & cannot be deducted. Visa, MC, AX, DC. English spoken (Elio), direct-dial phone, satellite TV w/English channel, wonderful charming quaint hotel w/antiquish furnished comfortable great rms., lots of ambiance & Italian character, #140 (quaint w/view) & 158 (romantic) are the best rms., #132 is a corner room w/2 windows, double-paned windows, central heating, air-conditioned, bar, elevator, 6 flrs. *10% rm. discount when you show owners/managers Alfonso & Elio Sasson or staff this book.* **Metro:** Termini. Exit the train station, turn left, walk down Via Giovanni Giolitti, turn right onto Via Gioberti, turn left onto Via Filippo Turati.

MORGANA: Via Filippo Turati 33. **Tel:** 06-4467230. **Fax:** 06-4469142. **Web site:** http://www.hotelmorgana.com/

E-mail: morganQtin.it (95 rms., all w/toilet & bath or shower.) 175,000-395,000L (90-203E) single; 195,000-395,000L (100-203E) double; 230,000-520,000L (118-267E) triple; 260,000-570,000L (133-292E) quad. Rooms range in categories from standard to superior. You have to ask for one of the 70 lower-priced standard rooms. Buffet breakfast (6:30-10:45am) is included in the rates & cannot be deducted but can be served in the room (11,500L extra pp). Visa, MC, AX, DC. English spoken (Ivor & Roberto), direct-dial phone, satellite TV w/English channel, wonderful 19th-century magnificent hotel, rooms vary from nicely to elegantly furnished comfortable rms., #111 & 112 are examples of standard rms., minibars (superior only), many rms. w/balconies, double-paned windows, central heating, air-conditioned, bar, elevator, 6 flrs., parking (45,000L per day). *5% rm. discount when you show owner/manager Roberto Dirienzo or staff this book.* If you reserve the room with enough notice, they will pick you up from the airport in their van. **Metro:** Termini. For directions, see Hotel Kennedy.

OCEANIA: Via Firenze 38, 3rd fl. **Tel:** 06-4824696. **Fax:** 06-4885586. **E-mail:** hoceania@tin.it (9 rms., all w/toilet & bath or shower.) 205,000L (105E) single; 260,000L (133E) double; 330,000L (169E) triple; 370,000L (190E) quad. Call for family rates. Buffet breakfast (8:30am) is included in the rates & can be served in the room but can be deducted in low season to reduce room price. Visa, MC, AX, DC. English spoken (Stephani), direct-dial phone, satellite TV w/English channel, beautiful quaint 19th-century palace w/elegantly furnished comfortable large pretty rms., #9 is wonderful, #6 is a corner rm. w/2 windows, central heating, air-conditioned, bar, elevator. **Metro:** Repubblica. From Termini train station, go diagonally left across Piazza Cinquecento (in front of station), turn left onto Via Viminale, take 2nd right to Via Firenze. Located near Via XX Settembre & the American Embassy.

ORLANDA: Via Principe Amedeo 76, 3rd fl. **Tel:** 06-4880124/ 4880637. **Fax:** 06-4880183.
Web site: http://www.traveleurope.it/h24htm/
E-mail: hotelorlanda@traveleurope.it (24 rms., 12 w/toilet & shower.) 65,000-135,000L (33-69E) single; 105,000-215,000L (54-110E) double; 140,000-290,000L (72-149E) triple; 180,000-360,000L (92-

185E) quad. Breakfast at 11,500L pp is not obligatory & can be served in the room. Visa, MC, AX, DC. English spoken, direct-dial phone, 12 rms. w/TVs, basic hotel, 3rd fl. renovated modern nicely furnished rooms are the best unless he renovates the 5th fl. by March '99, nice flrs., hair driers, double-paned windows, elevator. *Free breakfast when you show owner/manager Marco Policheni or staff this book.* **Metro:** Termini. For directions, see Hotel Fiorini.

SWEET HOME: Via Principe Amedeo 47, 1st fl. **Tel:** 06-4880954. **Fax:** 06-4817613. (11 rms., 8 w/toilet & bath or shower.) 75,000-135,000L (38-69E) single; 105,000-195,000L (54-100E) double; 125,000-260,000L (64-133E) triple; 140,000-300,000L (72-154E) quad. Children under 6 free. Breakfast (8:30-10:30am) at 9,500L pp is not obligatory & can be served in the room. Visa, MC, AX, DC. English spoken (Daniele), direct-dial phone, TV, wonderful charming hotel w/old-fashioned furnished pretty nice-size rms., wooden flrs., double-paned windows, central heating, elevator, 2 flrs. This warm family also has another hotel w/4 rms. & no bathrooms (3 bathrooms in the hall) for 80,000L double on Via Filippo Turati. **Metro:** Termini. For directions, see Hotel Fiorini.

TETI: Via Principe Amedeo 76, 2nd fl. **Tel/Fax:** 06-48904088. **E-mail:** hotelteti@iol.it (13 rms., all w/toilet & bath or shower.) 85,000-155,000L (44-79E) single; 115,000-200,000L (60-103E) double; 140,000-240,000L (72-123E) triple; 170,000-310,000L (87-159E) quad. Visa, MC, AX, DC. Breakfast (8-9:30am) at 9,500L pp is not obligatory & can be served in the room. English spoken (Giordana & Sergio), direct-dial phone, TV, modern hotel w/nicely furnished comfortable nice-size rms., #2 & 7 are the best rms., nice flrs., double-paned windows, central heating, walk up 15 steps to elevator, 1 fl., parking (30,000L per day). *10% rm. discount when you show owner/ manager Sergio Trotta or staff this book.* **Metro:** Termini. For directions, see Hotel Fiorini.

Hotels north of Stazione Termini
Right side (near track 1)
Please see Neighborhood surrounding Stazione Termini at the beginning of this chapter.

✔**ASCOT:** Via Montebello 22, 2nd fl. **Tel:** 06-4741675. **Fax:** 06-4740165. (21 rms., 19 w/toilet & bath or shower.) 85,000-95,000L (44-50E) single; 105,000-125,000L (54-64E) double; 140,000-170,000L (72-87E) triple; 180,000-210,000L (92-108E) quad. Breakfast (8-10am) at 11,500-16,500L pp is not obligatory & can be served in the room. Visa, MC, AX, DC. English spoken (Paris), direct-dial phone, satellite TV w/English channel (11,000L per day), basic hotel w/simply furnished dark rms., #24 (large), 28 & 29 have balconies & bathrooms, #27 & 30 are the best rms., 4 rms. have handicapped access, double-paned windows, central heating, ceiling fans, 15 rms. w/air-conditioning, terrace, bar, elevator, 3 flrs., parking (25,000-35,000L per day). Don't be concerned about the X-rated cinema around the corner, although I did get approached by a pimp for a job. *5% rm. discount when you show owners/managers Paris, Maria & Fernando Melato or staff this book.* **Metro:** Termini. Exit station, turn right onto Via Marsala, which becomes Via Volturno; after 3 blocks, turn right onto Via Montebello.

BOLOGNESE: Via Palestro 15. **Tel/Fax:** 06-490045. (21 rms., 7 w/toilet & bath or shower.) 65,000L (33E) single; 95,000-115,000L (50-60E) double; 130,000-160,000L (67-82E) triple; 170,000L (87E) quad. No breakfast is served. Cash only. English spoken, basic hotel w/simply furnished large rms., no elevator, 3 flrs. Owned/managed by cheerful George who is an artist. **Metro:** Termini. Exit the train station to the right, walk 4 blocks up Via Marghera, turn left onto Via Palestro, walk up about 7 blocks, hotel is just before Via XX Settembre.

✗**CASTELFIDARDO:** Via Castelfidardo 31, 3rd fl. **Tel:** 06-4464638. **Fax:** 06-4941378. (28 rms., 14 w/toilet & bath or shower.) 85,000-105,000L (44-54E) single; 110,000-135,000L (60-69E) double; 135,000-180,000L (69-92E) triple. Call for quad rates. No breakfast served. Visa, MC, AX, DC. English spoken (Luisella), satellite TV, charming hotel w/nicely furnished airy rms., #509 (balcony) & 514 (terrace) w/bathrooms are the best rms., #510 is huge w/bathroom, double-paned windows, central heating, elevator, 4 flrs. *5% rm. discount when you show owners/managers Massimo Piacentini, Luisella Lazzari or staff this book.* The above information includes the rooms in Hotel Lazzari in the same bldg. He also turned his private apt. into rooms for rent. 3 of the 4 rms. have to share one bathroom but you have access to the refrigerator. **Metro:** Termini. Exit the train station to the right, walk up Via Marghera, left on Via Varese which becomes Via Vittorio Bachelet when you cross Via Vicenza, continue straight as it becomes Via Castelfidardo.

CORALLO: Via Palestro 44, 6th fl. **Tel/Fax:** 06-4456340. (12 rms., all w/toilet & bath or shower.) 75,000-95,000L (38-50E) single; 115,000-145,000L (60-74E) double; 200,000L (103E) triple. Breakfast (8-10am) at 11,500L pp is not obligatory & can be served in the room. Visa, MC. Limited English spoken (Giuseppe), charming hotel w/simply furnished rms., #1, 2 & 3 w/balconies are the best rms., #5-8 share a large balcony, central heating, bar, walk to the back of the bldg. to catch elevator, 1 fl. Lots of ambiance. *Free breakfast when you show owner/manager Antonio Celestino or staff this book.* **Metro:** Termini. Exit the train station to the right, walk up Via Marghera (4 blocks), turn left onto Via Palestro.

DOLOMITI: Via San Martino Battaglia 11, 1st fl. **Tel:** 06-4957256/ 491058. **Fax:** 06-4454665. **Web site:** http://www.hotel-dolomiti.it **E-mail:** dolomiti@hotel-dolomiti.it (30 rms., 20 w/toilet & bath or shower.) 95,000-115,000L (50-59E) single; 120,000-210,000L (62-108E) double; 150,000-230,000L (77-118E) triple; 180,000-245,000L (93-126E) quad. Children under 8 free. Breakfast (8:30-10am) at 11,500L pp is not obligatory & can be served in the room. Visa, MC. English spoken (Gaetano & Sabrina), direct-dial phone, TV (on request), wonderful charming hotel w/nicely furnished comfortable rms., 5 rms. w/balconies, double-paned windows, central heating, bar, renovated rooms on the 2nd & 4th fl. have minibars, a/c, TV & hair driers, elevator, 4 flrs. Owned/managed by Gaetano & Sabrina Ensabella. They also own Hotel Lachea in the same bldg. which they plan to renovate in '99. **Metro:** Termini. Exit the train station to the right, walk 3 blocks up Via Marghera, turn left onto Via Varese, walk up 2 blocks to Piazza Indipendenza, turn right onto Via San Martino Battaglia.

ERCOLI: Via Collina 48, 3rd fl. **Tel:** 06-4745454. **Fax:** 06-4744063. **Web site:** http://italmarket.com/hotels/ercoli/ (14 rms., all w/toilet & bath or shower.) 115,000L (60E) single; 175,000L (90E) double;

220,000L (113E) triple; 270,000L (138E) quad. Breakfast (7-10am) is included in the rates & can be served in the room. Visa, MC. English spoken (Flavio & Giorgio), direct-dial phone, TV, wonderful charming modern hotel w/nicely furnished comfortable pretty rms., minibars ('99), hair driers, lots of ambiance, nice flrs., central heating, quiet location, elevator, 1 fl. *10% rm. discount when you show owner/manager Aurelio Biasotti or staff this book.* The same wonderful family manages Hotel Piave. From Termini train station, go diagonally left across Piazza Cinquecento (in front of station) to Piazza Repubblica, walk to the right around Piazza Repubblica, walk down Via Vitt. Em. Orlando, turn right onto Via XX Settembre, turn left onto Via Aureliana, turn right onto Via Flavia, turn right onto Via Collina. **Metro:** Repubblica.

FENICIA: Via Milazzo 20. **Tel/Fax:** 06-490342. (11 rms., all w/toilet & bath or shower.) 95,000-115,000L (50-60E) single; 135,000-175,000L (69-90E) double; 160,000-200,000L (82-103E) triple; 180,000-220,000L (92-113E) quad. Breakfast (7-9:30am) at 9,500L pp is not obligatory & can be served in the room. Visa, MC, AX. English spoken (Anna), TV, wonderful charming hotel w/nicely furnished comfortable bright rms., hair driers, nice flrs., rooms on the 4th fl. are larger, 3 rms. w/balconies, #6 is the best rm., double-paned windows, central heating, air-conditioned, no elevator, 2 flrs. *10% rm. discount when you show owners/managers Anna & Giorgio Brancadoro or staff this book.* Upon request, the hotel will organize a sightseeing tour. **Metro:** Termini. Exit station, turn right onto Via Marsala, then left onto Via Milazzo.

HARMONY: Via Palestro 13. **Tel:** 06-486738. **Fax:** 06-4743904. (26 rms., all w/toilet & bath or shower.) 135,000L (69E) single; 175,000L (90E) double. Breakfast is included in the rates & can be served in the room but can be deducted to reduce the room price. Cash only. English spoken, direct-dial phone, nice hotel w/simply furnished nice-size bright rms., most rms. w/view of park, double-paned windows, terrace, central heating, bar, noisy location, elevator, 4 flrs. (elevator goes to 3 flrs.) *10% rm. discount when you show owner/manager Rino Imperato or staff this book.* **Metro:** Termini. For directions, see Hotel Bolognese.

GABRIELLA: Via Palestro 88. **Tel:** 06-4450120. **Fax:** 06-4450252. **Web site:** http://www.micanet.it/hotelgabriella/ **E-mail:** gabriel@micanet.it (24 rms., all w/toilet & bath or shower.) 135,000-185,000L (69-95E) double; 180,000-240,000L (92-123E) triple; 220,000-300,000L (113-154E) quad. Children under 8 free. Buffet breakfast (7-10am) is included in the rates & can be served in the room. Visa, MC, AX, DC. English spoken (Barbara), direct-dial phone, satellite TV w/English channel, charming modern hotel w/ nicely furnished comfortable pretty rms., 8 rooms on the 1st fl. will be renovated 5/99, hair driers, nice flrs., double-paned windows, central heating, air-conditioning (21,000L per day), bar, parking (35,000L per day). *10% rm. discount when you show owner/manager Romolo Nardelli or staff this book.* **Metro:** Termini. Exit the train station to the right, walk up Via Marghera, turn right onto Via Palestro.

GALLI: Via Milazzo 20, 2nd fl. **Tel:** 06-4456859. **Fax:** 06-4468501. (12 rms., 11 w/toilet & bath or shower.) 75,000-95,000L (38-50E) single; 95,000-135,000L (50-69E) double; 125,000-170,000L (64-87E) triple; 160,000-180,000L (82-92E) quad. Breakfast (8-10am) at 13,500L pp is not obligatory & can be served in the room. Visa, MC, AX. Limited English spoken (Antonella), direct-dial phone, wonderful charming hotel, rooms #201-205 on the 2nd fl. have been newly renovated into nicely furnished comfortable pretty rms. w/ minibars, TVs, modern bathrooms & nice flrs., the rooms on the 4th fl. are cheaper & not as nice, 2 rms. w/balconies, double-paned windows, central heating, no elevator, 2nd & 4th fl. *10% rm. discount when you show the warm, wonderful owners/managers Pino, Antonello, Maria Cavezza or staff this book.* I stayed in a room on the 2nd fl. It was comfortable and relaxing. Conveniently located next to Termini train station for my day trips. **Metro:** Termini. For directions, see Hotel Fenicia.

MAGIC: Via Milazzo 20, 3rd fl. **Tel/Fax:** 06-4959880. (15 rms., 14 w/toilet & bath or shower.) 65,000-85,000L (33-44E) single; 95,000-135,000L (50-69E) double; 130,000-160,000L (67-82E) triple; 160,000-170,000L (82-87E) quad. Breakfast (7-10am) at 7,500L pp is not obligatory & can be served in the room. Visa, MC. Limited English spoken, satellite TV, charming hotel w/nicely furnished comfortable bright rms., nice flrs., double-paned windows, central heating, bar, 1:00 am curfew, no elevator. *5% rm. discount when you show owner/manager Carmelo Riso or staff this book during off-season.* **Metro:** Termini. For directions, see Hotel Fenicia.

PAPA GERMANO: Via Calatafimi 14A. **Tel:** 06-486919 (17 rms., 7 w/bath or shower). 50,000-65,000L (26-33E) singles (sinks only); 85,000-105,000L (44-54E) double; 110,000-140,000L (56-72E) triple; 120,000-160,000L (62-82E) quad. Children under 3 free. Visa, MC, AX. English spoken (Gino), direct-dial phone, satellite TV w/ English channel, nice hotel w/simply furnished airy nice-size rms., hair driers, #7 & 8 are the best rms., clientele is mostly European, double-paned windows, central heating, terrace, no elevator, 3 flrs. He keeps guest sign-in books that go back 10 yrs. Don't be concerned about the X-rated cinema down the street, although I did get approached by a pimp for a job. *10% rm. discount when you show owner/manager Gino Tomasso or staff this book from Nov.-March.* Gino is a wonderful & informative owner. **Metro:** Termini. Exit station, turn right onto Via Marsala, which becomes Via Volturno; turn right onto the backward L-shaped Via Calatafimi.

PIAVE: Via Piave 14. **Tel:** 4743447. **Fax:** 06-4873360. (12 rms., 10 w/toilet & bath or shower.) 70,000L (36E) single; 95,000-125,000L (50-64E) double; 155,000L (79E) triple; 180,000L (92E) quad. Breakfast (7:30-10am) at 6,500L pp is not obligatory & can be served in the room. Visa, MC. English spoken (Stephano), direct-dial phone, nice hotel w/simply furnished rms., central heating, no elevator, 1 flr. The same wonderful family manages Hotel Ercoli. From Termini train station, go diagonally left across Piazza Cinquecento (in front of station) to Piazza Repubblica, walk to the right around Piazza Repubblica, walk down Via Vitt. Em. Orlando, turn right onto Via XX Settembre, turn left onto Via Aureliana, turn right onto Via Flavia, turn right onto Via Collina. **Metro:** Repubblica.

TIZI: Via Collina 48, 1st fl. **Tel:** 06-4820128. **Tel/Fax:** 06-4743266. (18 rms., 8 w/toilet & bath or shower.) 70,000L (36E) single (no bathrooms); 95,000-115,000L (50-60E) double. Call for triple & quad rates. Breakfast (8-9am) at 10,500L pp is not obligatory. Cash only.

Limited English spoken (Tizirna), basic hotel w/simply furnished nice-size airy rms., nice flrs., elevator, 2 flrs. **Metro:** Repubblica. For directions, see Hotel Ercoli.

HOTELS OVER $100 A NIGHT FOR TWO
These hotels may have rooms under $100 a night for two because it is low season or the rooms do not have private bathrooms.

ASTORIA GARDEN: Via Vittorio Bachelet 8/10. **Tel:** 06-4469908. **Fax:** 06-4453329. **E-mail:** astoria.garden@flashnet.it (33 rms., 24 w/toilet & bath or shower.) 140,000-200,000L (72-103E) single; 165,000-265,000L (85-136E) double; 195,500-357,500L (100-183E) triple; 220,000-445,000L (113-228E) quad. Rooms range in categories from rooms w/o toilets, standard to superior. You have to ask for the lower priced rooms. Buffet breakfast (7:30-10am) is included in the rates but can be deducted to reduce room price. Breakfast can be served in the room at extra cost of 6,500L pp. Visa, MC, AX, DC. English spoken, direct-dial phone, satellite TV w/English channel, 18th-century hotel, rooms vary in size, decor & brightness, most rms. are on the dark side, #22 (w/bathtub) is a simply furnished standard rm., #32 is a nicely furnished superior dark room w/Jacuzzi (4 more in '99), 12 rms. w/air-conditioning (21,000L extra per day), lots of character, 4 rms. have balconies, double-paned windows, central heating, bar, beautiful terrace/garden, no elevator, 3 flrs., parking (25,000L per day). *15% rm. discount or free breakfast when you show owner/ manager Giuseppe Gallina or staff this book.* **Metro:** Termini. Exit the train station to the right, walk up Via Marghera, left on Via Varese which becomes Via Vittorio Bachelet when you cross Via Vicenza.

CAMBRIDGE: Via Palestro 87. **Tel:** 06-4456821. **Fax:** 06-49384917.Web site: http://space.tin.it/viaggi/vfuggett/ **E-mail:** hcambrrm@tin.it (29 rms., 23 w/toilet & bath or shower.) 75,000-140,000L (38-72E) single; 115,000-205,000L (60-105E) double; 140,000-230,000L (72-118E) triple; 180,000-290,000L (92-149E) quad. Breakfast (7:30-9:30am) is included in the rates & can be served in the room (6,500 extra pp) but can be deducted to reduce room price. Visa, MC, AX, DC. English spoken (Ellon), TV w/CNN, wonderful charming beautiful hotel w/nicely furnished pretty rms., the 9 rooms that were not renovated are old-fashioned furnished & cheaper,

6 rooms w/o toilets have showers, hair driers, #26 w/bathtub is beautiful, 1 rm. has handicapped access, 9 rms. w/minibars, central heating, 20 rms. w/air-conditioning (21,000L per day), double-paned windows, bar, elevator, 4 flrs. *10% rm. discount or free breakfast when you show owner/manager Vicenzo Fuggetta or staff this book.* They offer half- (40,000L pp) and full-board (70,000L pp) rates. **Metro:** Termini. Exit the train station to the right, walk up Via Marghera, turn right onto Via Palestro.

CONTINENTALE: Via Palestro 49. **Tel:** 06-4450382/4462855. **Fax:** 06-4452629 (14 rms., all w/toilet & bath or shower.) 115,000-165,000L (60-85E) single; 155,000-215,000L (79-110E) double; 170,000-260,000L (87-133E) triple; 220,000-280,000L (113-144E) quad. Breakfast (7-10am) is included in the rates & cannot be deducted but can be served in the room. Visa, MC, AX, DC. English spoken (Stephanie), direct-dial phone, TV, newly renovated hotel w/ nicely furnished comfortable rms., minibars, central heating, air-conditioned, elevator. *10% rm. discount when you show owner/manager Stephanie Restivo or staff this book.* **Metro:** Termini. Exit the train station to the right, walk up Via Marghera (4 blocks), turn left onto Via Palestro.

LEALE: Via Milazzo 4. **Tel:** 06-4455661. **Fax:** 06-4462965. **Web site:** http://www.emmeti.it/Welcome/Lazio/Roma/Alberghi/ Leale/index.it.html/ **E-mail:** hotel_leale@yahoo.com (7 rms., all w/ toilet & bath or shower.) 140,000L (72E) single; 200,000L (103E) double; 260,000L (133E) triple. Breakfast (8-9am) is included in the rates & is served in the room but can be deducted to reduce the room price. Visa, MC, AX, DC. English spoken (Maria), direct-dial phone, satellite TV, wonderful charming modern hotel w/a mixture of old-fashioned furnished & nicely furnished comfortable pretty rms., #101, 103-105 w/hair driers are newly remodeled & #102, 106 & 107 are older rms. but I like them better, nice flrs., elevator, 4 flrs. *10% rm. discount when you show owners/managers Maria Quagliarella, Concentta or staff this book.* Maria also manages a lesser-priced hotel on the same street w/7 rooms but no private bathrooms. **Metro:** Termini. Exit station, turn right onto Via Marsala, then left onto Via Milazzo.

POSITANO: Via Palestro 49. **Tel:** 06-490360. **Fax:** 06-4469101. **E-mail:** hotposit@tin.it (19 rms., 14 w/toilet & bath or shower.) 115,000-165,000L (60-85E) single; 155,000-215,000L (79-110E) double; 170,000-260,000L (87-133E) triple; 220,000-280,000L (113-144E) quad. Breakfast (7-10am) is included in the rates & cannot be deducted but can be served in the room. Visa, MC, AX, DC. English spoken (Thi), direct-dial phone, TV, newly renovated hotel w/nicely furnished comfortable rms., minibars, central heating, air-conditioned, 5 rms. on the 6th flr. are w/o bathrooms, elevator, 4 flrs. *10% rm. discount when you show owner/manager Ercole or staff this book.* **Metro:** Termini. For directions, see Hotel Continentale.

RIMINI: Via Marghera 17. **Tel:** 06-4461991. **Fax:** 06-491289. **Web site:** http://www.travel.it/roma/rimini/rimini.html/ **E-mail:** rimini@travel.it (35 rms., all w/bath or shower). 105,000-135,000L (54-69E) single; 145,000L-205,000L (74-105E) double; 220,000-250,000L (113-128E) triple; 240,000-270,000L (123-138E) quad. Breakfast (7-10:30am) is included in the rates & cannot be deducted but can be served in the room. Visa, MC, AX, DC. English spoken (Massimo), direct-dial phone, TV, basic hotel w/simply furnished rms., #28, 36 (balcony) & 26 w/bathtubs are the best rms., #34 has a balcony, #38, 40 & 42 have terraces, hair driers, double-paned windows, central heating, 14 rms. w/air-conditioning, bar, garden, elevator, 6 flrs. *5% rm. discount when you show owner/manager Massimo Alessi or staff this book.* **Metro:** Termini. Exit the train station to the right, cross the street and walk up Via Marghera.

Hotels in/near Piazza Campo de' Fiori
(Historic center)

This is central Rome's most picturesque outdoor market. It is a great, safe, historic, fascinating area to stay and explore on foot. Some of the best restaurants and open-air vegetable & flower markets are in this area. Although centrally located to many of the sites, it is not near any metro line. If you have a lot of luggage, I recommend you taxi to your hotel because the buses are extremely crowded.

LUNETTA: Piazza Paradiso 68. **Tel:** 06-6861080/6877630. **Fax:** 06-6892028. (35 rms., 19 w/toilet & bath or shower.) 95,000-115,000L (50-60E) single; 135,000-175,000L (69-90E) double;

185,000-230,000L (95-118E) triple; 220,000-280,000L (113-144E) quad. No breakfast is served. Visa & MC. English spoken (Michela), direct-dial phone, basic hotel w/simply furnished nice-size dark cheerless rms., tiny bathrooms, 2 rms. w/balconies, no elevator, 3 flrs. Great location. This hotel is not family-owned and attracts a lot of students and creative types. **Bus:** #64. Stop: Piazza Navona. From Corso Vittorio Emanuele, turn down Via Paradiso to Piazza Paradiso.

PICCOLO: Via Chiavari 32. **Tel:** 06-68802560/6892330. (16 rms., 10 w/toilet & bath or shower.) 115,000-135,000L (60-69E) single; 135,000-165,000L (69-85E) double; 160,000-180,000L (82-92E) triple; 190,000L (97E) quad. Breakfast (7-11am) at 9,500L pp is not obligatory. Visa, MC, AX. Limited English spoken (Mario & Anna), direct-dial phone, nice charming hotel w/simply furnished rms., 10 rms. w/air-conditioning (11,000L per day), 1:30am curfew, bar, great quiet location, no elevator, 5 flrs. **Bus:** #64. Stop: Largo Torre Argentina. Start walking west, in the same direction that the bus is going, along Corso Vittorio Emanuele II, turn left onto Via Chiavari, the hotel is 3 blocks ahead on your right.

SMERALDO: Vicolo Chiodaroli 9. **Tel:** 06-6875929/6892121. **Fax:** 06-68805495. (35 rms., 24 w/toilet & bath or shower.) 110,000-145,000L (56-74E) single; 145,000-185,000L (74-95E) double; 170,000-215,000L (87-110E) triple. Breakfast (8-10am) at 10,500L pp is not obligatory & can be served in the room (6,500L extra pp). Visa, MC, AX. English spoken, direct-dial phone, TV, nice charming hotel w/simply furnished rms., the 2 rms. w/balconies are for 1 & have no bathrooms, 2 rooftops w/views of Rome's rooftops (one you share w/hotel's laundry), air-conditioned (11,000L per day), bar, elevator, 5 flrs. This hotel is not family-owned & will be totally renovated in 1999. **Bus:** #64. Stop: Largo Torre Argentina. Start walking west, in the same direction that the bus is going, along Corso Vittorio Emanuele II, turn left onto Via Torre Argentina, turn right onto Via Santa Anna, look for the narrow street Vicolo Chiodaroli on your left.

HOTELS OVER $100 A NIGHT FOR TWO

These hotels may have rooms under $100 a night for two because it is low season or the rooms do not have private bathrooms.

ARENULA: Via Santa Maria Calderari 47. **Tel:** 06-6879454. **Fax:** 06-6896188. (50 rms., all w/toilet & bath or shower.) 125,000-185,000L (64-95E) single; 155,000-235,000L (79-121E) double. Call for triple rates. Buffet breakfast (7-10am) is included in the rates & cannot be deducted but can be served in the room (6,500L extra pp). Visa, MC. English spoken, direct-dial phone, satellite TV w/English channel, charming beautiful 19th-century hotel w/simply furnished large airy soft-pink pretty rms., nice flrs., rooms on the 4th fl. are larger, double-paned windows, white marble & wrought iron oval staircase, make sure the bathroom is enclosed and not stationed in the rm. w/no privacy, hair driers, central heating, air-conditioned (20,000L per day), bar, noisy location, no elevator, 5 flrs. (You'd better be in shape if you want to stay at this hotel.) Owned by Pino Patta & managed by Paolo Chiodi. **Bus:** #64. Stop: Largo Torre Argentina. Start walking west, in the same direction that the bus is going, along Corso Vittorio Emanuele II, turn left onto Via Torre Argentina, which becomes Via Arenula when you walk straight through Largo Arenula & Piazza Cairoli, turn left onto Via Santa Maria Calderari.

CAMPO FIORI: Via Biscione 6. **Tel:** 06-68806865/6874886. **Fax:** 06-6876003. (27 rms., 9 w/toilet & bath or shower.) 155,000-220,000L (79-113E) double; 195,000-270,000L (100-138E) triple. Call for quad rates. Breakfast (7:30-10am) is included in the rates & cannot be deducted. Visa, MC. English spoken (Edith & Andy), direct-dial phone, charming picturesque cozy hotel w/nicely furnished comfortable rms. which vary in size from claustrophobic to large, #601 (small room w/view of rooftops) & 602 (romantic room w/ canopy bed) are on the 6th fl., split-level rooftop garden terrace w/ wonderful panoramic view of Rome, no elevator, 6 flrs. (You'd better be in good physical shape if you want to stay at this hotel & enjoy the rooftop view.) They also have 9 fully equipped apts. for 270,000L & up. This hotel is not family-owned. **Bus:** #64. Stop: Piazza San Pantaleo. Located around the corner from Piazza Paradiso. From

Piazza San Pantaleo, cross the street, walk down Via Baullari, turn left at the clothing store, walk down the street, turn left into Piazza Teatro Pompeo, turn left past the barbershop to hotel.

CASA SANTA BRIGIDA: Piazza Farnese 96.
Tel: 06-68892596/68892497. **Web site:** http://www.brigidine.org/ **E-mail:** brigida@mclink.it (24 rms., all w/toilet & bath or shower.) 165,000L (85E) single; 270,000L (138E) double; 230,000-300,000L (118-154E) triple; 280,000-360,000L (144-185E) quad. Breakfast is included in the rates. Cash only. English spoken, nice hotel (convent) w/simply furnished rms. No curfew. They offer half- and full-board rates. I didn't get a chance to revisit this convent. **Bus:** #64. Stop: Palazzo Cancelleria. Located in the beautiful Piazza Farnese. From Palazzo Cancelleria, walk straight to your right through Piazza Campo Fiori, onto Via Corda to Piazza Farnese.

POMEZIA: Via Chiavari 12. **Tel/Fax:** 06-6861371. (24 rms., 12 w/ toilet & bath or shower.) 75,000-145,000L (38-74E) single; 95,000-195,000L (50-100E) double; 105,000-260,000L (54-133E) triple. Call for quad rates. Children under 8 free. Breakfast (8-11am) at 11,500L pp is not obligatory & can be served in the room. Visa, MC, AX, DC. English spoken (Maurizio), direct-dial phone, basic hotel w/simply furnished small rms., #11-19, 28, 37 & 38 have bathrooms, rooms on the 1st fl. have been renovated, double-paned windows, noisy location but rooms in the back are quiet, central heating, bar, no elevator, 4 flrs. *Free breakfast when you show owner/manager Flora Fiori or staff this book.* **Bus:** #64. Stop: Largo Torre Argentina. Start walking west, in the same direction that the bus is going, along Corso Vittorio Emanuele II, turn left onto Via Chiavari, the hotel is 3 blocks ahead on your right.

SOLE: Via Biscione 76. **Tel:** 06-68806873. **Fax:** 06-6893787. **E-mail:** sole@italyhotel.co (60 rms., 32 w/toilet & bath or shower.) 110,000-135,000L (56-69E) single; 155,000-195,000L (79-100E) double; 210,000L (108E) triple; 300,000L (154E) quad. Children under 3 free. No breakfast is served. Cash only. English spoken (Angeletti & Pera), direct-dial phone, old pleasant hotel w/old-fashioned furnished bright large rustic rms., top floor rooms (#418 &

419 which share a terrace & 421 w/terrace) are the best w/minibars, new bathrooms & wonderful views, #408 has a balcony, central heating, roof garden terrace w/view, elevator, 5 flrs. but there is a long flight of stairs from street level to the reception, garage parking (35,000L). The hotel is not family-owned & does not have a friendly staff. *10% rm. discount when you show managers Luigi & Iris or staff this book in off-season.* **Bus:** #64. Stop: Piazza San Pantaleo. For directions, see Hotel Campo Fiori.

Hotels near Piazza Navona
(Medieval historic center)
A great, safe, fascinating area to stay and explore on foot. Although centrally located to many of the sites, it is not near any metro line. If you have a lot of luggage, I recommend you taxi to your hotel because the buses are extremely crowded.

MIMOSA: Via Santa Chiara 61, 2nd fl. **Tel:** 06-68801753. **Fax:** 06-6833557. (12 rms., 1 w/toilet & bath or shower.) 100,000-105,000L (51-54E) single; 135,000-145,000L (69-74E) double; 190,000-205,000L (97-105E) triple; 240,000-250,000L (123-128E) quad. Breakfast (8-9am) at 6,500L pp is not obligatory & can be served in the room (4,500L extra pp). Cash only. English spoken (Romano), basic old-fashioned hotel w/simply furnished large rms., #11 has a bathroom, #4 will have a bathroom Feb. '99, access to refrigerator, attracts lots of students, tranquil location, no elevator, 2 flrs. **Bus:** #64. Stop: Largo Torre Argentina. Start walking west, in the same direction that the bus is going, along Corso Vittorio Emanuele II, turn right onto Via Torre Argentina, turn left onto Via Santa Chiara.

NAVONA: Via Sediari 8. **Tel:** 06-6864203. **Tel/Fax:** 06-68803802. (31 rms., 21 w/toilet & bath or shower.) 125,000-145,000L (64-74E) single; 145,000-185,000L (74-95E) double. Call for triple & quad rates. Breakfast (8:30-9:30am) is included in the rates & cannot be deducted. Cash only. English spoken (Patricia & Corry, the Australian-Italian architect owners), wonderful charming 15th-century Roman style hotel w/simply furnished bright rms., high ceilings, rooms on the 4th fl. are newly renovated w/wonderful decor & modern bathrooms, 10 rms. w/balconies (3 w/view of the noisy square), 7 rms. w/ air-conditioning (costs extra), double-paned windows, no elevator (maybe by mid '99). Hotel attracts lots of students. Read the posted rules: Pay in advance, no washing laundry, no guests and you must leave your room every day by 10:00am. **Bus:** #70 or 492. Stop: Corso Rinascimento. From Corso Rinascimento, turn right (McDonald's clock) at Largo Sapienza, walk straight through onto Via Sediari. The same family owns & manages the new Hotel Zanardelli Residence.

PRIMAVERA: Piazza San Pantaleo 3, 1st fl. **Tel:** 06-68803109. **Fax:** 06-6869265. (16 rms., 14 w/toilet & bath or shower.) 105,000-125,000L (54-64E) single; 145,000-185,000L (74-95E) double; 200,000L (103E) triple. Buffet breakfast is included in the rates. Cash only. English spoken (Serena & Victorio), satellite TV w/English channel, grand small 19th-century hotel w/simply furnished large airy bright comfortable rms., nice flrs., the best rooms are on the 5th floor (#13-19) which are beautiful, newly renovated & are air-conditioned, #11 has a wonderful view w/private bathroom in the hall, marble floors in hallway, hair driers, double-paned windows, central heating, magnificent entrance, marble stairs, terrace, elevator, 2 flrs. *10% rm. discount or free breakfast when you show owner/manager Maria Sena or staff this book.* **Bus:** #64. Stop: Piazza San Pantaleo.

HOTEL OVER $100 A NIGHT FOR TWO
ZANARDELLI: Via Zanardelli 7. **Tel:** 06-6864203. **Tel/Fax:** 06-68803802. 7 rms., all w/toilet & shower.) 145,000L (74E) single; 195,000-215,000L (100-110E) double. Call for triple & quad rates. Breakfast (8:30-9:30am) is included in the rates & cannot be deducted. Cash only. English spoken (Patricia & Corry, the Australian-Italian architect owners), wonderful charming newly renovated palazzo hotel w/beautifully furnished romantic bright rms., double-paned windows, central heating, air-conditioned, elevator, 1st fl. The owners of this hotel are trying to attract people who want to get married in Rome. **Bus:** #70 or 87. Stop: Napoleonico Museum Via Zanardelli. The same family owns & manages Hotel Navona.

Hotel near Piazza Venezia

A great safe area to stay. Although centrally located to many of the sites, it is not near any metro line. If you have a lot of luggage, I recommend you taxi to your hotel because the buses are extremely crowded.

HOTEL OVER $100 A NIGHT FOR TWO

CORONET: Piazza Grazioli 5, 3rd fl. **Tel:** 06-6790653. **Tel/Fax:** 06-69922705. (13 rms., 10 w/toilet & bath or shower.) 185,000-215,000L (95-110E) double; 260,000L (133E) triple; 320,000L (164E) quad. Breakfast (7:30-9:30am) is included in the rates & can be served in the room (6,500 extra pp) but can be deducted in low season to reduce room price. Visa, MC, AX. English spoken (Alex), 17th-century wonderful renovated palace hotel w/old-fashioned furnished large rms., high ceilings, #33 & 34 (jr. suite) w/bathtubs are the best rms. but are noisy at night, 2 rms. have handicapped access, noisy location, elevator, free parking. The palace belongs to Princess Doria Pamphili & the royal family who still live on the premises. If you are looking for rooms to rent in Positano, ask Alex about his fisherman friend Pietro Pane who rents rooms in his home at a reasonable price. **Bus:** #64. Stop: Piazza Venezia. From Piazza Venezia, take Via Plebiscito, turn right on Via Astalli into Piazza Venezia. Located inside the Palazza Doria.

Hotels near Piazza Spagna
(Spanish Steps)

A safe, stylish area to explore on foot. Some of the best shops and attractions are located here or within a 5-minute walk, convenient to public transportation. To get to this general area take any of the following buses from the Termini train station: #46, 62 or 64. However, if you have a lot of luggage, I recommend you taxi to your hotel because the buses tend to be very crowded.

HOTELS OVER $100 A NIGHT FOR TWO

These hotels may have rooms under $100 a night for two because it is low season or the rooms do not have private bathrooms.

DODGE: Via Due Macelli 106, 4th fl. **Tel:** 06-6780038. **Tel/Fax:** 06-6791633. (18 rms., all w/toilet & bath or shower.) 165,000L (85E) single; 220,000L (113E) double; 290,000L (149E) triple; 340,000L

(174E) quad. Breakfast (8-10am) is included in the rates & cannot be deducted but can be served in the room. Visa, MC, AX. Limited English spoken (Romano), direct-dial phone, TV, wonderful hotel w/nicely furnished comfortable rms., nice flrs., new bathrooms, rooms on 4th fl. have balconies, hair driers, central heating, air-conditioned, bar, steps to elevator, 2 flrs. Entrance located through a retail sports store. **Metro:** Spagna. Turn left onto Piazza Spagna, walk out onto Via Macelli.

ERDARELLI: Via Due Macelli 28.
Tel: 06-6791265/6784010. **Fax:** 06-6790705.
Web site: http://www.italyhotel.com/roma/erdarelli/erdarelli/html/
E-mail: erdarelli@italyhotel.com (28 rms., 22 w/toilet & bath or shower.) 165,000L (85E) single; 220,000L (113E) double. Call for triple & quad rates. Breakfast (7:30-9:30am) is included in the rates & cannot be deducted but can be served in the room. You can order American/English breakfast. Visa, MC, AX, DC. Limited English spoken (Franco), direct-dial phone, wonderful basic hotel w/old-fashioned furnished comfortable rms., high ceilings, rooms on top fl. have balconies but no views, rooms on the inner courtyard are more quiet, the view from #11 is wonderful, 10 rms. w/air-conditioning (21,000L per day), laundry services available, quiet ambiance, elevator, 6 flrs. **Metro:** Spagna. For directions, see Hotel Dodge.

MARCUS: Via Clementino 94, 2nd fl.
Tel: 06-68300320/6873679. **Fax:** 06-68300312.
Web site: http://www.venere.it/roma/marcus/ (17 rms., all w/toilet & bath or shower.) 135,000-155,000L (69-79E) single; 185,000-205,000L (95-105E) double; 220,000-250,000L (113-128E) triple; 250,000-270,000L (128-138E) quad. Breakfast (7:30-10am) is included in the rates & cannot be deducted but can be served in the room. Visa, MC, AX. English spoken (Marcus) direct-dial phone, TV, 16th-century charming palace w/simply old-fashioned furnished nice-size pretty rms., lots of ambiance, #12 & 18 have balconies, #9 (large) & 6 are the best rms., 1 rm. has private bathroom in hall, some rms. have antique fireplaces, central heating, air-conditioned, bar, double-paned windows, minibars ('99), elevator, 2 flrs. Owned/managed by Salvatore DeCaro. **Metro:** Spagna. From Piazza Spagna, turn left, then right onto Via Condotti, follow this street which becomes Via Fontanella Borghese and eventually becomes Via Clementino.

PARLAMENTO: Via Convertite 5, 3rd fl.
Tel: 06-6792082/69941697. **Fax:** 06-69921000. (22 rms., all w/toilet & bath or shower.) 145,000-185,000L (74-95E) single; 165,000-215,000L (85-110E) double; 246,000-295,000L (126-151E) triple; 300,000-330,000L (154-169E) quad. Buffet breakfast (7-10:30am) is included in the rates & cannot be deducted but can be served in the room. Breakfast is served in the garden in warm weather. Visa, MC, AX, DC. English spoken (George & Tiziano) direct-dial phone, satellite TV w/English channels, charming hotel w/old-fashioned furnished comfortable pretty rms., #106 (honeymoon), 107 & 104 (honeymoon) share the breakfast terrace, #108 has a balcony, #82 (huge), 108, 106 & 107 are some of the best rms., hair driers, lots of ambiance, double-paned windows, central heating, air-conditioned (21,000L per day), flowered rooftop garden terrace, steps to elevator, 2 flrs. The hotel is not family-owned but is managed by Plinio Chini. Located between Piazza Colonna and the Spanish steps. **Metro:** Spagna. From Piazza Spagna, walk down Via Condotti, turn left onto Via Corso, walk about 4 blocks, turn left onto Via Convertite.

SUISSE: Via Gregoriana 54-56, 4th fl.
Tel: 06-6783649/6786172. **Fax:** 06-6781258. (13 rms., 9 w/toilet & bath or shower.) 135,000-165,000L (69-85E) single; 165,000-215,000L (85-110E) double; 285,000L (146E) triple. Breakfast (8-10am) is included in the rates & is served in the room but can be deducted to reduce room price. Visa, MC. (You may be able to charge half your bill on a Visa or MC.) English spoken (Andrian), direct-dial phone, basic hotel w/old-fashioned furnished comfortable large rms., top-floor rms. have views, terrace, central heating, elevator, 3 flrs. **Metro:** Barberini. From Piazza Barberini, look for Pepi's bar & Planet Hollywood, opposite that corner is Via Sistina, walk up Via Sistina, turn left on Via Crispi, turn far right onto Via Gregoriana.

Hotel near Piazza Popolo

A safe, great historic area to shop and explore on foot.
It's very close to the Spanish steps and convenient to public transportation. **Metro:** Flaminio.

BROTZKY: Via Corso 509, 3rd fl. **Tel/Fax:** 06-3612339. **Tel:** 06-3236641. (25 rms., 20 w/toilet & bath or shower.) 85,000-105,000L

(44-54E) single; 145,000-175,000L (74-90E) double; 210,000L (108E) triple; 240,000L (123E) quad. Breakfast (8-11am) at 9,500L pp is not obligatory & can be served in the room. Cash only. English spoken (Marco), direct-dial phone, 50% w/TVs, basic hotel w/simply furnished rms., 1st floor rooms are renovated w/new bathrooms, 2nd fl. will be completed by '99, all rooms have names of painters, Toulouse & 3 others on the 2nd fl. have arched wood-beamed ceiling & bathrooms, 2 rms. w/balconies, panoramic view from rooftop terrace, hotel attracts lots of students, elevator, 2 flrs. There always seems to be a lot of dusty construction going on in this bldg. Great location. **Metro:** Flaminio. Walk through the large Roman arch (Porta Popolo), continue straight across Piazza Popolo to Via Corso (the middle street).

Hotels near Citta Vaticano (Vatican City)

Vatican City perches on the right bank of the Tiber river. A very charming, Italian neighborhood feel to this section of Rome. This location is convenient only for enjoying the Vatican and watching local families performing their daily routines, not for seeing the other sites or shopping. Metro: Ottaviano or Bus #64. Stop: St. Peter's. If you have a lot of luggage, I recommend you taxi to your hotel because the buses & metros are extremely crowded. Taxi 25,000-30,000L.

BAR CRISTALLO: Viale Giulio Cesare 114-116. **Tel:** 06-3723916. Hrs.: Daily 7am-8pm. Stop in here if you need to pick up some affordable freshly made delicious sandwiches and gelateria before you tour the Vatican. As always, the food is cheaper if you stand than if you sit at a table. Owned/managed by Giacomo, the charming old man at the cash register.

ADRIATIC: Via Vitelleschi 25. **Tel:** 06-68808080/68806386. **Fax:** 06-6893552. **E-mail:** adriatic@ats.it (32 rms., 26 w/toilet & shower.) 105,000-145,000L (54-74E) single; 135,000-175,000L (69-90E) double; 180,000-235,000L (92-121E) triple; 290,000L (149E) quad. No breakfast served. Visa, MC, AX. English spoken (Marino), direct-dial phone, satellite TV w/English channel, basic quaint hotel w/simply furnished comfortable rms., 7 rms. w/balconies, 19 rms. have handicapped access, double-paned windows, central heating, air-conditioned, small terrace garden, elevator, 4 flrs. Owned/managed by Franco & Mencucci. **Bus:** #64. Stop: Bgo. Sant' Angelo (near St. Peter's, pass under the nearby portal). Walk 1 block along Via Porta Castello, turn left onto Via Vitelleschi.

BENJAMIN 1: Via Boezio 31, 4th fl. **Tel/Fax:** 06-68802437. (7 rms., 1 w/toilet & bath or shower.) 75,000L (38E) single; 115,000-145,000L (60-74E) double; 140,000L (72E) triple; 160,000L (82E) quad. Children under 5 free. No breakfast is served. Cash only. Limited English spoken (Franca & Fabrizio), basic hotel w/simply furnished bright airy rms., #7 has the bathroom, #1 & 2 have free-standing showers inside the room but also share 3 bathrooms w/the other 4 rms. on the same flr., no elevator, 3 flrs. Franca also manages hotel Benjamin #2 in the same bldg. on the 1st fl. but only #6 has a private bathroom out of the 6 rms. although #1, 2 & 3 have free-standing showers inside the rooms. *10% rm. discount when you show owners/ managers Franca & Fabrizio Foudi or staff this book.* You can reserve a room by credit card but must pay in cash. Located on the corner of Via Terenzio at Via Boezio 31. **Bus:** #64 or **Metro:** Ottaviano. From metro stop, look for the exit sign "Via Barletta-Viale Giulio Cesare." Exit, walk down Viale Giulio Cesare, turn right on Via Massimo, walk for about 6 blocks, turn left on Via Boezio.

GIUGGIOLI: Via Germanico 198, 1st fl.
Tel: 06-3242113/3243697. (5 rms., 1 w/toilet & bath or shower.) 130,000-150,000L (67-77E) double. No breakfast is served. Cash only. No English spoken, basic hotel w/antique furnished large rms., #4 w/the private bathroom is the best rm., elevator, 1 flr. **Metro:** Lepantro. From Viale Giulio Cesare, take Via Marcantonio Colonna, turn right onto Via Pompeo Magno, walk straight through Piazza Quiriti to Via Germanico.

MARVI: Via Pietro Valle 13, 3rd fl. **Tel:** 06-68802621/6865652. **Fax:** 06-6865652. (8 rms., all w/toilet & bath or shower.) 105,000-145,000L (54-74E) single; 135,000-165,000L (69-85E) double; 210,000L (108E) triple; 240,000L (123E) quad. Breakfast (7:30-9am) is included in the rates & cannot be deducted but can be served in the room. Cash only. Limited English spoken (Max), direct-dial phone, basic hotel w/simply furnished rms., quiet street, elevator, 3 flrs. **Bus:** #64. Stop: Piazza Pia. From Piazza Pia, walk to Piazza Adriana, look for #12/13 Piazza Adriana, walk around the corner to the right of the square to Via Alberico, turn right onto Via Pietro Valle.

SAN PIETRO: Viale Giulio Cesare 62, 1st fl. **Tel:** 06-3725617. **Fax:** 06-3725463. (13 rms., 0 w/toilet & bath or shower.) 65,000-85,000L (33-44E) single; 125,000-155,000L (64-79E) double. Breakfast (7-10am) is included in the rates but can be deducted to reduce room price. Breakfast can be served in the room at extra cost of 6,500L pp. Visa, MC. I broke my rules about not including hotels that offer no private bathrooms, because this is a charming place. English spoken (Stephano), nice hotel w/nicely furnished comfortable large pretty rms., 11 rms. share 5 bathrooms on the 1st fl. & #512 & 513 on the 5th fl. have wonderful views of St. Peter's & share 1 bathroom, nice flrs., double-paned windows, central heating, elevator, 2 flrs. *5% rm. discount or free breakfast when you show owners/managers Stefano & Simone or staff this book.* **Metro:** Ottaviano. Look for the exit sign "Via Barletta-Viale Giulio Cesare." Hotel is on the corner.

HOTELS OVER $100 A NIGHT FOR TWO
These hotels may have rooms under $100 a night for two because it is low season or the rooms do not have private bathrooms.

ALIMANDI: Via Tunisi 8,
Tel: 06-39723948/39726300/314457. **Fax:** 06-39723943.
Web site: http://www.travel.iol.it/alberghi/alimandi/
E-mail: alimandi@tin.it (35 rms., all w/toilet & bath or shower.) 165,000L (85E) single; 210,000L (108E) double; 245,000L (126E) triple. Buffet breakfast (8-10am) at 16,500L pp is not obligatory. Breakfast is served on the terrace in warm weather. Visa, MC, AX, DC. English spoken, direct-dial phone, satellite TV w/CNN, wonderful charming modern hotel w/nicely furnished nice-size airy comfortable bright rms., 30 rms. w/bathtubs, 1 rm. has handicapped access, hair driers, laundry services available, nice flrs., double-paned windows, central heating, air-conditioned, spectacular panoramic view from rooftop garden/terrace, enjoy the rooftop view w/the exotic fish & Papagallo the parrot, pool room, bar, quiet location, 2 elevators, 4 flrs., parking (35,000L per day). *5% rm. discount when you show owners/managers/brothers Enrico, Paolo, Luigi Alimandi or staff*

this book and pay in cash. This bldg. has been in the family for years. There are 7 brothers and 4 sisters in the family. Their mother was born on the 3rd fl. of the hotel. The family tries to make sure all your needs are met. Guests from all over send back special plates to hang on the walls of the hotel. If you call in advance, they can arrange to have you catch their free scheduled bus to and from the airport. If you want your own schedule then you'll have to pay. Located just down the steps off Viale Vaticano in front of the Vatican Museum. **Metro:** Ottaviano. Viale Giulio Cesare becomes Via Candia at the corner of Via Barletta, walk down Via Candia for about 5 blocks, turn left at Via Tunisi.

AMALIA: Via Germanico 66, 2nd fl.
Tel: 06-39723354/39723356. **Fax:** 06-39723365
Web site: http://www.hotelamalia.com/ **E-mail:** hotelamalia@iol.it
(30 rms., 18 w/toilet & bath or shower.) 115,000-195,000L (60-100E) single; 165,000-265,000L (85-136E) double; 230,000-348,000L (118-178E) triple; 300,000-445,000L (154-228E) quad. Buffet breakfast (7-9:30am) is included in the rates & cannot be deducted but can be served in the room. Visa, MC, AX, DC. After June '99, the hotel will be totally renovated to include 12 more bathrooms. The lower rates will no longer be available. English spoken (Rudolfo), direct-dial phone, TV, 19th-century hotel w/elegantly furnished modern large bright rms., marble bathrooms, #20 is the best rm., #204 has a balcony, hair driers, beautiful courtyard entrance, minibars, most rms. have double-paned windows, central heating, bar, elevator, 5 flrs. You have a choice of quiet rms. in the back with depressing views or noisy rms. in the front with better views. *10% rm. discount when you show owner/manager Amalia Consoli or staff this book and pay in cash.* **Metro:** Ottaviano. Walk down Via Ottaviano for 2 blocks, turn right onto Via Germanico.

BRAMANTE: Vicolo Palline 24.
Tel: 06-68806426. **Tel/Fax:** 06-6879881. **Web site:** http://www.travel.it/ **E-mail:** bramante@excalhq.it (20 rms., 12 w/toilet & bath or shower.) 147,000L (75E) single; 191,000L (98E) double; 257,000L (132E) triple; 315,000L (162E) quad. Breakfast (8-10am) at 13,500L pp is not obligatory & can be served in the room. Breakfast is served on the terrace in warm weather. Visa, MC, AX, DC.

English spoken, direct-dial phone, satellite TV w/English channel, charming old quaint hotel w/old-fashioned furnished comfortable rms., terrace has a view of Colonnato Vaticano, front rooms have double-paned windows, central heating, air-conditioned ('99), bar ('99), no elevator, 3 flrs. **Bus:** #64. Stop: Via Corridor. Vicolo Palline intersects Via Corridor next to the Vatican wall.

LADY: Via Germanico 198, 4th fl. **Tel:** 06-3242112. **Fax:** 06-3243446. (8 rms., 4 w/toilet & bath or shower.) 150,000L (77E) single; 165,000-190,000L (85-97E) double; 195,000L (100E) triple (no bathrooms); 240,000L (123E) quad. Breakfast (8-10am) at 16,500L pp is not obligatory & can be served in the room. Cash only. English spoken (Dario), direct-dial phone, TV, basic hotel w/old-fashioned furnished nice-size rms., #1, 2, 5 & 6 have bathrooms, double-paned windows, elevator, 1 flr. **Metro:** Lepantro. From Viale Giulio Cesare, take Via Marcantonio Colonna, turn right onto Via Pompeo Magno, walk straight through Piazza Quiriti to Via Germanico.

SANT'ANGELO: Via Marianna Dionigi 16. **Tel:** 06-3242000. **Fax:** 06-3204451. **Web site:** http://www.novaera.it/hsa/ **E-mail:** hsa@novaera.it (30 rms., all w/toilet & bath or shower.) 85,000-185,000L (44-95E) single; 135,000-235,000L (69-121E) double; 190,000-290,000L (97-149E) triple; 220,000-320,000L (113-164E) quad. Visa, MC, AX, DC. Buffet breakfast (7:30-10:30am) is included in the rates & cannot be deducted. English spoken (Alex & Eric), direct-dial phone, satellite TV w/English channel, beautiful charming hotel w/elegantly furnished large rms., modern bathrooms, nice flrs., double-paned windows, central heating, 15 rms. w/air-conditioning (cost extra), minibars (1999), bar, elevator, 3 flrs., parking (40,000L per day). *10% rm. discount when you show owner/manager Mr. Torre or staff this book.* **Bus:** #492. Stop: Piazza Cavour. Via Marianna Dionigi runs off Piazza Cavour.

Still unable to find a room?
If you don't feel like walking up and down Via Principe Amedeo where there are dozens of hotels, then try the following services:

Accommodation Planet 29: Via Gaeta, 29. **Tel:** 06-486520. **Fax:** 06-484141. **Web site:** http://www.mclink.it/com/travel/

E-mail: cristina@mclink.it 105,000L single; 125,000-140,000L double; 155,000-165,000L triple. Call for family rates. English spoken (Cristina Pignataro). **Cell phone:** 393477863895.

Enjoy Rome: Via Varese 39. **Tel:** 06-4451843.
Fax: 06-4450734. **Web site:** http://www.enjoyrome.com/
E-mail: enjoyrome.com Summer hrs.: Mon.-Fri. 8:30am-6pm; Sat. 8:30am-2pm. Winter hrs.: 8:30am-1pm and 3:30-6pm. Sat. 9am-1pm.
Metro: Termini. Exit the train station to the right, walk 3 blocks up Via Marghera, turn right onto Via Varese. English spoken, maps, free accommodation services, English-only tours and bike tours. They'll work with your budget.

Hotel Reservation (H.R.) Tel: 06-6991000. Daily: 7am-10pm. Free hotel reservation service with locations at Leonardo da Vinci Airport and Termini train station (located at the end of track #10). They usually require that you pay first night's stay in advance.

MONEY
Banca Nazionale Communicazioni: Termini train station between tracks, the entrance to tracks 8 & 11 and 12 & 15. **Tel:** 06-5219730. Hrs.: Mon.-Sat. 8:30am-7pm. The rates are sometimes better than the center. Compare the rates with the exchange rates at the post office.

Central Post Office: Piazza San Silvestro 19. Located close to the Piazza Spagna. **Tel:** 055-672225. Hrs.: Mon.-Fri. 8:30am-7pm.

LAUNDROMATS (Lavanderia)
Daily: 8am-10pm. 13,000L for 14 lbs. of wash, dry and soap. Self-service.

North of the train station
Acqua & Sapone: Via Montebello 66. **Tel:** 06-4883209.
Onda Blu: Via Milazzo 20b. **Tel:** 06-4441665.
Oblo: Via Vicenza 50. **Tel:** 06-4463194.
Bolle Blu: Via Palestro 59/61. **Tel:** 06-4465864.
Bolle Blu: Via Milazzo 20b. **Tel:** 06-4465864.
Laundry: Castelfidardo 31.

South of the train station
Onda Blu: Via Principe Amedeo 70b. **Tel:** 06-47446647.
Onda Blu: Via Lamarmora 10.

Vatican City
Onda Blu: Via Vespasiano 50. **Tel:** 06-39724255.

RESTAURANTS

Please check page 20 for my criteria for selecting restaurants. The true challenge for me was finding an affordable restaurant with delicious food near the train station. There are plenty of fabulous restaurants in the historic area of Rome, but my hotel was near the train station and sometimes I just didn't feel like trekking back to my hotel from the center.

GROTTO D'ABRUZZO: Via Palermo 45. **Tel:** 06-4740980. Mon.-Sat. Hrs.: Lunch 12pm-3pm; dinner 7pm-11pm. Closed Sun. No English spoken. Visa, MC, AX. Wonderful little Roman favorite that serves great homemade food & desserts and hasn't been discovered by the tour groups. Located in a quiet neighborhood. Lovely ambiance. Menu in English. A full dinner complete with a liter of house wine and homemade dessert will cost about 80,000L for two people. I tried four other restaurants that were recommended by other guidebooks and was dissatisfied before a local friend recommended this place. The food was so fresh and delicious. I ate here three times trying different dishes each time and was totally content. *Show Bruno, Valentino or Nicola this book and they will give you a complimentary limoncello.* **Metro:** Termini. From Termini train station, go diagonally left across Piazza Cinquecento (in front of station), turn left onto Via Viminale to the end, turn right onto Via Quattro Fontane, cross the street, turn left onto Via Palermo.

VINCENZO: Via Castelfidardo 4-6. **Tel:** 06-484596. **Fax:** 06-4870092. Mon.-Sat. Hrs.: Lunch 12pm-3pm; dinner 7pm-11pm. Closed Sun., holidays & Aug. No English spoken. Visa, MC, AX, DC. Extensive menu in English. This restaurant specializes in fresh fish but they also serve meat dishes. This was my last day and my last city to research for the book. I wanted to treat myself to an expensive fish dinner before I headed back to the States. I ordered a whole lobster (35,000L), still cheaper than in the U.S. I still remember the ecstasy I experienced as I slowly ate my shellfish. The *spaghetti arrabiatta* was great. Although I was full, I couldn't pass up the homemade dessert. *Show Rita or Vincenzo this book and they will give you a complimentary limoncello or sambucca.* **Metro:** Termini. Exit the train station to the right, walk up Via Marghera, left on Via Varese which becomes Via Vittorio Bachelet when you cross Via Vicenza, continue straight as it becomes Via Castelfidardo. Located just before you reach Via XX Settembre.

SOFFITTA PIZZERIA: Via Villini 1E/1F. **Tel:** 06-4404642. Mon.-Sat. Hrs.: Dinner 7pm-12 midnight. Closed Sun. Visa, MC, AX. Ask any Italian which city makes the best pizza in the country and they will tell you Naples. Ask any local in Rome and they will tell you Soffitta pizzeria. The family who owns this pizzeria are from Naples. Whenever the mayor of Naples is in town, he stops by this pizza place. Get there early or make reservations. You can watch as they make and serve large, fresh, delicious pizzas. I ordered a *Napoli* pizza, carrot salad and a house bottle (9,000L) of wine. The pizza was the best I'd ever had in Italy. There is an Italian sign that hangs on their wall which translates "You are what you eat." You can't really relax and eat slowly because of the hungry locals waiting in the long line outside. If my hotel had a rooftop terrace or a place to bring food, I would order a pizza to go, buy a bottle of wine and slowly eat my pizza. *Show Massimo, Stephano, Rosalba or Luigi this book and they will give you a complimentary after-dinner drink.* Exit the train station to the right, walk 4 blocks up Via Marghera, turn left onto Via Palestro, walk straight until it ends at Via XX Settembre, turn right, continue straight on Via XX Settembre through Porta Pia where it becomes Via Nomentana, turn right onto Via Villini. Or catch **Bus:** #36. Stop: Porta Pia. Walk straight up Via Nomentana, turn right onto Via Villini. There is another location at Via Piave 62/64. **Tel:** 06-42011164. Tues.-Sun. Closed Mon. Hrs.: Lunch 12pm-3pm; dinner 7pm-12 midnight.

SANTA MARGHERITA
Italian Riviera, zip code 16038
Area code 39, City Code 0185

Orientation: A beautiful classic affordable resort village which makes a great base for exploring the Italian Riviera or the Cinque Terre coastline. The town is in the shape of an arc surrounding its small port. The train station is in **Piazza Raul Nobili** which is located on **Via Trieste** overlooking the village. From Piazza Raul Nobili (train station), turn right, take the stairs to the right of the stop sign in front of the train station and take **Via Stazione** toward the **Lungomare** (waterfront). There are two main squares that line the Lungomare: the **Piazza Martiri Liberta** and **Piazza Vittorio Veneto** (where the main bus terminal for local buses is located). As you face the Lungomare, **Via Gramsci** winds around the port to the left, while **Via XXV** Aprile (tourist office) continues on to become **Corsco Matteotti**. Many of the events and holidays that take place in Genoa affect the availability of hotel rooms in Santa Marguerita.

Santa Margherita's Tourist Information Center
Via XXV Aprile 2B. **Tel:** 0185-287485. **Fax:** 0185-283034. Hrs.: Mon.-Sat. 9am-12:30pm & 2:30-5:30pm. Sun. 9:30am-12:30pm. Longer hrs. in the summer. Located just off Piazza Caprera. Turn right from the train station onto Via Roma, then turn right onto Via XXV Aprile.

Hotels
AZALEA: Via Roma 60. **Tel/Fax:** 0185-288160. (10 rms., all w/ toilet & bath or shower.) 65,000-80,000L (33-41E) single; 95,000-110,000L (50-56E) double. Call for triple & quad rates. Breakfast (8-9am) is included in the higher rates but can be deducted to reduce room price. Cash only. English spoken (Sirmoine), nice hotel w/ simply furnished comfortable large rms., all w/views & balconies, #8, 10, 12 & 14 are the best rms., one of the rooms has a private bathroom in the hall, central heating, bar, elevator, 2 flrs. They offer half- and full-board rates. Owned/managed by Lodovica Maffeis. Hotel has two entrances. Located 1/2 block down across from the train station. Turn right from the train station, Via Trieste becomes Via Roma, walk down Via Roma past the stairs towards the hotel

sign hanging over the green doors. Ring the buzzer to the elevator which is locked at both entrances. Someone will bring the elevator up to get you. It is better to call first to make sure they have a room available. (Closed Nov.)

CONTE VERDE: Via Zara 1. **Tel:** 0185-287139. **Fax:** 0185-284211. **Web site:** http://www.it/ftpcv/index.html/
E-mail: cverde@zeus.newnetworks.it (34 rms., 27 w/toilet & bath or shower.) 105,000-175,000L (54-90E) single; 115,000-205,000L (60-105E) double; 150,000-240,000L (77-123E) triple; 180,000-270,000L (92-138E) quad. Children under 10 free. Buffet breakfast (8-10am) is included in the rates but can be deducted to reduce room price. Breakfast can be served in the room at extra cost of 6,500L pp & is served in the garden in warm weather. Visa, MC, AX, DC. English spoken (Alessandro), direct-dial phone, 15 rms. w/satellite TV w/English channel, modern hotel w/nicely furnished rms., hotel could use new carpeting in some of the rms., #24 & 25 are the best rms., #1, 2, 24 & 25 have balconies, 3 rms. have handicapped access, double-paned windows, central heating, garden, bar, restaurant, elevator, 5 flrs., parking (25,000L per day). *Depending on the season you can get 5-10% rm. discount when you show owner/manager Alessandro Pizzi or staff this book.* Turn right on Via Trieste directly in front of the train station, Via Trieste becomes Via Roma. Via Zara is about 1/2 block down on the right-hand side opposite the post office. (Closed Nov.-Dec.)

EUROPA: Via Trento 5. **Tel:** 0185-287187. **Fax:** 0185-280154. (18 rms., 16 w/toilet & bath or shower.) 105,000-135,000L (54-69E) double; 135,000-185,000L (69-95E) triple. Breakfast (8-9:30am) at 11,500L pp is not obligatory. Visa, MC, AX. English spoken (Piero & Guido), direct-dial phone, charming old-fashioned hotel w/nice simply furnished comfortable large rms., tiled flrs., #24 & 34 are the best rms., 12 rms. w/balconies, central heating, tranquil location, bar, no elevator, 3 flrs., parking (15,000 lire per day). Owned/managed by Guido Carota. Located at the bottom of the stairs below the Duomo. This hotel & hotel Minerva are located on the other side of Santa Margherita. To walk from the train station, take the stairs to the right of the stop sign in front of the train station, take Via Stazione down to the waterfront, walk along the waterfront for about 25 minutes passing Piazza Martiri Liberta & Hotel Laurin, turn right onto Via Favale, when you see the Q8 gas station on your left, turn right onto Via Trento. About a 30-minute walk or catch bus. Stop: Mercato del Pesce. Taxi 20,000L. (Closed Nov.-Feb.)

FASCE: Via Luigi Bozzo 3. **Tel:** 0185-286435. **Fax:** 0185-283580. **E-mail:** fasc001@pn.itnet.it (16 rms., all w/toilet & bath or shower.) 105,000-145,000L (54-74E) single; 155,000-183,000L (79-94E) double; 200,000-240,000L (103-123E) triple; 220,000-260,000L (113-133E) quad. Breakfast (8-9:30am) is included in rates & cannot be deducted but can be served in the room (11,500L extra pp). Breakfast is served on the terrace in warm weather. Visa, MC, AX, DC. English spoken (Jane), direct-dial phone, satellite TV w/English channels, charming hotel w/large nicely furnished modern comfortable rms., lots of ambiance, hotel could use new carpeting in some of the rms., plenty of storage space, 4 rms. w/private balconies, #28 has 2 balconies (there are 3 other rooms like #28 but she wouldn't give me the numbers), minibars, double-paned windows, central heating, pretty rooftop terrace w/panoramic view of the surrounding hillside, laundry services, 12 new bikes available free for guests, back courtyard perfect for a picnic, bar, no elevator, 3 flrs., parking (30,000L per day). Owned/managed by husband and wife, Aristide Fasce (Italian) & Jane McGuffie (Scottish). It is a shame that such a lovely hotel is managed by Jane, who seems to have a difficult time being warm to her guests. Many readers who really loved the hotel wrote me about her snobbish and superior attitude. I kept their hotel in the book because it's so wonderful. Turn right from the station onto Via Roma, turn right onto Via XXV Aprile, which becomes Corso Matteotti. Via Luigi Bozzo is off Corso Matteotti. (Closed Jan.-Feb.) Taxi 22,000L.

FIORINA: Piazza Mazzini 26. **Tel:** 0185-287517. **Fax:** 0185-281855. (55 rms., 50 w/toilet & bath or shower.) 100,000-125,000L (51-64E) single; 130,000-155,000L (67-79E) double; 220,000-270,000L (113-138E) triple. Buffet breakfast (8-10am) at 16,500L pp is not obligatory & can be served in the room. Visa, MC, AX. English spoken (Marisa & Roberto), direct-dial phone, TV, wonderful charming hotel w/large modern furnished rms., 29 rms. w/balconies, #105 & 506 large rms. w/balconies are the best rms., #206 is beautiful w/balcony,

#209 & 201 are also large, double-paned windows, tiled flrs., central heating, hair driers, laundry services, bar, restaurant (closed Oct.-Dec.), elevator, free parking. They offer half- (135,000 lire pp) and full-board (160,000 lire pp) rates. *5% rm. discount when you show owners/managers Paola Pendola, Mino Queirolo or staff this book.* To walk from the train station, take the stairs to the right of the stop sign in front of the train station, take Via Stazione down to the waterfront, cross the street when you see bus stop on the left and the little Esso gas station on the corner, follow the road up and around the little square to Largo Giusti, cross the street, turn left onto Via Torino towards the church, turn right onto Via Cavour, continue walking on Via Cavour, turn left onto Via Cairoli, the hotel is on the corner of Via Cairoli & Piazza Mazzini. Taxi 18,000. (Closed Nov.Dec.)

MINERVA: Via Maragliano 34/D.
Tel: 0185-286073. **Fax:** 0185-281697.
Web site: http://www.topwork.com/turismo/it/minerva.htm/
E-mail: hminerva@promix.it (28 rms., all w/toilet & bath or shower.) 100,000-143,000L (51-73E) single; 155,000-195,000L (79-100E) double; 200,000-260,000L (103-133E) triple. Buffet breakfast (7:30-9am) is included in the rates & cannot be deducted but can be served in the room. Breakfast is served in the garden in warm weather. Visa, MC, AX, DC. Limited English spoken (Franco), direct-dial phone, satellite TV w/English channel, charming wonderful hotel w/nicely furnished comfortable rms. & modern bathrooms, fabulous rooftop terrace w/magnificent view worth the price of the room, 14 rooms in front have balconies, most w/views of the sea or surrounding hills, #305 (large jr. suite), 201, 101 & 202 are so special that they are usually booked for the year but try anyway, although they require a 3-night minimum stay, 10 rms. have bathtubs, all the rooms ending in #1-5 face the water, rooms ending in #6-10 (12) face the back & are not as bright as the front, most rms. w/hair driers, central heating, air-conditioned, minibars, laundry services, beautiful tranquil location, bar, restaurant, garden/terrace, elevator, 4 flrs., parking (20,000L per day). *One day free parking when you show owners/managers Metaldi & Devoto, Franco or staff this book.* They offer half- and full-board rates w/minimum stay requirement of 3 nights. This hotel & hotel Europa are located on the other side of Santa Margherita. To walk from the train station, take the stairs to the right of the stop sign

in front of the train station, take Via Stazione down to the waterfront, walk along the waterfront for about 30 minutes passing Piazza Martiri Liberta & Hotel Laurin as Via Marconi becomes Via Bottaro, turn right onto Via Maragliano. Hotel is located up the hill. About a 35-minute walk. Taxi 20,000L.

NUOVA RIVIERA: Via Belvedere 10/2. **Tel/Fax:** 0185-287403. **Web site:** http://space.tin.it/viaggi/gsabin
E-mail: gisabin@tin.it (9 rms., 2 w/bath or shower.) 100,000-115,000L (51-60E) single; 125,000-160,000L (64-82E) double; 160,000-210,000L (82-108E) triple; 180,000-270,000L (92-138E) quad. Buffet breakfast (7-10am) is included in the rates & cannot be deducted but can be served in the room (6,500L extra pp).Visa, MC. English spoken (John Carlo), TV, charming hotel w/old-fashioned furnished large rms. which vary quite a bit, #6 & 12 which have the bathrooms & 8 (balcony) are the best rms., #7, 2 & 3 also have balconies, lots of character, high ceilings, central heating, garden, bar, restaurant, no elevator, 3 flrs., parking. They offer half- and full-board rates (delicious meals including homemade pasta & great family wine) w/minimum stay requirement of 3 nights. Restaurant is also open to the public but you have to reserve in the morning for a 7:30 seating. Owned & managed by John Carlo & his family, who are warm, unbelievably accommodating and very friendly. The hotel offers lots of information on tours, bus & train schedules. If they'd had a room available with a bathroom, I would have stayed here. To walk from the train station, take the stairs to the right of the stop sign in front of the train station, turn right onto Via Gramsci, bear to your right, turn right onto Via Arco, follow signs to Via Belvedere. Taxi 15,000L.

TERMINUS: Piazza Raul Nobili 4. **Tel:** 0185-286121. **Fax:** 0185-282546. (24 rms., 20 w/toilet & bath or shower.) 85,000-95,000L (44-50E) single; 155,000-175,000L (79-90E) double; 230,000-260,000L (118-133E) triple; 300,000-340,000L (154-174E) quad. Children under 6 free. Large English buffet breakfast (7:30-10am) is included in the rates but can be deducted to reduce room price. Breakfast can be served in the room at extra cost of 21,500L pp. Breakfast is served on the terrace in warm weather. Visa, MC, AX, DC. English spoken (Angelo), direct-dial phone, TV, modern furnished comfortable nice-size bright rms. & large bathrooms, great views of the water, #220 & 222 are the best rms. w/views, 4 rms. w/balconies, double-paned windows, hair driers, laundry services, central heating, garden terrace, bar, restaurant, no elevator, 3 flrs., free parking. Owned/managed by the wonderful and charming Angelo Calo, who owned his own restaurant in London for 20 years. He goes out of his way to make you feel comfortable and to make sure all your needs are met. They offer half- (105,000L pp) and full-board (135,000L pp) rates. Angelo brings out buffet appetizers around 7pm and his own wine which comes from his vineyards in the south of Italy (Feb.-Sept.). It's less than a 2-minute walk from the train station. Just make a left as you exit the train station and you will walk right into it. Less than a 10-minute walk from the waterfront. My husband and I stayed here on one of our trips. (Closed Jan-Feb. for 1999 only because of renovations.)

ULIVI: Via Maragliano 28, I attempted to visit the Hotel Ulivi and the blond women at the desk were two of the rudest women I encountered in Italy. They refused to talk to me or show me any of their rooms.

MONEY
Carige Cassa Risparmio Genova Imperia: Largo Antonio Giusti 17. **Tel:** 0185-286034. Hrs.: Mon.-Fri. 8:30am-1pm & 2:30-4pm. Great rates but double-check on the commission.

RESTAURANTS
Please check page 20 for my criteria for selecting restaurants.

NUOVA RIVIERA: Via Belvedere 10/2. **Tel/Fax:** 0185-287403. Visa, MC. Homey-type hotel/restaurant with a tranquil ambiance. This simple restaurant with only nine tables serves wonderful fresh fish, homemade pasta & dessert. You can have a 2nd helping of pasta which you won't get at any of the other restaurants. I ate here the night as one of the patrons celebrated her birthday. Owner, John Carlo's mother made the birthday cake. I was pleasantly surprised at the attention to detail John Carlo exhibits to make sure you are content, while John Carlo's father stands at attention to make sure no one needs anything. Dinner costs approximately 35,000-40,000L which includes a 3-course meal plus dessert w/o wine. Wine costs from 15,000-20,000L per bottle. The best thing about the restaurant is no smoking is allowed. *Show John Carlo this book and he will give you a complimentary after-dinner drink.* You have to call the hotel in the morning to reserve for a 7:30 seating and to find out what is on the menu for the evening.

PEZZI (Da): Via Cavour 21. **Tel:** 0185-285303. Hrs: Lunch 10-2:15pm & Dinner 5-9:15pm. Closed Sat. & Dec. 20-Jan. 20. Cash only. Dinner: 60,000L for two which includes appetizers, pasta, main course, dessert and a liter of house wine. A simple cozy neighborhood restaurant that serves traditional local nonfancy food to a loyal clientele which consists of workmen and businessmen. Delicious fresh vegetables & fish, pesto, homemade pasta and good quality local wine. Mama makes the desserts. If you are looking for a romantic ambiance, it is not at this restaurant.

SAN SIRO: Corso Matteotti 137. Hrs.: 12-2pm & 7pm-12am. Closed June & Sat. except in Aug. Cash only. Since 1967, this simple cozy neighborhood restaurant has served traditional local non fancy food to a loyal clientele which consists of only working-class Italians. Delicious fresh vegetables & fish, pesto, homemade pasta and good quality local wine. This restaurant is a good 15-minute walk away from the waterfront and the tourists. Don't forget to bring your *Eating and Drinking in Italy* menu reader to read the specials on the blackboard since there is no menu. If you are looking for a romantic ambiance, it is not at this restaurant either.

Note: Baicin: Via Algeria 5 is a local trattoria that is quite popular.

SIENA
Tuscany, zip code 53100
Area code 39, city code 0577

Orientation: Magnificent Siena sits on top of three hills. It is one of the most beautiful cities in Italy. It manages to maintain its medieval appearance with its narrow winding streets and noble buildings. Siena makes a great base for visiting the Tuscany area including San Gimignano & Volterra. Once you get settled in your hotel, Siena is a perfect place to explore by foot with its narrow alleys and steep streets. Most people arrive in Siena by bus from Florence. The buses from Florence drop you off at the long-distance bus terminal at **Piazza San Domenico**. I prefer taking the train from Florence to Siena because there are no toilets on the buses. Most of the trains departing from Florence to Siena leave from track #1. Siena's train station is located in **Piazza Fratelli Rosselli**, 2 km northeast in a valley below town, with about a 50-minute strenuous uphill climb to town. If you arrive by train to Siena, I recommend you taxi (16,000L) to your hotel. If you decide to catch a bus from the station to the center, purchase your bus ticket inside the train station from the automatic machine. (Make sure you have plenty of coins for the machine.) There was a lot of construction happening in front of the Siena train station, so when you exit the station, turn left and follow the construction site to the top of the hill. Look for the bus stop where you catch the orange bus #4, 7, 8, 17 or 77 to **Piazza Sale**. It is a 10-minute walk from Piazza Sale or Piazza San Domenico to the fabulous car-free **Il Campo/Piazza Campo** where the magnificent **Duomo** is located. The Il Campo/Piazza Campo is the city's heart and central square.

Siena Tourist Information Centers
1.) Il Campo/ Piazza Campo 56. **Tel:** 0577-280551. **Fax:** 0577-270676. Hrs.: Mon.-Fri. 8:30am-1pm & 3:30-6:30pm; Sat. 8:30am-1pm. Longer hours in-season. **2.)** Via Citta 43. **Tel:** 0577-42209. **Fax:** 0577-281041. Hrs.: Mon.-Fri. 9am-1pm. Via Citta is south of the Il Campo/Piazza Campo. Look for the yellow change sign. **3.)** Train station. Hrs.: Mon.-Fri. 9am-1pm and 4-7pm. **4.)** Prenotazioni Alberghiere, a small hotel-information counter in Piazza San Domenico that charges a fee for its services.

SIENA

Low season: Nov. 3-Dec. 24. & Jan. 7-March 10.
You must have hotel reservations if you are attending "Il Palio delle Contrade" (Palio horse race) which takes place July 2 and August 16.

Hotels near Il Campo/Piazza Campo

CENTRALE: Via Cecco Angiolieri 26, 3rd fl. **Tel:** 0577-280379 **Fax:** 0577-**42152.** (7 rms., 6 w/toilet & bath or shower.) 130,000-135,000L (67-69E) double. Call for triple rates. Breakfast (8-10am) at 9,500L pp is not obligatory & is served in the room. Visa, MC. English spoken (Lucia), direct-dial phone, TV, wonderful hotel w/ nicely furnished comfortable nice-size pretty rms., #41 & 42 wonderful rms. w/terraces, #35 & 37 have views, quiet location, central heating, ceiling fans, no elevator, 4 flrs. Located a block from Il Campo/Piazza Campo. From Il Campo/Piazza Campo, with your back to the tower, exit right, take the stairs next to the tourist office, turn right onto Banchi Sotto, turn left on Via Donzelle, left onto Via Angioleri. (Closed Christmas & 10 days in Jan.)

DUOMO: Via Stalloreggi 38. **Tel:** 0577-289088. **Fax:** 0577-43043. **E-mail:** hduomo@comune.siena.it
(23 rms., all w/toilet & bath or shower.) 115,000-155,000L (60-79E) single; 175,000-235,000 (90-121E) double; 220,000-310,000L (113-159E) triple; 250,000-350,000L (128-179E) quad. Buffet breakfast (7:30-10am) is included in the rates & cannot be deducted. Visa, MC, AX, DC. English spoken, direct-dial phone, satellite TV w/ English channel, classy 17th-century mansion w/nicely furnished comfortable large rms., #61 & 62 w/balconies & magnificent views are the best rms., other rooms have views of the Duomo and the hills, wonderful rooftop terrace w/beautiful view of Tuscany, central heating, air-conditioned, quiet location, elevator, free parking. The hotel is not family-owned but is managed by Adriano Davitti. *5% rm. discount when you show manager Adriano or staff this book during low season.* Take Via Citta south of the Il Campo/Piazza Campo which becomes Via Stalloreggi.

PERLA: Via Terme 25, 2nd fl. **Tel:** 0577-47144. (13 rms., all w/ toilet & bath or shower.) 75,000L (38E) single; 105,000L (54E) double; 145,000L (74E) triple. No breakfast is served. Cash only. No English spoken, basic hotel w/simply furnished small rms. & tiny bathrooms,

2 rms. w/balconies, some beds are too soft, #6 view of square, laid-back atmosphere, no elevator, 1 fl. Located in Piazza Indipendenza.

PICCOLO ETRURIA: Via Donzelle 3.
Tel: 0577-288088/283685. **Fax:** 0577-288461.
E-mail: H.Etruria@sienanet.it (13 rms., 12 w/toilet & bath or shower.) 80,000-85,000L (41-44E) single; 125,000L (64E) double; 165,000L (85E) triple. Children under 4 free. Breakfast (8-11am) at 8,500L pp is not obligatory & can be served in the room. Visa, MC, AX, DC. English spoken (Lucia), direct-dial phone, TV, basic hotel w/simply furnished rms., hair driers, #4 & 13 are the best rms., 1 rm. has handicapped access, rooms are divided between the main bldg. (9 rms. w/a 12:30am curfew) & an annex w/4 nicer rms. directly across from the hotel, no views, central heating, restaurant (2/99), no elevator, 3 flrs., nearby parking (15,000-20,000L per day). Owned/managed by Paolo & Giorgio Fattorini, a wonderful family. The hotel hopes to acquire 6 more rms. by 7/99. From Il Campo/Piazza Campo, with your back to the tower, exit right, take the stairs next to the tourist office, turn right onto Banchi Sotto, left on Via Donzelle. (Closed 1 week around Christmas.)

TOSCANA (La): Via Cecco Angioleri 12. **Tel:** 0577-46097. **Fax:** 0577-270634. (42 rms., 33 w/toilet & bath or shower.) 105,000L (54E) single; 145,000L (74E) double; 180,000L (92E) triple; 210,000L (108E) quad. Breakfast (7:30-10am) at 16,500L pp is not obligatory & can be served in the room. Visa, MC, AX. English spoken (David), direct-dial phone, TV, 13th-century hotel, charming palazzo w/wonderfully furnished large rms., all the rms. vary in size & decor, #441, 432 & 548 are the best rms., #326 & 324 are huge, front rms. have double-paned windows, central heating, bar, elevator, 6 flrs., garage parking (25,000L per day). Owned/managed by Germano Mazzini. For directions, see Hotel Centrale. Located on an alley behind Piazza Tolomei on Banchi Sopra.

TRE DONZELLE: Via Donzelle 5. **Tel:** 0577-280358. **Tel/Fax:** 0577-223933. (26 rms., 5 w/toilet & bath or shower.) 65,000L (33E) single (no toilets); 86,000-105,000L (44-54E) double; Call for triple & quad rates. No breakfast is served. Cash only. English spoken (Valentina), basic hotel w/simply furnished large rms., #2, 4, 5, 10

& 16 have bathrooms, quiet location, no elevator, 4 flrs. This hotel is not family-owned. Located just off Banchi Sotto, north of the Campo. For directions, see Hotel Piccolo Etruria.

Hotels near Piazza Sale
CANNON D'ORO: Via Montanini 28. **Tel:** 0577-44321. **Fax:** 0577-280868. (30 rms., all w/toilet & bath or shower.) 85,000-121,000L (44-62E) single; 105,000-150,000L (54-77E) double; 130,000-185,000L (67-95E) triple; 180,000-220,000L (92-113E) quad. Breakfast (8-10am) at 13,500L pp is not obligatory. Visa, MC, AX. English spoken, direct-dial phone, stylish hotel w/simply furnished large airy rms., some w/views, double-paned windows, central heating, views of gardens & hills, quiet location, no elevator, 3 flrs. Make sure you ask for a renovated rm. w/new bathrooms. The hotel is not family-owned but is managed by Luca Buccianti. *10% rm. discount when you show Luca or staff this book.* Catch bus #4, 7, 8, 17 or 77 from train station to Piazza Sale. Walk up the hill on Via Giuseppe Garibaldi from Piazza Sale, turn left onto Via Montanini. Hotel is located near the end of Via Montanini.

IL PALIO: Piazza Sale 19. **Tel:** 0577-281131. **Fax:** 0577-281142. (26 rms., all w/toilet & bath or shower.) 80,000-165,000L (41-85E) single; 105,000-175,000L (54-90E) double; 140,000-236,000L (72-121E) triple. Buffet breakfast (7-10:30am) at 9,500L pp is not obligatory & can be served in the room (5,500L extra pp). Visa, MC, AX, DC. English spoken, direct-dial phone, TV, comfortable dark rms., #226 & 224 are the best rms., 2 rms. w/balconies, 2 rms. have handicapped access, minibars, double-paned windows, central heating, noisy location, bar, elevator, 3 flrs. *Free breakfast when you show owner Sopra Vedi, manager Luciana Pescini or staff this book.* Catch bus #4, 7, 8 or 77 from train station to Piazza Sale.

Hotels near Piazza Domenico
These hotels are located close to the long-distance bus terminal at the western edge of the old city near the church of San Domenico. I recommend you taxi (16,000L) to these hotels.

ALMA DOMUS: Via Camporegio 37. **Tel:** 0577-44177/44487. **Fax:** 0577-47601. (27 rms., all w/toilet & bath or shower.) 110,000L (56E) double; 140,000L (72E) triple; 160,000L (82E) quad. Breakfast (8-9am) at 13,500L pp is not obligatory. Cash only. No English spoken, nice hotel w/simply furnished large pretty rms., 10 rms. w/balconies, great views of the Duomo, elevator, 4 flrs. This hotel is owned/managed by nuns who have a 10:00am checkout, 11:30pm curfew and no double beds.

BERNINI: Via Sapienza 15. **Tel/Fax:** 0577-289047. (9 rms., 5 w/toilet & bath or shower.) 120,000L (62E) single; 150,000L (77E) double. Call for triple rates. Buffet breakfast (8-10am) at 11,500L pp is not obligatory. Cash only. Limited English spoken, nice hotel w/simply furnished bright airy rms., some w/postcard views of the village, #4 is great, #10 view & bathroom, #11 view of Siena for 4 people w/o bathroom, private rooftop terrace w/spectacular view but can only be used by guests during the day, midnight curfew, no elevator, 1 fl. Owned/managed by Alessandro Saracini. Alessandro will renovate the hotel in March '99. (Closed Dec. 27-Jan. 3.)

CHIUSARELLI: Viale Curtatone 9. **Tel:** 0577-280562. **Fax:** 0577-271177. **E-mail:** chiusare@box1.tin.it (50 rms., all w/toilet & bath or shower.) 115,000L (60E) single; 180,000L (92E) double; 247,000L (127E) triple; 332,000L (170E) quad; suites 260,000 (133E) quad. Breakfast (7:30-10:30am) is included in the rates & can be served in the room (6,500 extra pp) but can be deducted to reduce room price. Breakfast is served on the veranda. Visa, MC, AX. English spoken, direct-dial phone, TV, 19th-century renaissance style villa hotel w/nicely furnished modern comfortable rms., 85% rms. have bathtubs, hair driers, 8 rms. w/balconies, #51 is a suite w/balcony, noisy location, veranda garden, bar, restaurant, no elevator, 2 flrs., free parking. They offer half-board rates at 35,000L extra pp. This hotel is not family-owned. Located across from the Piazza Domenico. 20-minute walk to the Duomo.

Hotel near Forte Santa Barbara
LEA: Viale XXIV Maggio 10. **Tel/Fax:** 0577-283207. (13 rms., all w/toilet & bath or shower.) 90,000L (46E) single; 135,000L (69E) double; 170,000L (87E) triple; 200,000L (103E) quad. Breakfast (7:30-10:30am) is included in the rates & cannot be deducted but can be served in the room (6,500L extra pp). Visa, MC, AX. English

spoken (Arianna), direct-dial phone, 10 rms. w/TVs, 18th-century cozy basic villa w/simply furnished airy bright rms., homey atmosphere, new bathrooms, #10 & 12 have views, only the one single rm. has a balcony, quiet location, garden, bar, no elevator, 4 flrs., street parking. Owned/managed by Renzo Sandrucci. If you are looking for the street on the map it is listed as Ventiquattro Maggio. Bus #9 or 10. The bus drops you off at the intersection of Via Trieste & Viale XXIV Maggio. Taxi 18,000L. Located in very nice residential neighborhood on a road looping around the Forte Santa Barbara. 25-minute walk to the Duomo.

Hotels outside the walls
Don't get turned off by the fact that these hotels are outside the walls. They are all conveniently located within a 15-minute walk to the Duomo without the noise of the inner city. I recommend you taxi (15,000L) to these hotels from the train station.

ALEX: Via Girolamo Gigli 5. **Tel:** 0577-282338. **Fax:** 0577-288776. (14 rms., all w/toilet & bath or shower.) 160,000L (82E) double; 200,000L (103E) triple; 240,000L (123E) quad. Children under 6 free. Breakfast (8-9:30am) is included in the rates & cannot be deducted. Visa, MC. English spoken (Alexandro), direct-dial phone, satellite TV w/English channel, wonderful charming hotel w/nicely furnished comfortable pretty rms., #8 is wonderful, minibars, double-paned windows, 1 rm. has handicapped access, hair driers, central heating, air-conditioned, terrace, bar, quiet location, no elevator, 2 flrs., parking (25,000L per day). *10% rm. discount when you show owner/manager Fracassi Chiara or staff this book.* If you don't taxi, then catch bus #17 from train station, ask bus driver for Porta Pispini stop. It is only a 15-minute walk from the hotel to the Duomo. Exit and enter through Porta Pispini to get to the Duomo. (Closed Dec. 20-March 18.)

IL GIARDINO: Via Baldassarre Peruzzi 35. **Tel/Fax:** 0577-221197. (9 rms., all w/toilet & bath or shower.) 95,000L (50E) single; 175,000L (90E) double. Children under 4 free. Breakfast (8-10am) is included in the rates & cannot be deducted. Visa, MC, AX, DC. English spoken (Gianna), direct-dial phone, TV, wonderful charming hotel w/nicely decorated comfortable bright rms., 1 rm. w/balcony, #6 & 7 are the best rms., central heating, air-conditioned, tranquil location, garden, pool/solarium, bar, restaurant, no elevator, 1 fl., free parking. This is a breathtaking oasis where you can enjoy magnificent views of Siena. Owned/managed by Umberto & Gianna Preve. The only problem I have with this hotel is Umberto & Gianna's rude & obnoxious son who is more interested in proving he can speak English than showing me any manners or respect. I suggest you only interact with Gianna, the warmest member of the family. *Gianna will extend a 10% discount to seniors over 55.* If you don't taxi, then catch bus #5 or 2 to hotel. It is a 20-minute walk from the hotel to the Duomo. Exit and enter through Porta Pispini to get to the Duomo.

MODERNO: Via Baldassarre Peruzzi 19. **Tel:** 0577-288453. **Fax:** 0577-270596. **Web site:** http://sienanet.it/moderno/
E-mail: moderno@sienanet.it (63 rms., all w/toilet & bath or shower.) 104,000L (53E) single; 149,000L (76E) double; 190,000L (97E) triple; 210,000L (108E) quad. Children under 8 free. Buffet breakfast (8-10am) at 17,500L pp is not obligatory & can be served in the room. Visa, MC, AX, DC. English spoken (David), direct-dial phone, TV, wonderful hotel w/nicely furnished comfortable rms., nice wooden flrs., #20bis & 50bis are the best rms., double-paned windows, no views, central heating, garden, bar, restaurant, elevator, parking (20,000L per day). They offer half- and full-board rates. *5% rm. discount when you show owner/manager Pierluigi Pagni or staff this book.* If you don't taxi, then catch bus #5 or 2 to hotel, ask bus driver for Porta Ovile or Hotel Moderno stop. It is a 20-minute walk from the hotel to the Duomo. Exit and enter through Porta Ovile to get to the Duomo.

MONEY
I like the exchange rates at the post office. Main post office: Piazza Matteotti 36-37, **Tel:** 0577-202000. Located between the bus station and Piazza Gramsci. Hrs.: Mon.-Fri.: 8:15am-6pm.

LAUNDROMATS (Lavanderia)
Daily: 8am-10pm. 13,000L for 14 lbs. of wash, dry and soap. Selfservice. **Wash & Dry Lavanderia:** Via Pantaneto 38.
Ondablu: Via Casato Sotto 17.

RESTAURANT
Please check page 20 for my criteria for selecting restaurants.

PAPEI: Piazza Mercato 6. **Tel:** 0577-280894. Tues.-Sun. Hrs.: Lunch 12-3pm; dinner 7pm-10:30pm. Open for lunch on Mon. but closed Mon. evenings. A full dinner complete with a bottle of house wine and dessert will cost about 85,000L for two people. Visa, MC, AX. Cover charge: 3,500L pp. Reservations are strongly recommended. Wonderful little 50-year-old local family restaurant that serves fabulous traditional recipes including homemade pasta and desserts accompanied with local wines. Owned/managed by Roberto Papei. Roberto's mother, brother & cousin do the cooking. Great ambiance with an outdoor street terrace. They serve only meat dishes, no fish. If you want fish, you have to order a day in advance. They don't have liters of wine. They put a bottle on your table and you pay for what you drink. A full bottle is 11,000L. Ask for Daniele, the charming waiter or Marina who only works from June-Oct. *Show owner Roberto Papei or staff this book and they will give you a complimentary Vin Santo or Grappa.* Located behind the duomo. Facing the duomo, turn right, turn left down the arched walkway to Piazza Mercato, bear left into the Piazza to the 2nd restaurant. This restaurant is so good that on one of my day trips to Siena from Florence, I made a reservation for 7pm, had a wonderful dinner, walked from the restaurant to Piazza Sale, caught a bus (every 15 min.) to the train station and caught the last train (9:22pm) back to Florence. You can always taxi back to the train station. If you decide to catch a bus, make sure you buy your bus ticket ahead of time and don't forget to confirm the train schedule.

Note: Many of the guidebooks raved about Osteria Chiacchera, Costa San Antonio 4. My husband, sister and I did not enjoy our meals at all. We felt like we were caught in a tourist trap and felt rushed as we tried to eat our dinner. It was one of the worst restaurant meals we have experienced in all our years of traveling to Italy.

SIRMONE
Lake Garda, zip code 25019
Area code 39, city code 030

Orientation: Located on the southernmost tip of Lake Garda, Sirmone is the most popular of the resorts on the lake. The picturesque, Disneyland-type village is charming, romantic and historic with its flower-lined streets and scenic archways despite the fact that hundreds of tourists bombard it constantly, especially in July & Aug. When you arrive by bus in Sirmone, you'll be dropped off at the post office, with your back toward the post office, walk to your left, make another left which puts you onto Viale Marconi which takes you through the arched wooden portal to the old city.

Transportation: Catch the train to Desanzano's train station. Don't look for a bus station at the train station-there isn't any. Walk across the street to Bar Olympia, where there should be some bus drivers hanging out. Ask them for the departure times to Sirmone, then go back to the train station and buy your bus ticket inside at the bar. It is a half-hour bus ride to Sirmone. Bus info tel: 045-8004129. Or you can walk (15 minutes) or taxi to Desanzano's port to catch a 30-minute boat ride to Sirmone. You can also catch a 2-hr. ferry boat ride from Riva del Garda to Sirmone. Navigazione Lago di Garda tel: 167-551801.

Sirmone's Tourist Information Center
Viale Marconi 2. **Tel:** 030-916114. **Fax:** 030-916222. **E-mail:** aptbs@gardanet.it. Nov.-March Hrs.: Mon.-Fri. 9am-12:30pm & 3-6pm. Sat. 9am-12:30pm. Later hrs. & Sun. in-season. Located outside the old city.

Low season March-May & Oct.-Nov.

Hotels inside the old city
CORTE REGINA: Via Antica Mura 11. **Tel/Fax**: 030-916147. **Tel/Fax**: 030-9196470. (14 rms., 12 w/toilet & bath or shower.) 80,000-95,000L (41-50E) single; 145,000-185,000L (74-95E) double. Call for triple rates. Buffet breakfast (7:30-10:30am) is included in the rates & cannot be deducted. Visa, MC, AX. English spoken (Lorenzo),

direct-dial phone, TV, newly renovated wonderful charming hotel w/ contemporary furnished large rms., new bathrooms w/telephones, beautiful tiled flrs., all rooms are named after flowers, pretty terrace, 4 rms. w/balconies, 1 rm. (Bouganvillea) has handicapped access, Ortensia & Camelia both w/balconies are the best rms., minibars, hair driers, tranquil location, central heating, air-conditioned, bar, restaurant w/Roman ruin under glass-covered floor (closed Thurs.), elevator, 2 flrs. Owned/managed by Alba Saceltella. Immediately after going through the gate of Sirmone, stay straight on the main road, turn right onto Via Antica Mura. Located next door to the restaurant Botte. (Closed Jan.-March.)

DEGLI OLEANDRI: Via Dante 31. **Tel:** 030-9905780. (20 rms., 16 w/toilet & bath or shower.) 80,000L (41E) single; 103,000-185,000L (53-95E) double. Call for triple rates. Breakfast (7:30-10am) is included in the rates & cannot be deducted. Visa, MC, AX. English spoken (Julio), direct-dial phone, wonderful charming old hotel w/comfortable rms., some w/TVs, great terrace w/view of the water, #21 & 25 are the best rms. w/views of the lake near the terrace, all the rooms on the 1st fl. have been renovated, they plan to work on the rest in the year 2000, central heating, bar, restaurant, no elevator, 2 flrs. They offer half- (90,000 lire pp) and full-board (105,000 lire pp) rates. The hotel is not family-owned but is managed by Paolo Cichello. Immediately after going through the gate of Sirmone, turn right, follow the wall on your right which curves around, when you see the Elle store make a left up the road, hotel will be on the left. (Closed Nov.-Easter.)

GRIFONE: Via Bocchio 4. **Tel:** 030-916014. **Fax:** 030-916548. (16 rms., all w/toilet & bath or shower.) 65,000L (33E) single; 95,000-103,000L (50-53E) double; 150,000L (77E) triple; 160,000L (82E) quad. No breakfast is served. Cash only. English spoken (Cristina), wonderful charming hotel w/simply furnished comfortable rms., #36 & 28 have balconies and beautiful views, tiled flrs., all rms. w/lakeside view, garden, central heating, elevator which only goes to 3 of the 4 flrs. The restaurant next door with the same name is not part of the hotel. (Different management.) You can choose to have your breakfast in the restaurant but it is not worth the 11,500L pp. I made the mistake of thinking breakfast came with the room. Owned/managed by Nicola & Cristina Marcolini. Immediately after going through the gate of Sirmone, turn right, follow the wall on your right which curves around, when you see the Elle store turn left up the road, make your first right to the hotel. (Closed Nov.-March.)

LUNA: Via Vittorio Emanuele 92. **Tel**: 030-9905836. **Fax**: 030-916381. (31 rms., all w/toilet & bath or shower.) 95,000-135,000L (50-69E) single; 135,000-155,000L (69-79E) double; 180,000L (92E) triple. Buffet breakfast (7:30-9:45am) at 11,500L pp is not obligatory. Visa, MC, AX. English spoken (Mario), direct-dial phone, TV, basic hotel w/simply furnished comfortable rms., all rms. w/balconies, central heating, air-conditioned, restaurant, elevator, 2 flrs. They offer half- and full-board rates with minimum-stay requirement of 3 nights. Owned/managed by Mario Lizzeri. Immediately after going through the gate of Sirmone, stay straight on the main road, hotel is located at the edge of the old city near the park. (Closed Nov.-March.)

PACE: Via Carpentini 17. **Tel**: 030-9905877. **Fax**: 030-9196097. (22 rms., all w/toilet & bath or shower.) 105,000L (54E) single; 165,000L (85E) double; 200,000L (103E) triple; 220,000L (113E) quad. Buffet breakfast (7:30-10:30am) is included in the rates & cannot be deducted but can be served in the room (6,500L extra pp). Breakfast is served on the veranda in warm weather. Visa, MC, AX. English spoken (Eleanor), direct-dial phone, TV, beautiful charming hotel w/nicely furnished comfortable rms., #50, 52, 58 & 60 are the best rms & have large balconies, ceiling fans, central heating, beautiful garden w/sunbathing private pier (worth the price of the rooms), bar, restaurant that overlooks the lake w/swans, elevator, 4 flrs. They offer half- and full-board rates. Owned/managed by Dino Barelli. The Barelli family also owns the higher price Hotel Catullo (185,000-205,000L double) across the street from the Hotel Pace. Immediately after going through the gate of Sirmone, stay straight on the main road, turn left onto Via Carpentini. (Closed Nov.-Dec. 20 & Jan.-Feb. 15.)

SPERANZA: Via Castello 6. **Tel**: 030-916116. **Fax**: 030-916403. (13 rms., all w/toilet & bath or shower.) 80,000L (41E) single; 125,000L (64E) double; 170,000L (87E) triple; 210,000L (108E) quad. Breakfast (8-10am) is included in the rates & can be served in the room but can be deducted to reduce room price. Visa, MC. English spoken (Franco & Aliza), direct-dial phone, TV, wonderful charming old hotel w/simply furnished airy large rms. & modern bathrooms, marble staircase & flrs. in lobby, #24 & 25 are the best rms., central heating, double-paned windows, elevator, 2 flrs., parking (25,000L per day). Owned/managed by Franco Sacchella. Immediately after going through the gate of Sirmone, stay straight on the main road, when you see the Donum store at the 1st traffic light, turn left, hotel will be on the right side of the street. (Closed Nov. 15-March 1.)

HOTELS I DIDN'T GET A CHANCE TO REVISIT
GIARDINO: Via Vittorio Emanuele 67. **Tel**: 030-916135. **Fax:** 030-916381. 165,000L (85E) double including breakfast. Visa, MC. I didn't get a chance to visit this hotel but how bad could it be for a 3-star.

MAGNOLIA (La): Via Vittorio Emanuele 59. **Tel**: 030-916135. 90,000L double. Hotel is open for 3 months. (July-Sept.)

RESTAURANT
Please check page 20 for my criteria for selecting restaurants.

BOTTE (La): Via Antiche Mura 25. **Tel:** 030-9196257. **Fax:** 030-916273. Hrs.: 12-2:45pm & 6:45-10:45pm. Closed Tues. Visa, MC, AX. Delicious food and wonderful ambiance. I had salad, pasta, chicken dish (w/extra garlic), 1/2 liter wine and homemade dessert for 45,000L. Make reservations or try to get to the restaurant when they first open. 10% gratuity is added to the check. Salvatore, the waiter, speaks limited English.

SORRENTO
Amalfi Coast, zip code 80067
Area code 39, city code 081

Orientation: Sorrento, located about 150 feet above the sea along the clifftop, is a beautiful charming resort town. It makes a great base for visiting Positano, Amalfi, Capri, Pompeii, Ischia and Naples. **Sorrento** *Circumvesuviana* train station is located directly in front of **Corso Italia**, which is the town's main avenue. From the train station, walk down the stairs, turn left onto Corso Italia, continue straight to **Piazza Tasso** (center/heart of town). To get to the port, turn left onto **Via Maio** from Piazza Tasso. To get to **Via/Punto Capo** (50-minute walk), continue straight through Piazza Tasso to the the edge of town where it becomes Via Capo (a highway), continue on Via Capo to Punta Capo. You can also catch Sita bus #A from the train station or Piazza Tasso to Via Capo. Taxi 23,000L. Night taxi 30,000L.

For those of you who don't know how to get to Sorrento by train, catch the independent local *Ferrovia Circumvesuviana* on the lower level of the Naples Centrale station. When you arrive at the Naples Centrale station, look for the large blue signs "*Circumvesuviana*." Follow the signs, go downstairs, buy your ticket at the *Circumvesuviana* window. Walk to the far left of the turnstiles, insert your ticket into the machine and walk downstairs to the tracks. Please keep in mind, there are no toilets on these local trains. (A fact I had to learn the hard way.) It takes about 70 min. to get to Sorrento (last stop) from Naples by train. Trains run about twice an hour from 4am-11pm. 5,000L pp. No rail passes. There are also hydrofoils that leave from Naples' Beverello port (15,000L for a 30-minute ride) to Sorrento's port. From the port you'll have to taxi to your hotel unless you want to take the long, winding very steep 15-minute climb uphill to the center of town.

Sorrento's Tourist Information Center
Web site: http://www.vol.it/sorrento. Via Luigi Maio 35. **Tel:** 081-8074033. **Fax:** 081-8773397. Hrs.: Mon.-Sat. 8:30am-6:30pm. Closed Sun. Longer hrs. in-season. From the station, go left on Corso Italia, walk 5 minutes to Piazza Tasso, turn right at end of square

down Via L. Maio. Go through Piazza Sant'Antonio, continue to the right toward the port. To the right is the Foreigners' Club Mansion #35. The tourist office is on the left as you enter the building.

The Hotel Nice at Corso Italia 257 sells bus tickets to nearby towns and other cities. If you catch a bus to Positano or Almafi, sit on the the right side of the bus to experience the most magnificent coastline of Italy and the scary ride. I admit, I had to close my eyes more than once on this ride because it upset my equilibrium.

Hotels near the center
A nice, safe but noisy area to stay in. All these hotels are within a 10-minute walk from the train station and bus station. Corso Italia is a busy noisy street even though they stop traffic from 8pm-12midnight.

ASTORIA: Via S. Maria Grazie 24. **Tel:** 081-8074030. **Fax:** 081-8771124. (34 rms., all w/toilet & bath or shower.) 90,000-100,000L (46-51E) single; 135,000-155,000L (69-79E) double; 160,000-190,000L (82-97E) triple. Breakfast (7-9am) is included in the rates & cannot be deducted. Visa, MC. English spoken (Josie), direct-dial phone, 17th-century wonderful charming hotel w/nicely furnished nice-size comfortable rms., 5 rms. w/balconies, terrace/garden, bar, restaurant (guests must reserve in advance), no elevator, 4 flrs. on one side & 1 fl. on the other side. They offer half- and full-board rates. *5% rm. discount when you show owner/manager Josie or staff this book.* From station, walk down the stairs to Corso Italia, turn left onto Corso Italia, continue straight through Piazza Tasso, turn right onto Via Archi, turn left onto Via S. Maria Grazie. (Closed Nov.-March but open for Christmas.)

CITY: Corso Italia 221. **Tel/Fax:** 081-8772210.(13 rms., all w/toilet & bath or shower.) 90,000L (46E) single; 110,000-120,000L (56-62E) double; 155,000-165,000L (79-85E) triple; 185,000-205,000L (95-105E) quad. Breakfast (8-10am) is included in the rates but can be deducted to reduce room price. Visa, MC, AX. English spoken (Gianni), basic hotel w/nicely furnished comfortable nice-size airy bright rms. w/tiny patio or terrace, nice flrs., modern bathrooms, #106 & 9 are the best rms., noisy location, no elevator, 2 flrs. Owned/managed by Gianni Magliulo. From station, walk down the stairs to

Corso Italia, turn left onto Corso Italia and walk for 1 1/2 blocks. (Closed Nov. or Jan.)

CORSO (Del): Corso Italia 134. **Tel:** 081-8073157. **Fax:** 081-8071016. **E-mail:** luda@syneme.it (20 rms., all w/toilet & bath or shower.) 115,000-130,000L (60-67E) double; 170,000-185,000L (87-95E) triple; 200,000-220,000L (103-113E) quad. Children under 5 free. Buffet breakfast (7-9am) at 11,500-16,500L pp is not obligatory. Breakfast is served on the terrace in warm weather. Visa, MC, AX, DC. English spoken (Luca), direct-dial phone, nice hotel w/ simply furnished comfortable nice-size airy rms., most of the rooms face the back, #68 & 69 are the best rms., #53 is nice w/balcony but faces the noisy front, 7 rms. w/balconies, 8 rms. have handicapped access, air-conditioned (1999), solarium terrace (1999), #7 is perfect for a family of six w/wonderful rooftop view of Naples, central heating, noisy location, bar, elevator, 2 flrs. They only serve dinner in Aug., cooked by Luca's mother. Owned/managed by Luca Marciano & his family for over 26 years. From station, walk down the stairs to Corso Italia, turn left onto Corso Italia, walk for 2 1/2 blocks. (Closed Dec.-mid.-Feb.)

MIGNON: Via Sersale 9. **Tel:** 081-8073824. (11 rms., all w/toilet & bath or shower.) 105,000L (54E) single; 125,000L (64E) double; 160,000L (82E) triple; 180,000L (92E) quad. Breakfast (7-10am) is included in the rates & cannot be deducted but can be served in the room. Visa, MC. English spoken (Dalmira), TV, nice hotel w/nicely furnished comfortable rms., #9 & 10 are the best rms., 10 rms. w/ balconies, central heating, noisy location, no elevator, 2 flrs. Dalmira, the housekeeper, has a wonderful & energetic personality. From station, walk down the stairs to Corso Italia, turn left onto Corso Italia, continue straight through Piazza Tasso, turn left at the Fortuna toy store onto Via Sersale.

NICE: Corso Italia 257. **Tel:** 081-8781650. **Fax:** 081-8071154. (20 rms., all w/toilet & bath or shower.) 90,000L (46E) single; 115,000L (60E) double; 160,000L (82E) triple; 200,000L (103E) quad. Breakfast (7:30-10am) is included in the rates but can be deducted to reduce room price. Visa, MC, AX, DC. English spoken (Alfonso), direct-dial phone, satellite TV w/English channels, wonderful hotel w/

simply furnished comfortable nice-size rms., 6 rms. w/balconies, central heating, air-conditioned (cost extra), no elevator, 3 flrs. Alfonso is very charming & accommodating and will make sure all your needs are met. From station, walk down the stairs to Corso Italia, turn left onto Corso Italia to the hotel. The hotel sells tickets to nearby towns and other cities. Owned/managed by the same family as Hotel Loreley & Londres. (Closed Dec.-Feb.)

Hotels near the center of town
LORELEY & LONDRES: Via Califano 2. **Tel/Fax:** 081-8073187. (27 rms., all rms., w/toilet & bath or shower.) 155,000L (79E) double; 200,000L (103E) triple; 230,000L (118E) quad. Children under 10 free. Rates are lower if you pay cash. Breakfast (7-10am) is included in the rates & cannot be deducted. Breakfast is served on the garden terrace in warm weather. Visa, MC, DC. English spoken, wonderful charming ancient villa w/beautifully furnished comfortable large bright rms., rooms facing the noisy street are cheaper, 15 rms. w/sea views, 8 of those rms. have balconies, #14 (corner), 12, 13 & 11 are the best rms., central heating, fabulous view from garden/terrace restaurant, elevator to private beach, bar, no elevator, 2 flrs., free parking. Owned/managed by Giuseppina Ereolan who also owns Hotel Mignon. The hotel is located high on the cliffs on the eastern edge of town. From station, walk down the stairs to Corso Italia, turn right on Corso Italia, an immediate left at the gas station onto Via Capasso, which becomes Via Califano. Taxi 18,000L. (Closed Nov.-March.)

MARA: Via Rota 5. **Tel:** 081-8783665. (10 rms., 3 w/toilet & bath or shower.) 55,000L (28E) single; 105,000L (54E) double; 140,000L (72E) triple; 180,000L (92E) quad. No breakfast is served. Cash only. No English spoken, basic hotel w/simply furnished rms., nothing special, #24, 28 & 26 have bathrooms, 5 rms. w/balconies, no elevator, 2 flrs., free parking. Located a couple blocks from the train station. From station, walk down the stairs to Corso Italia, turn right on Corso Italia, an immediate left at the gas station onto Via Capasso, turn right onto Via Rota, just past the main police station.

Hotel above the train station
LINDA: Via Aranci 125. **Tel:** 081-8782916. (15 rms., all w/toilet & bath or shower.) 65,000L (33E) single; 95,000-105,000L (50-54E)

double. Call for triple rates. Breakfast (7:30-10am) at 6,500L pp is not obligatory & is served in the room. Cash only. No English spoken, ugly exterior bldg. but nice hotel w/simply furnished comfortable pretty airy rms., large bathrooms, 10 rms. w/balconies, #16 is pretty, elevator, 3 flrs. Owned/managed by charming Giannovi & Anna. This residential nontourist neighborhood is only convenient for the train station, located just below. From the station, make an immediate left, turn left again onto Via Marziale, follow this curved road up as it ends into Via Aranci (main road), turn left to the hotel.

Hotels near Punta Capo/Via Capo
Wonderful peaceful cliffside located outside of town. It is not a centrally located area but it is perfect for relaxing and doing nothing while you enjoy the exquisite views of Sorrento. You will not regret staying at any of these hotels. Just make sure you request a room with a view. It is a 50-minute walk from the train station and a 25-minute walk from Piazza Tasso to these hotels. From the train station, walk down the stairs, turn left onto Corso Italia, continue straight through Piazza Tasso to the edge of town where it becomes Via Capo (a highway) straight to Punta Capo. You can also catch Sita bus #A from the train station or from Piazza Tasso to Via Capo. Taxi 23,000L. Night taxi 30,000L.

DESIREE: Via Capo 31. **Tel/Fax:** 081-8781563. (22 rms., all w/ toilet & bath or shower.) 95,000L (50E) single; 155,000L (79E) double; 185,000L (95E) triple; 210,000L (108E) quad. Breakfast (7:30-9:30am) is included in the rates but can be deducted to reduce room price. Cash only. English spoken (Michele, Imma & Joseph), direct-dial phone, wonderful charming hotel w/nicely furnished comfortable airy rms., walk down the stairs to the rms., #14 & 1 have magnificent views, 11 rms. w/balconies, 7 of those rooms have a view, charming Michele didn't want to show me more rooms because he didn't want me to mention the room numbers, 2 rms. have handicapped access, nice flrs., terrace, elevator to private beach, fabulous peaceful location, free parking, no elevator, 2 flrs., free parking. Owned/managed by Corinna Gargiulo. Same driveway & private beach as Hotel Tonnarella. Don't believe Michele if he says there is no room #14. Ask Michele about the restaurant his family owns. I didn't get a chance to eat there. Please let me know if it is any good. (Closed Nov. 5-March 10.)

ELIOS: Via Capo 33. **Tel:** 081-8781812. (14 rms., 12 w/toilet & bath or shower.) 60,000L (31E) single; 85,000-100,000L (44-51E) double. Breakfast (7-9am) at 9,500L pp is not obligatory. Breakfast is served on the terrace in warm weather. Cash only. English spoken (Gianna), wonderful charming hotel w/simply furnished comfortable rms., 4 rms. w/balconies & 8 rms. w/terraces, #7 & 8 are the best rms., #5 & 6 have views but no bathrooms, only #1, 4, 10 & 11 are w/o sea views, beautiful rooftop terrace w/magnificent panoramic view, fabulous peaceful location, central heating, no elevator, 3 flrs., free parking. If this hotel took credit cards, I would be in heaven. Owned/managed by Luigi & Maria Aiello. Ask bus driver for Hotel Elios. (Closed Nov.-Feb.)

MINERVETTA (La): Via Capo 25. **Tel:** 081-8773033. **Fax:** 081-8073069. **Web site:** http://www.sabah.it/aziende/laminervetta/ **E-mail:** jobcity@sabah.it (12 rms., all w/toilet & bath or shower.) 165,000L (85E) double; 230,000L (118E) triple; 270,000L (138E) quad. Breakfast (7:30-10am) at 22,500L pp is not obligatory & can be served in the room. Breakfast is served in the beautiful veranda. Visa, MC, AX, DC. English spoken (Salvatore), direct-dial phone, TV, wonderful hotel w/nicely furnished comfortable rms., terrace, 9 rms. w/balconies, all the rooms have wonderful sea views, #105 & 204 have wonderful views, bunk beds, balcony & large bathroom, central heating, private steps to the beach, terrace w/fabulous view, bar, restaurant, no elevator, 3 flrs., free parking. Owned/managed by Salvatore & Antonino Morvillo. The same family has owned the restaurant for 65 years. They offer half- and full-board rates.

TONNARELLA (La): Via Capo 31.
Tel: 081-8781153/8781016. **Fax:** 081-8782169.
Web site: http://www.geocities.com/hotsprings/3194/
E-mail: pippo@syrene.it (21 rms., all w/toilet & bath or shower.) 205,000-225,000L (105-115E) double; 250,000-260,000L (128-133E) triple; 270,000L (138E) apt. Breakfast (7:30-9:30am) is included in the rates & cannot be deducted but can be served in the room. Breakfast is served in the beautiful veranda. Visa, MC, AX. English spoken (Pippo & Giuseppe), direct-dial phone, satellite TV w/English channel, wonderful charming villa w/beautifully furnished comfortable rms., the lower rates are for rooms w/o views, 15 rms.

w/balconies, many w/sea views, #1-5 are the most luxurious rms., #2 w/huge terrace, #4 has 2 balconies w/views, #13 (arched wood-beamed ceiling) & 14 have views & Jacuzzi bathtubs, #12 has a balcony w/view & Jacuzzi shower, 3 rms. have Jacuzzi showers, #15 no view but Jacuzzi bathtub, hair driers, wonderful terrace, elevator to private beach, central heating, air-conditioned, bar, restaurant, fabulous peaceful location, elevator, 2 flrs., free parking. They offer half- and full-board rates. Same driveway & private beach as Hotel Desiree. Owned/managed by Cristina & Giuseppe Gargiulo.

Still looking for a room? Try **Hotel Ascot:** Via Capo 6, **Tel/Fax:** 081-8783032 & **Hotel Rivage:** Via Capo 11, **Tel:** 081-8781873. **Fax:** 081-8071253. Each about 180,000L double including buffet breakfast.

MONEY
Sometimes the exchange rates are better at the post office. **Post Office:** Corso Italia 210/S-V. **Tel:** 081-8781636. Hrs.: Mon.-Sat. 8:15am-6pm. Located near Piazza Lauro. From station, walk down the stairs to Corso Italia, turn right onto Corso Italia.

LAUNDROMAT (Lavanderia)
Terlizzi: Corso Italia 30. **Tel:** 081-8781185. Daily: 9am-9pm. 17,000L per load. Self-service. Drycleaning is closed Sat. & Sun.

RESTAURANTS
Please check page 20 for my criteria for selecting restaurants.

GATTO NERO: Via Santa Maria Pieta 36. **Tel:** 081-8781582. Tues.-Sun. Hrs.: Lunch 1-3pm; dinner 7pm-12am. Closed Mon. Visa, MC. A great hole-in-the-wall cozy restaurant with wonderful homemade food & tiramisu. A full dinner complete with a liter of house wine and dessert will cost about 60,000L for two people. English menu. 8 tables. Owned/managed by Marcello & his family. Maria, his wife, does all the cooking. *Show owner/waiter Marcello or son/waiter Nino this book and they will give you a complimentary limoncello.* The only down side about the restaurant is it seems all the tourists know about it. Get here at 7pm when they open or make advance reservations. From Piazza Tasso, bear left over to Via Santa Maria Pieta which parallels Corso Italia.

SORRENTO

RED LION: Via Marziale 25. **Tel:** 081-8073089. Hrs.: Daily lunch 11am-3pm; dinner 7pm-2am. (Closed Tues. from Oct.-March.) Visa, MC, DC. This plain restaurant with an English name but very Italian food & an extensive menu (including pizza) is a fun place to enjoy a simple, affordable meal. Ask which of the pastas are homemade. *Show owner/manager Tonino Maresca this book and he will give you a complimentary after-dinner drink.* From station, walk down the stairs to Corso Italia, turn left onto Corso Italia, turn left to restaurant.

VARENNA
Lake Como, zip code 23829
Area code 39, city code 031

Orientation: Varenna, a beautiful ancient waterfront fishing village has a romantic promenade, tiny harbor and lots of steep steps that substitute for streets. From the train station take the curvy road downhill, as you go around the curve, look for the steps (shortcut) on your right, take the steps down to the Via Per Esino (main road), make a right onto Via Per Esino and just follow the road, when you get to Via Croce make a left, then a quick right down to the waterfront.

Varenna's Tourist Information Center
Piazza San Giorgio. **Tel:** 0341-830367. Hrs.: May 15-Oct. 1 9am-12pm; 3-6pm. Sun. 10am-12:30pm & 3-6pm. Off-season mornings only. These hours are not etched in stone. Located in the main square.

Low season March 21-April, & Sept. 27-Oct. 24; mid-season May, June 21-July 18, high season July 19-Sept 19.

Hotels
For walking directions to hotels, look under Orientation above.

BERETTA: Via Per Esino 1. **Tel/Fax:** 0341-830132. (7 rms., 3 w/ toilet & bath or shower.) 65,000L (33E) single; 135,000L (69E) double; 150,000L (77E) triple. Breakfast (8:30am) at 11,500L pp is not obligatory & can be served in the room (2,500L extra pp). Breakfast is served on the outdoor patio in warm weather. Visa, MC, AX, DC. Limited English spoken (Giulia), direct-dial phone, satellite TV w/English channel, basic hotel w/nicely furnished rms., #9 (huge balcony) & 5 (balcony) w/views but no bathrooms & 4 are the best rms., double-paned windows, central heating, hotel has view of the lake, outdoor patio, bar, restaurant (discount if you eat in the restaurant), no elevator, 2 flrs. #5, 8, 9 & 10 have no bathrooms but they plan to renovate these rms. in spring of 1999 to include bathrooms. Don't get discouraged by the outside of the bldg. *Free breakfast when you show owner/manager Tosca Proto or staff this book.* They offer half- (90,000L pp) and full-board (120,000L pp) rates.

MILANO: Via XX Settembre 29. **Tel/Fax:** 0341-830298.
Web site: http://www.welcome.to/varenna/
E-mail: varenna@welcome.to (8 rms., all w/toilet & bath or shower.)
90,000-165,000L (46-85E) single; 170,000-225,000L (87-115E)
double. Buffet breakfast (8-10am) at 16,500L pp is not obligatory &
can be served in the room. Breakfast is served on the beautiful terrace or veranda in warm weather. Visa, MC, AX, DC. English spoken (Giovanni), direct-dial phone, wonderful charming hotel w/sim-
ply furnished comfortable nice-size rms. & modern bathrooms, all
rms. w/balconies, #1 & 2 which have huge terraces and face the front
are the best rms., #5 & 6 have smaller balconies, face the street and
have better views, #3 has a private bathroom outside the rm., central
heating, bar, no elevator, 3 flrs. *5% rm. discount when you show
owner/manager Amelia Bernardoni or staff this book.* Located just
off the main square overlooking the lake off Contrada Alla Cortesella.
(Closed Nov.)

MONTE CODENO: Via Croce 2. **Tel:** 0341-830123. **Fax:** 0341-
815227. (11 rms., all w/toilet & bath or shower.) 155,000-165,000L
(79-85E) double; 200,000-215,000L (103-110E) triple; 240,000-
260,000L (123-133E) quad. Buffet breakfast (8-9:30am) at 16,500L
pp is not obligatory & can be served in the room (6,500L extra pp).
Visa, MC, AX, DC. English spoken (Marina & Rudolpho), direct-
dial phone, satellite TV w/English channel, nice basic hotel w/simply
furnished rms., #10 has a balcony, 2 rms. have handicapped access,
#6 & 7 are the best rms., double-paned windows, central heating,
small garden, bar, great restaurant (discount if you eat in the restaurant), no elevator, 2 flrs. *Free breakfast when you show owner/man-
ager Ferruccio Castelli or staff this book.* They offer half- (105,000L
pp) and full-board (120,000L pp) rates. The specialty of the restaurant is the fresh fish of Lake Como. Award-winning Chef Castelli
prides himself on fabulous recipes. (Closed Wed. & Dec. 15-Jan. 15.)

OLIVEDO: Piazza Martiri. **Tel/Fax:** 0341-830115. (15 rms., 6 w/
toilet & bath or shower.) 90,000-105,000L (46-54E) single; 105,000-
170,000L (54-87E) double; 140,000-210,000L (72-108E) triple.
Breakfast (8-10am) is included in the rates but can be deducted to
reduce the price of the room. Breakfast is served on the garden terrace
in warm weather. Visa, MC. English spoken (Laura), old-world charm-

ing Victorian hotel w/old-fashioned furnished rms. & hardwood flrs., 11 rms. w/balconies, #18 & 26 w/balconies, great views & bathrooms are the best rms., #21, 11, 1 & 3 also have great views & bathrooms but #1 & 3 are on the 1st flrs., double-paned windows, central heating, bar, good restaurant (discount if you eat in the restaurant), no elevator, 5 flrs., free parking. *5% rm. discount when you show owners/managers Laura & Antonia Columbo or staff this book during off-season. They will also extend a free breakfast to seniors over 55.* They offer half-board rates at 95,000-130,000L pp which may be required in summer. Facing the ferry dock. (Closed Nov.-Dec. 3.)

RESTAURANT
Please check page 20 for my criteria for selecting restaurants.

SOLE (Del): Piazza San Giorgio. **Tel:** 0341-23829. Cash only. Hrs.: 12-2:30pm & 7-10pm. Closed Wed. Delicious pizza. No English spoken. Cover charge 3,500L pp. 11,000L for pizza. Located in the same square as the tourist office.

VENICE (Venezia)
The Veneto, zip code 30121
Area code 39, city code 041

Orientation: Venice is a beautiful city that can easily be managed by foot, once you are settled in your hotel. The **Santa Lucia** train station is located on the northwestern edge of the city. The two main means of transportation in Venice are walking or *vaporetto* (water bus). It is about a 45-minute walk to the **Piazza San Marco** (St. Mark's Square, the heart of Venice). I won't even begin to give you directions to walk from the train station to St. Mark's Square. Either use the map you hopefully purchase prior to your arrival in Venice or pick one up at the always crowded tourist office in the train station. You can begin walking to the left of the station along **Lista di Spagne**, follow the yellow signs and tourists. Remember *ponte* means bridge and vaporetti means water buses. The water buses drop you off at **Piazzale Roma** (bus station), which is just across the **Grand Canal** from the train station. It is a long walk from here to any of the hotels that are not near the train station so I suggest you catch a vaporetto.

Venice is divided into six districts (*sestieri*): **Cannargio** (from the station to Rialto), **San Marco** (St. Mark's square and the immediate surrounding area), **Castello** (behind San Marco) are all on one side of the canal and **San Polo**, **Dorsoduro** and **Santa Croce** are on the other side. Venice also consists of 117 small islands and has 410 bridges but if you want to cross over the Grand Canal, Venice's main artery, there are only three bridges that cross over it: **1.)** Ponte Scalzi (near the train station), **2.)** Ponte Rialto (connects San Marco and San Polo at the center of town) and **3.)** Ponte Accademia (connects the Campo Santo Stefano in the San Marco area with the Accademia museum in the Dorsoduro area). If you are too far from these bridges to cross over the canal, look for the convenient *traghetti* (little picturesque ferry gondolas) that shuttle locals across the Grand Canal from about 8 locations for under 1,000L pp. (The fare is regulated by the government.) There will be a traghetto station at the end of any street named "Calle Traghetto" that has a yellow sign with the black symbol of a gondola. Expect to stand up the entire trip. Walk to the back of the gondola, turn around so that your back is to the water. The gondola will then turn around and you end up with a view. Ask the tourist office for a map that shows the traghetto stations or have them mark the locations on your map. Hrs.: Not all the gondolas work every day. Some work on mornings only.

Parking: Be prepared for a long wait to park your car. There are three parking garages in Venice. Two are located on Tronchetto. **1.)** Garage Communal on Piazzale Roma. **Tel:** 041-5222308 and **2.)** Venice Terminal. **Tel:** 041-5207555. Call and confirm their rates. (About 45,000L per day.) Also check with your hotel to see if they can get you a discount voucher to use at these garages. Submit the voucher to the garage before you leave Venice. **3.)** Garage San Marco is the most expensive (about 55,000L per day) on Piazzale Roma. They don't take any discount vouchers. **Tel:** 041-5232213. Catch vaporetto #82 to your hotel stop. Stay away from those expensive private boats. They come up with all kinds of devious explanations as to why you should use them to get to your hotel.

Venice Tourist Information Centers (APT)
Indirizzo Internet Web site:
http://www.portve.interbusiness.it/wetvenice/wetvenice.html/
1.) Santa Lucia Train Station. **Tel:** 041-5298727. **Fax:** 041-719078. Hrs.: 8:10am-6:50pm, located on the left side of the train station. **2.)** Palazzina del Santi, San Marco. **Tel:** 041-5226356. **Fax:** 041-5298730. Hrs.: June-Sept. Mon.-Sat. 9:30am-6:30pm, Oct. to May, Mon.-Sat. 9:30am-12:30pm. **3.)** Aeroporto Marco Polo/Tessera. **Tel/Fax:** 041-5415887. **4.)** Calle dell'Ascensione 71C, San Marco. **Tel:** 041-5208964.

VAPORETTO STOPS FOR VENICE HOTELS
Web site: *Venice transport system:* http://www.actv.it/
I have included vaporetto stops with all the hotel listings. You will notice that some hotels have two vaporetto stops. That is because the hotel is easily accessed from both stops. Please refer to the master vaporetto list below. This list will make it convenient for you when you arrive in Venice without reservations. You might end up walking around the city and will need to know what hotels are listed near your vaporetto stop. As you exit the train station facing the water, line #1 is to the right & lines #82 & N are to the left. Purchase your 6,500L boat ticket before you board or you'll pay a little extra to the

conductor if you board without a ticket. There is a charge of about 7,000L for luggage. Vaporetto drivers are known for their rudeness. They won't wait for you if they see you running and won't help you to climb on the boat with your bags. If you plan to visit any of the other islands, inquire about the one-day boat ticket that will take you in one direction on line #12 including the islands, which costs a little bit more than the regular boat ticket . Also, if you don't like to or can't walk a lot then inquire about the 24-hr. (19,000L) or 72-hr. (36,000L) unlimited usage tickets on sale at the ticket offices by the boat stations. Check your guidebook for more details on catching the different vaporetti.

Finding street addresses: There is no logic to their numbering system and many streets share the same names but are in different districts. Invest in a good map with an index. I was able to find every hotel without any problems using the Hallwag map for Venice. (See maps in index for more information on purchasing maps.) I have tried to include walking directions under each hotel from the vaporetto stop. When trying to find your hotel, look for the vaporetto stop on the map and follow the directions with your fingers. When looking for restaurants or stores, it is important to identify the district then look for the street name. Some streets in Venice have two names. When using the index of a map to look up the street name, look up the second name of the street address first. If you can't find the name, then try the street's first name. If you write to a hotel in Venice, make sure you include the district of the hotel in the mailing address.

STOP/VAPORETTI
Accademia: Lines #82Red, 1, 3, 4 & N
Hotels: Fiorita, Galleria

Arsenal: Lines #1, 52Red
Hotel: Bucintoro

Ca' d'Oro: Lines #1, N
Hotels: Bernardi Semenzato, Mignon

Ca' Rezzonico: Line #1
Hotels: Antico Capon, Pausania

VENICE

Ferrovia: Lines #82Red, 1, 3, 4 & N
Hotels: Abbazia, Adua, Al Gobbo, Caprera, Casa Gerrotto, Dolomiti, Marin, Marte & Biasin, Minerva E Nettuno, Rossi, San Geremia, Santa Lucia, Villa Rosa

Giglio: Line #1
Hotel: Do Pozzi

Rialto: Lines #82Red, 1, 3 & N
Hotels: Al Gambero, Al Gazzettino, Alla Scala, Canada, Caneva, Casa Petrarca, Gallini, San Salvador, San Zulian, Serenissima

Salute: Line #1
Hotels: Alla Salute Cici, Messner

San Angelo: Line #1
Hotels: Fiorita, Gallini, San Giorgio, San Samuele

San Marco: Lines #82Red, 1, 3, 4 & N
Hotels: Ai do Mori, Canal, Riva, San Zulian, Silva

San Samuele: Lines #82Red, 1, 3, 4
Hotel: San Samuele

San Toma: Lines #82Red, 1, N
Hotel: Ca' Foscari, Casa Peron, Dalla Mora, Falier, Tivoli

San Zaccaria: Lines #82Red, 1, 4 & N
Hotels: Al Piave, Campiello, Casa Fontana, Casa Verardo, Doni, Paganelli

Zattere: Lines #82Red, 82Green, 1 & N
Hotels: Calcina, Seguso

Low season Jan.-Feb. & Nov.12-Dec.24; mid-season March, June-Aug.; high season April, May, Sept.-Nov. 11, Carnivale (2 wks. before Lent), Christmas & New Year's.

VENICE

Please note: This is Venice; there really isn't a low season. The *minimum* rate quoted for a hotel room usually applies to one or all of the following: off-season, the smallest room, one large double bed, a room with no shower or toilet or no phone or TV. You can assume it will be missing something. For your convenience, I have divided the hotels into two price categories for each district. If I included only the hotels under $99 a night for two, there would only be 23 hotels listed for the Venice chapter. If you travel without hotel reservations, you will need more than 23 hotels to choose from when trying to find a room.

Floods: When I was in Venice researching the hotels, it rained for five days in a row. Each of those days, the water in the canals overflowed into the streets and lobbies of hotels. In order to be able to continue my work, I was forced to buy fisherman's boots that came up to my knees because most of the hotels that were located near the canals had at least one foot of water in their reception areas. I apologize in advance for any errors I might have made due to the unusual circumstances surrounding my trip to Venice.

Venice hotels listed alphabetically

Hotels in/near Cannaregio
(Lista di Spagne)

Located to the immediate left as you exit the station. Not very close to the major sights of Venice but you usually get the best lodging prices in this area. It stretches from the train station to the Jewish ghetto and into part of Ca' d'Oro and the Rialto Bridge. Not a lot of tourists here but can be quite noisy nonetheless.

ADUA: Lista Spagna 233A. **Tel/Fax:** 041-716184. **Fax:** 041-2440162. (20 rms., 2 w/toilet & bath or shower.) 80,000-140,000L (41-72E) single; 95,000-175,000L (50-90E) double; 130,000-226,000L (67-116E) triple; 160,000-290,000L (82-149E) quad. Breakfast (8-10am) at 11,500L pp is not obligatory & can be served in the room. Visa, MC, AX, DC. English spoken (Luciano), small hotel w/large comfortable unusually decorated rms., some rooms w/ views but not the back rms., 2 rms. w/balconies & 2 w/terraces, #2 & 11 are the best rms., central heating, no elevator, 2 flrs. He has 9 new rms. in the next bldg. *5% rm. discount when you show owner/manager Luciano Stefani or staff this book.* The hotel closed in Nov. '98 for renovations and will reopen in Feb. '99. I have not seen the hotel with its improvements. Air-conditioning will be available for 11,500L extra per day as well as direct-dial phone and TV in some rooms. **Vaporetto:** Ferrovia. Exit the train station, turn left and walk straight up Lista Spagna, hotel is about 2 blocks up on your right.

AL GOBBO: Campo San Geremia 312.
Tel: 041-715001/714765. (10 rms., 8 w/toilet & bath or shower.) 110,000-120,000L (56-62E) single; 115,000-155,000L (60-79E) double; 190,000L (97E) triple; 230,000L (118E) quad. Breakfast (8-10am) is included in the rates & cannot be deducted. Visa. Limited English spoken (Silvia), nice hotel w/simply furnished rms., some w/views., 3 rms. w/balconies, #7 is the best rm., central heating, bar (1999), restaurant, no elevator, 3 flrs. Owned/managed by Maria Vinco. **Vaporetto:** Ferrovia. Exit the train station, turn left and walk straight up Lista Spagna, continue straight into Campo San Geremia. (Closed mid-Dec.-mid-Jan.)

BERNARDI SEMENZATO: Calle dell'Oca, SS. Apostoli 4363-66. **Tel:** 041-5227257. **Fax:** 041-5222424. (Including the annex, 25 rms., 13 w/toilet & bath or shower.) 85,000-110,000L (44-56E) single; 140,000-180,000L (72-92E) double; 165,000-220,000L (85-113E) triple; 190,000-240,000L (97-123E) quad/suite. Breakfast at 10,000L pp. Visa, MC, AX. English spoken (Maria & Leonardo), direct-dial phone, satellite TV (5,000L), newly renovated wonderful charming hotel w/nicely furnished rms. & modern bathrooms, #7 (wonderful), 25 & 26 (arched wood-beamed ceiling) are the best rms., air-conditioned, nice flrs., summer rooftop terrace (ask permission to visit), garden, the rooms in the annex which are old-fashioned furnished are cheaper & have better views, #5, 2 & 3 are the best in the annex, they turned 2 rooms into a private suite (#6) w/1 bathroom & view of canal, no elevator. **Vaporetto:** Ca' d'Oro. From the water stop, walk up Calle Ca' d'Oro, turn right onto Strada Nova, continue straight to Campo SS. Apostoli, turn left at the church of Santi Apostoli onto Campiello Salizzada Pistor, then left onto Calle dell'Oca. Located in a small alleyway. (Closed 1st 2 wks. in Dec. & mid-Jan. to Feb.)

CAPRERA: Calle Gioacchina 219/220.
Web site: http://www.gpnet.caprera.it/ **E-mail:** caprera@gpnet.it **Tel:** 041-715271. **Fax:** 041-715927. (20 rms., 4 w/toilet & bath or shower.) 65,000-95,000L (33-50E) single; 95,000-135,000L (50-69E) double; 110,000-170,000L (56-87E) triple; 200,000-270,000L (103-138E) quad. Children under 5 free. Breakfast (8-10am) at 13,500L pp is not obligatory & can be served in the room. Visa, MC, AX, DC. English spoken (Massimo), direct-dial phone, basic hotel w/simply furnished rms., 9 w/balconies, #12 is the best rm., 1 rm. has handicapped access, double-paned windows, central heating, no elevator, 4 flrs. *Free breakfast when you show owner/manager Corrado Bico or staff this book.* **Vaporetto:** Ferrovia. Exit the train station, turn left and walk straight up Lista Spagna, turn left onto Calle Gioacchina, just before the hotel Adua. (Closed Dec.-Jan.)

CASA GEROTTO CALDERAN: Campo San Geremia 283.
Tel: 041-715562. **Tel/Fax:** 041-715361. (34 rms., 12 w/toilet & bath or shower.) 50,000-70,000L (26-36E) single (no toilets); 80,000-110,000L (41-56E) double; 100,000-140,000L (51-72E) triple; 140,000-160,000L (72-82E) quad. Breakfast (8:30-10:30am) at 7,500L pp is not obligatory & can be served in the room. Cash only. English spoken, charming simple hotel w/wonderful simply furnished

airy bright large rooms, #310 & 210 are the best rms. w/balconies & bathrooms, #211 has a balcony but no bathroom, #312 has a balcony, #212 w/a huge balcony is a perfect room for 4/5 people, double-paned windows, central heating, no elevator, 4 flrs. They will accept a reservation via fax. Owned/managed by Olindo Milani & her wonderful family. **Vaporetto:** Ferrovia. Located in charming square. For walking directions, see Hotel Al Gobbo.

DOLOMITI: Calle Priuli Cavalletti 72-74. **Tel:** 041-715113/716635. **Tel/Fax:** 041-716635. (49 rms., 19 w/toilet & bath or shower.) 135,000-155,000L (69-79E) single (no bathrooms); 185,000-220,000L (95-113E) double; 230,000-255,000L (118-131E) triple. Breakfast (7:30-10am) is included in the rates but can be deducted in low season to reduce room price. Visa, MC. English spoken (Carlo), basic hotel w/simply furnished comfortable large rms., #16 (huge w/ bathtub) is the best rm., you can't tell from the room number what floor you are on, no elevator, 5 flrs. Charming Carlo will make sure you have a good stay. Owned/managed by Basaldella. **Vaporetto:** Ferrovia. Exit the train station, turn left onto Lista Spagna, turn left on the first alley onto Calle Priuli Cavalletti. (Closed Nov. 15-Jan.)

MINERVA E NETTUNO: Lista Spagna 230.
Tel: 041-715968/5242366. **Fax:** 041-5242139.
E-mail: lchecchi@tin.it (30 rms., 11 w/toilet & bath or shower.) 160,000L (82E) single/double. Call for triple rates. Breakfast (8-10am) at 5,500L pp is not obligatory. Visa, MC, AX. English spoken (Memo), basic hotel w/simply furnished nice-size rms., 11 rms. w/balconies, #12 & 25 are the best rms., rms. in front are noisy, hair driers in rms. w/bathrooms, central heating, double-paned windows, restaurant nearby the hotel, no elevator, 3 flrs. They may renovate in 1999 to include phones, TVs and more bathrooms. The hotel is not family-owned but is managed by Memo Checchini. *10% rm. discount when you show him or staff this book.* They offer half- (28,000L extra pp) and full-board (46,000L extra pp) rates at a restaurant nearby. **Vaporetto:** Ferrovia. Exit the train station, turn left onto Lista Spagna.

ROSSI: Calle Procuratie 262. **Tel:** 041-715164. **Tel/Fax:** 041-717784. (14 rms., 10 w/toilet & bath or shower.) 75,000-100,000L (38-51E) single (no bathrooms); 105,000-165,000L (54-85E) double;

150,000-200,000L (77-103E) triple; 180,000-240,000L (92-123E) quad. Children under 4 free. Breakfast (7:30-10am) is included in the rates & cannot be deducted. Visa, MC, AX. English spoken (Francesco), direct-dial phone, pleasant hotel w/simply furnished rms., 2 rms. w/balconies, #103, 104, 206 & 208 are the best rms., central heating, fans, quiet location, no elevator, 4 flrs. *10% rm. discount when you show owner/manager Francesco Cozzarini or staff this book.* Located in a cul-de-sac. **Vaporetto:** Ferrovia. Exit the train station, turn left and walk straight up Lista Spagna, after you pass the hotel Adua, turn 1st left under the arch onto Calle Procuratie, just before you get to Campo San Geremia. (Closed Jan.)

SANTA LUCIA: Calle Misercordia 358. **Tel:** 041-715180. **Tel/Fax:** 041-710610. (15 rms., 7 w/toilet & bath or shower.) 65,000-95,000L (33-50E) single; 135,000-175,000L (69-90E) double; 160,000-210,000L (82-108E) triple; 210,000-260,000L (108-133E) quad. Children under 3 free. Breakfast (8-10am) is included in the rates but can be deducted to reduce room price. Breakfast can be served in the room & in the garden in warm weather. Visa, MC, AX, DC. English spoken (Gianni & Maurizio), nice hotel w/simply furnished nice-size comfortable rms., #14, 15, 18 (balcony) & 23 are the best rms., #21 & 25 have balconies, no-smoking rms., double-paned windows, central heating, sunny garden patio, quiet location, no elevator, 1 fl. Owned/managed by Gianni Parcianello. **Vaporetto:** Ferrovia. Exit the train station, turn left onto Lista Spagna, Calle Misercordia will be the 2nd left turn. (Closed Dec.-Jan.)

VILLA ROSA: Calle Misercordia 389. **Tel:** 041-718976. **Tel/Fax:** 041-716569 (33 rms., all w/toilet & bath or shower.) 90,000-135,000L (46-69E) single; 145,000-165,000L (74-85E) double; 200,000L (103E) triple; 240,000L (123E) quad. Breakfast (8-10am) is included in the rates & cannot be deducted but can be served in the room. Breakfast is served on the terrace in warm weather. Visa, MC, AX, DC. English spoken (Martina), direct-dial phone, TV, quaint wonderful hotel w/old-fashioned furnished nice-size rms., 9 rms. w/balconies, #33 (terrace) & 39 (wood-beamed ceiling) are the best rms., tile flrs., 2 rms. have handicapped access, quiet location, 12 rms. w/ air-conditioning, central heating, no elevator, 3 flrs. Owned/managed by Ugo Marazzi. **Vaporetto:** Ferrovia. Exit the train station, turn left onto Lista Spagna, Calle Misercordia will be the 2nd left turn. (Closed Nov.-March 1.)

HOTELS OVER $100 A NIGHT FOR TWO

These hotels may have rooms under $100 a night for two because it is low season or the rooms do not have private bathrooms.

ABBAZIA: Calle Priuli Cavalletti 66/68. **Tel:** 041-717333. **Fax:** 041-717949. (39 rms., all w/toilet & bath or shower.) 135,000-305,000L (69-156E) single; 175,000-328,000L (90-168E) double. The minimum rates are for Jan., Feb., 2 wks. in Nov. & Dec. except New Year's Eve, Carnivale & Christmas. Only if you are going to Venice during those times should you continue reading about the hotel. Buffet breakfast (7:30-10am) is included in the rates & cannot be deducted but can be served in the room (4,500L extra pp). Visa, MC, AX, DC. English spoken (Mirko), direct-dial phone, satellite TV w/English channel, stylish wonderful charming converted monastery w/nicely furnished large rms. & new bathrooms, rms. vary in size & all w/chandelier lights, #205 (huge w/bathtub) & 203 are the best rms., minibars, hair driers, wonderful sitting area, central heating, air-conditioned, bar, beautiful garden, no elevator, 2 flrs. The hotel is not family-owned. **Vaporetto:** Ferrovia. Exit the train station, turn left onto Lista Spagna, turn left on the first alley onto Calle Priuli Cavalletti.

MARTE & BIASIN: Ponte Guglie 338. **Tel:** 041-716351/717231. **Fax:** 041-720642. (15 rms., 13 w/toilet & bath or shower.) 135,000-195,000L (69-100E) double; 190,000-250,000L (97-128E) triple; 220,000-270,000L (113-138E) quad. Breakfast (8-10am) at 9,500L pp is obligatory & can be served in the room. Visa, MC, AX, DC. English spoken (Antonella), pleasant charming hotel w/nicely furnished comfortable rms., #101 & 102 are the best rms., #103 has a balcony w/view of the bridge, nice flrs., no elevator, 2 flrs. **Vaporetto:** Ferrovia. Exit the train station, turn left onto Lista Spagna, walk straight up Lista Spagna through Campo San Geremia, from the square take Salazzada Geremia to Ponte Guglie (bridge), turn left at the bridge onto Fondamenta Savorgnan and to the hotel.

MIGNON: Campo SS. Apostoli 4535. **Tel:** 041-5237388. **Fax:** 041-5208658. (17 rms., 13 w/toilet & bath or shower.) 85,000-175,000L (44-90E) single; 115,000-215,000L (60-110E) double; 170,000-280,000L (87-144E) triple; 200,000-320,000L (103-164E) quad. Children under 8 free. Breakfast (8-10am) at 11,500L pp is not obligatory & can be served in the room (11,500L extra pp). Breakfast is served in the garden in warm weather. Visa, MC, DC. English spoken (Flavio & Gabriele), nice hotel/simply furnished small rms., #31 & 34 are small rms. w/bathrooms & large balconies, double-paned windows, central heating, 5 rms. w/minibars, all rooms on 3rd fl. have air-conditioning, garden, no elevator, 4 flrs. *5% rm. discount when you show owner/manager Franco Convilli or staff this book.* **Vaporetto:** Ca' d'Oro. From the water stop, walk up Calle Ca' d'Oro, turn right onto Strada Nova, continue straight onto Campo SS. Apostoli. (Closed Jan.-Feb. until Carnivale.)

SAN GEREMIA: Campo San Geremia 290/A. **Tel:** 041-716245/716260. **Fax:** 041-5242342. (20 rms., 16 w/toilet & bath or shower.) 125,000-155,000L (64-79E) single; 160,000-235,000L (82-121E) double. Breakfast (7-10am) at 16,500L pp is obligatory (not in off-season) & can be served in the room (11,500L extra pp). Visa, MC, AX, DC. English spoken (Claudio), direct-dial phone, satellite TV w/English channels, wonderful charming hotel w/nicely decorated small rms., 3 rms. on top floor have small private terraces, avoid #204 & 203 which are tiny rooms, most of the rooms overlook Campo San Geremia, hair driers, double-paned windows, central heating, bar, street terrace, no elevator, 5 flrs. The hotel is not family-owned but is managed by Claudio Casagrande & his family. *10% rm. discount when you show Claudio Casagrande or staff this book.* **Vaporetto:** Ferrovia. Exit the train station, turn left onto Lista Spagna, walk straight up Lista Spagna into Campo San Geremia.

Hotels in/near San Polo
With your back to the train station, this area is located less than 5 minutes from the right side across the bridge. It stretches all the way to Piazzale Roma. The least visited section of Venice.

CASA PERON: Calle Vinanti/Salizzada San Pantalon 84/85. **Tel:** 041-710021. **Tel/Fax:** 041-711038. (11 rms., 7 w/toilet & shower.)

90,000-115,000L (46-60E) single; 125,000-155,000L (64-79E) double; 170,000-210,000L (87-108E) triple. Breakfast (8-10am) is included in the rates but can be deducted in low season to reduce room price. Visa, MC, AX. English spoken (Gianrico), basic hotel w/simply furnished large airy bright rms., tiled flrs., #5 w/balcony & bathroom is the best rm., #6 large & w/bathroom, both on the top fl., #8 is large w/ balcony that faces the street w/shower only, fans, central heating, no elevator, 3 flrs. Peter the parrot speaks Italian. Owned/managed by Gianrico Scarpa. From train station, cross Ponte Scalzi, turn right on Fondamenta San Simeon Piccolo, left on Fondamenta Tolentini, left onto Fondamento Minotto which becomes Calle Vinanti/Salizzada San Pantalon. **Vaporetto:** San Toma. Walk down Calle Traghetto Vecchio, turn left onto Calle Campaniel, turn right onto Fondamenta Forner, left onto Calle Donna Onesta, turn right onto Crosera S. Pantalon which becomes Calle Preti, continue straight over Rio Mosche as it becomes Calle Vinanti/Salizzada San Pantalon. (Closed Jan.)

DALLA MORA: Calle Vinanti/Salizzada San Pantalon 42/A. **Tel:** 041-710703. **Fax:** 041-723006. (14 rms., 6 w/toilet & bath or shower.) 90,000-100,000L (47-51E) single; 110,000-150,000L (56-77E) double; 140,000-190,000L (72-97E) triple; 160,000-220,000L (82-113E) quad. Breakfast (8-10am) is included in the rates but can be deducted in low season to reduce room price. Visa, MC, DC. English spoken (Francesco), 2 bldgs. in one hotel, the rms. in the main house are better & have renovated bathrooms, basic hotel w/simply furnished airy rms., 1 rm. has handicapped access but there is one step up to get to the room, #6 & 7 w/views of the canal are the best rms. in the main house, #5 & 2 also in the main house have views of the canal, the 8 rms. in the annex have no private bathrooms, #10 in the annex has view of the water & no bathroom, terrace, double-paned windows, central heating, no elevator, 3 flrs. Owned/managed by Francesco & Alessandro Aidome. **Vaporetto:** San Toma. For directions, see Hotel Casa Peron. (Closed Jan.)

MARIN: Calle Traghetto di Santa Lucia 670/B.
Tel: 041-718022/721485. **Tel/Fax:** 041-718022.
Web site: http://www.gpnet.it/hotels/DB/HOTELS/ve_marin.htm/
E-mail: htlmarin@gpnet.it (19 rms., 13 w/toilet & bath or shower.)
105,000L (54E) single; 130,000-165,000L (67-82E) double; 175,000-

215,000L (90-110E) triple; 200,000-250,000L (103-128E) quad. Breakfast is included in the rates but can be deducted in low season to reduce room price. Breakfast can be served in the room at extra cost of 6,500L pp. MC, Visa, AX. English spoken (Scotton Bruno, Nadia & Samuel), direct-dial phone, wonderful no-smoking hotel w/ nicely furnished bright airy comfortable rms., beautiful flrs., central heating, quiet location, no elevator, 3 flrs. *Free breakfast when you show owner/manager Scotton Bruno or staff this book.* **Vaporetto:** Ferrovia. Exit the train station, cross the bridge, turn right, walk along the waterfront, when you see the pink Hotel Carlton turn left just before it and go down the alley (Calle Traghetto di Santa Lucia) to the hotel. (Closed 20 days between Nov. & Dec.)

HOTEL OVER $100 A NIGHT FOR TWO
This hotel may have rooms under $100 a night for two because it is low season or the rooms do not have private bathrooms.

FALIER: Salizzada San Pantalon 130.
Tel: 041-710882/711005. **Fax:** 041-5206554.
Web site: http://www.hotelfalier.com/ **E-mail:** falier@tin.it (19 rms., all w/toilet & bath or shower.) 85,000-205,000L (44-105E) single; 115,000-245,000L (60-126E) double. Breakfast (8-10am) is included in the rates but can be deducted to reduce room price. Breakfast can be served in the room at extra cost of 4,000L pp & is served in the garden/patio in warm weather. Visa, MC, AX. English spoken (Sutera), direct-dial phone, wonderful charming hotel w/nicely furnished rms., #41 a lovely quaint room w/arched wood-beam ceiling & fabulous terrace is the best rm., #23 is also lovely, central heating, bar, garden/patio, quiet location, no elevator, 4 flrs. *10% rm. discount when you show owner/manager Salvatore Sutera Sardo or staff this book.* **Vaporetto:** San Toma. For directions, see Hotel Casa Peron.

Hotels in/near Castello
Located east of San Marco and beyond Cannaregio is a quiet residential area away from the tourist hordes of Venice. If you want a place to escape the nonstop action, this is it. However, the hotels can be on the expensive side.

CANAL: Fondamenta Rimedio 4422/C. **Tel:** 041-5234538. **Fax:** 041-2419138. (7 rms., 2 w/toilet & bath or shower.) 135,000-185,000L (69-95E) double; 170,000-230,000L (87-118E) triple; 190,000-270,000L (97-138E) quad. Children under 3 free. Breakfast (8-9:30am) is included in the rates & cannot be deducted but can be served in the room (10,000L pp). Cash only. English spoken (Pasquale & Silvia), pleasant basic 13th-century hotel w/simply furnished large bright rms. & balconies, nice flrs., #1 (beautiful large rm., chandelier, view of canal, shower only) & 6 (bathroom) are the best rms., #2 has a bathroom, #3 & 7 have showers only, 4,000L extra pp to use hall showers, double-paned windows, central heating, quiet location. Owned/managed by Pasquale Tortorella since Jan. '98. Same family owns Hotel Campiello. **Vaporetto:** San Zaccaria or San Marco. From San Marco square, walk under the Torre l'Orologio clock tower, turn right onto Calle Larga San Marco, turn left onto Call dell'Anzelo, cross the bridge on the right and it becomes Calle Rimedio, turn left at the canal onto Fondamenta Rimedio.

CANEVA: Ramo dietro La Fava 5515. **Tel:** 041-5228118. **Fax:** 041-5208676. (23 rms., 14 w/toilet & bath or shower.) 65,000-130,000L (33-67E) single; 95,000-180,000L (50-92E) double; 140,000-240,000L (72-123E) triple; 180,000-300,000L (92-154E) quad. Buffet breakfast (7:30-10am) is included in the rates & cannot be deducted. Visa, MC, AX. English spoken (Mario), TV, pleasant hip hotel w/ simply furnished nice-size bright rms., 10 rms. have views of the canal, you have to give your credit card # & expiration date to reserve any of these rms., #33 (balcony), 30 & 34 are wonderful rms. w/views of the canal, 6 rms. w/balconies, some rms. have double-paned windows, central heating, air-conditioned, quiet courtyard, no elevator, 2 flrs. *15% rm. discount when you show owner/manager Massimo Cagnato or staff this book and pay in cash.* **Vaporetto:** Rialto. Walk straight ahead on Calle Larga Mazzini, turn left onto Calle San Salvatore Merceria to Campo San Bartolomeo, take Calle Stagneri from Campo San Bartolomeo, cross the bridge to Campo Fava, turn right, Calle Ramo dietro La Fava starts to the right after the church of the Fava. (Closed Jan.)

DONI: Calle Vin 4656. **Tel/Fax:** 041-5224267. (13 rms., 3 w/toilet & bath or shower.) 90,000L (46E) single (no toilets); 125,000-

165,000L (64-85E) double; 205,000L (105E) triple. Breakfast (8-10am) at 6,500L pp is not obligatory. Cash only but you can reserve with a credit card. English spoken (Nikos & Gina), 18th-century quaint hotel w/simply furnished airy rms., wooden flrs., #8 & 15 (large) have views of courtyard & have bathrooms, #3 (wonderful), 12 & 21 have views of the canal but no bathrooms, #22 has a bathroom, quiet location, the rms. either have a view of the canal or a courtyard, ceiling fans, central heating, no elevator, 4 flrs. *5% rm. discount when you show owner/manager Annabella Doni or staff this book.* **Vaporetto:** San Zaccaria. For directions, see Hotel Campiello. (Closed Jan.)

SILVA: Fondamenta Rimedio 4423. **Tel:** 041-5227643/5237892. **Fax:** 041-5286817. (24 rms., 13 w/toilet & bath or shower.) 77,000L (40E) single (sinks only); 109,000-159,000L (56E) double; 156,000L (80E) triple; 228,000L (117E) quad. Children under 3 free. Large breakfast (8-10am) at 9,500L pp is obligatory. Cash only. English spoken (Sandra), direct-dial phone, basic hotel w/simply furnished large rms., #1 & 2 are the best rms., #17 has a bathroom & view of the rooftops, #20 has a balcony but you share it w/the laundry, central heating, no elevator, 3 flrs. Owned/managed by Ettore Perut, a very unusual elderly man who speaks no English. **Vaporetto:** San Zaccaria or San Marco. For directions, see Hotel Canal. (Closed Dec.-Jan.)

HOTELS OVER $100 A NIGHT FOR TWO
These hotels may have rooms under $100 a night for two because it is low season or the rooms do not have private bathrooms.

AL PIAVE: Ruga Giuffa 4838/4840.
Tel: 041-5285174/5296468. **Fax:** 041-5238512.
Web site: http://www.elmoro.com/alpiave/
E-mail: hotel.alpiave@iol.it (15 rms., 12 w/toilet & bath or shower.) 135,000-175,000L (69-90E) single; 175,000-255,000L (90-131E) double; 290,000-380,000L (149-195E) triple; 370,000-420,000L (190-215E) quad. Family suites available. Children under 4 free. Buffet breakfast (7:30-10am) is included in the rates & cannot be deducted but can be served in the room. Visa, MC, AX, DC. English spoken (Mirella & Paolo), direct-dial phone, satellite TV w/English channel, newly remodeled cozy hotel w/nicely furnished nice-size

comfortable rms., #106 has a balcony, #313 is a large suite w/balcony, 3 rms. w/minibars (1999), central heating, double-paned windows (1999), air-conditioned, bar, no elevator, 4 flrs. He also has very large family suites to accommodate 3 to 5 people. *10% rm. discount when you show owners/managers Paolo & Mirella Puppin or staff this book.* **Vaporetto:** San Zaccaria. Walk straight ahead on Calle Rasse, turn left on Salizzada Provolo to Campo SS Filippo e Giacomo, turn right from the Campo onto Calle Rimpetola Sacrestia, continue over first small footbridge (Ponto Storto),which becomes Calle Castagna and intersects with Ruga Giuffa. (Closed Jan.)

BUCINTORO: Riva Schiavoni Biagio 2135. **Tel:** 041-5223240. **Fax:** 041-5235224. (28 rms., 23 w/toilet & bath or shower.) 135,000-158,000L (69-81E) single; 245,000-270,000L (126-138E) double; 320,000-360,000L (164-185E) triple. Breakfast (7:30-9:30am) is included in the rates & cannot be deducted but can be served in the room (4,500L extra pp). Cash only. English spoken (Donatello), direct-dial phone, wonderful beautiful hotel w/charming nicely furnished pretty rms., great flrs., some rms. w/bathtubs, #6 is beautiful w/magnificent view & bathtub, hair driers, double-paned windows, central heating, all the rooms have a view of the Venetian lagoon, #8, 9, 10, 16, 18 & 30 on the side of the bldg. have view of water & San Marco, no elevator, 5 flrs. Great location for visiting the other islands. Owned/managed by Augusta Bianchi. **Vaporetto:** Arsenal. Walk to your right along the waterfront over the bridge to the hotel. (Closed mid-Dec.-Jan. 1. Call to confirm.)

CAMPIELLO: Calle Vin 4647.
Tel: 041-5239682/5205764. **Fax:** 041-5205798.
Web site: http://www.hcampiello.it/
E-mail: campiello@hcampiello.it (16 rms., all w/toilet & bath or shower.) 125,000-185,000L (64-95E) single; 155,000-285,000L (79-146E) double; 230,000-350,000L (118-179E) triple; 270,000-405,000L (138-208E) quad. Children under 2 free. Breakfast (7:30-9:30am) at 11,500L pp is obligatory & can be served in the room (4,000L extra pp). Visa, MC, AX, DC. English spoken (Monica), direct-dial phone, satellite TV w/English channels, wonderful charming hotel w/beautifully Spanish furnished rms., some rms. w/modern bathrooms, some rms. w/nice views, 1 rm. has handicapped ac-

cess, #7 is wonderful w/balcony accessible only by climbing out your window, #8 w/inner balcony, #14 is large, great flrs., hair driers, double-paned windows, central heating, air-conditioned, bar, no elevator, 3 flrs. Owned/managed by Monica & Nicoletta Bianchini. This hotel is located in quiet little piazza on a little canal. In case the canals overflow, the hotel has 2 entrances. Same family owns Hotel Canal. **Vaporetto:** San Zaccaria. Turn right, walk along the waterfront over 2 bridges, Calle Vin will be the first left turn. (Closed Jan.)

CANADA: Campo San Lio 5659. **Tel:** 041-5229912. **Fax:** 041-5235852. (25 rms., all w/toilet & bath or shower.) 185,000L (95E) single; 245,000L (126E) double; 310,000L (159E) triple; 380,000L (195E) quad. Breakfast (7:30-10am) is included in the rates & cannot be deducted but can be served in the room. Visa, MC. English spoken (Guiseppe), direct-dial phone, typical Venetian hotel w/nice-size comfortable pretty rms., 15 rms. are newly renovated, the rest are old-fashioned furnished, #12B is a beautiful airy bright rm. w/ balcony & view of rooftops, #6, 9, 17 & 21 have views of the canal, #8 is pretty, #18 has a terrace & a/c but no view, 2 rms. w/balconies, 6 of the 10 rms. w/air-conditioning (22,500L extra per day) have no views, bar, no elevator, 2 flrs. Located on a small pleasant square. **Vaporetto:** Rialto. Walk straight ahead on Calle Larga Mazzini, turn left onto Calle San Salvatore Merceria through Campo San Bartolomeo, turn right after Calle Pirietta, turn left past Calle Zocca into Calle Calle Ponte Antonio which becomes Salizzada San Lio, look to your left for the hotel on Campo San Lio.

CASA FONTANA: Campo San Provolo 4701.
Tel: 041-5220579/5210533. **Fax:** 041-5231040.
Web site: http://www.hotelfontana.it/ **E-mail:** Htcasa@gpnet.it (15 rms., all w/toilet & bath or shower.) 115,000-165,000L (60-85E) single; 165,000-265,000L (85-136E) double; 230,000-320,000L (118-164E) triple; 270,000-350,000L (138-179E) quad. Breakfast (7:30-9:30am) is included in the rates & can be served in the room (13,500 extra pp) but can be deducted in low season to reduce room price. Visa, MC, AX, DC. English spoken (Gabriela), direct-dial phone, TV, wonderful hotel w/nicely furnished nice-size rms., lots of Italian ambiance, #11 (view of the garden) & 2 have private terraces, #14 is a 2-room suite, #2 & 3 have small bathtubs, central heating, bar, no elevator, 5 flrs.

Owned/managed by Gabriela Stainer who is charming. Great location. **Vaporetto:** San Zaccaria. Turn right, walk along the waterfront over 2 bridges, turn 1st left after Calle Vin into Campo San Zaccaria, walk through the square to the left straight onto Campo San Provolo.

CASA VERARDO: Ponte Storto 4765.
Tel: 041-5286138/5286127. **Fax:** 041-5232765. (9 rms., 7 w/toilet & bath or shower.) 95,000-145,000L (50-74E) single; 135,000-195,000L (60-100E) double; 200,000-260,000L (103-133E) triple; 250,000-310,000L (128-159E) quad w/private terrace. Children under 3 free. Buffet breakfast (8-9:30am) is included in the rates & cannot be deducted but can be served in the room (4,500L extra pp). Breakfast is served on the terrace in warm weather. Visa, MC. English spoken (Massimo & Sandra), direct-dial phone, quaint charming 14th-century grand style palazzo w/eclectically nicely furnished bright large rms. & tiny bathrooms, impressive sitting room, top-floor suite w/terrace, #1, 2 & 6 are huge, wonderful & are the best rms., #3 is the smallest w/large bathroom, 2 rms. have handicapped access, high ceilings, most rms. have floor-to-ceiling windows, some rms. have double-paned windows, central heating, bar, garden terrace overlooking canal, quiet location, no elevator, 2 flrs. Owned/managed by Massimo & Sandra Filippi. Sometimes they will meet you at the vaporetto dock. **Vaporetto:** San Zaccaria.Walk straight ahead on Calle Rasse, turn left on Salizzada Provolo to Campo SS Filippo e Giacomo, turn right from the Campo onto Calle Rimpetola Sacrestia, cross the first small footbridge (Ponto Storto), the hotel is located on the right facing the bridge. Ask hotel to fax you a map.

PAGANELLI: Campo San Zaccaria 4687. **Tel:** 041-5224324. **Fax:** 041-5239267. (22 rms., 19 w/toilet & bath or shower.) 115,000-165,000L (60-85E) single; 165,000-265,000L (85-136E) double; 290,000-357,000L (149-183E) triple; 445,000L (228E) quad. Children under 6 free. Buffet breakfast (8-11am) is included in the rates & cannot be deducted but can be served in the room (8,500L extra pp). Breakfast is served in the garden in warm weather. Visa, MC, AX. English spoken (Mario Schiavoa), direct-dial phone, satellite TV w/English channel, enchanting hotel w/18th-century Venetian-style decorated rms. except #11, 10 & 1, the hotel is divided into 2 sections (canal and the annex): the rms. on the canal side are the largest and have the best views of the lagoon, #16 & 18 are the best rms. on the canal side; the rms. in the annex are more modern, air-conditioned, hair driers, #22 w/arched wood-beamed ceiling & view of the square is the best rm. in the annex, some rooms have double-paned windows, bar, garden, quiet location. They offer half-board rates at 40,000L extra pp. This hotel is owned/managed by Francesco Paganelli. **Vaporetto:** San Zaccaria. Located near the vaporetto stop.

RIVA: Ponte dell'Anzelo 5310. **Tel:** 041-5227034. **Fax:** 041-5285551. (24 rms., 22 w/toilet & bath or shower.) 155,000-195,000L (79-100E) double; 260,000L (133E) triple. Breakfast (8:30-9:30am) is included in the rates & cannot be deducted. Cash only. English spoken (Sandro), beautiful charming hotel w/beautifully furnished bright modern rms., marble staircase, #27 is huge w/view of canal & wood-beamed ceiling, #4 is small but has 2 windows w/view of the canal & wood-beamed ceiling, #8 has 2 windows that overlook the canal, nice flrs., central heating, quiet location, no elevator, 4 flrs. Located on a delightful side of a canal at the junction of 3 canals where you can watch the gondolas go by. Owned/managed by Sandro Nart who is a wonderful & charming doctor of medicine. **Vaporetto:** San Marco. Exit Piazza San Marco by walking under the clock tower, turn right onto Calle Larga San Marco, then left onto Calle l'Anzelo, follow the street straight over 2 small bridges to the hotel. On some maps Calle l'Anzelo is spelled Calle d'Angelo. (Closed mid-Nov.-Jan.)

Hotels in/near Dorsoduro
Located on the opposite side of the Accademia Bridge from San Marco. A very colorful and characterful section of Venice. It is a university area, plenty of students, cafés and a great place to get away from the hordes of tourist.

ANTICO CAPON: Campo Santa Margherita 3004/B. **Tel/Fax:** 041-5285292. (12 rms., 9 w/toilet & bath or shower.) 80,000-155,000L (41-79E) single; 100,000-160,000L (51-82E) double. Check for off-season prices. Breakfast is included in the rates but can be deducted to reduce room price. Visa, MC. English spoken (Elias), simple charming hotel w/large nicely furnished rms. & tiny bathrooms (the shower is above the toilet), the hotel is 2 bldgs.: 7 rms. w/private bathrooms in the main house, #3, 4 & 5 have views of the square & are nicer than the annex; 5 rms. w/2 bathrooms in the annex w/no views, fans, central heating, no elevator, 3 flrs. The hotel has an arrangement with 2 restaurants in the square to serve breakfast to his guests. Owned/managed by the wonderful and very accommodating Elias Menna since Jan. '98. He even had galoshes on hand to loan to his guests when the canals flooded. I didn't see any 3-star hotels handing out galoshes to their guests. Elias will be renovating the entire hotel in Dec. '98. Located above a pizzeria-restaurant in a lovely square with a great local neighborhood feeling far away from the hordes of tourists. Most mornings there is a fruit and vegetable market in the square which becomes a playground for children in the late afternoons. The hotel is located opposite my favorite sandwich shop. **Vaporetto:** Ca' Rezzonico. Walk towards Campo Santa Margherita.

CA' FOSCARI: Calle Frescada 3887/B. **Tel:** 041-710401. **Fax:** 041-710817. (11 rms., 5 w/toilet & bath or shower.) 100,000L (51E) single; 125,000-155,000L (64-79E) double; 158,000-197,000L (81-101E) triple; 188,000-228,000L (96-117E) quad. Breakfast (8-9:30am) is included in the rates & cannot be deducted. Visa, MC. English spoken (Valter & Giuliana Scarpa), basic hotel w/simply furnished large bright airy rms, most rms. have huge windows, all the rms. vary in decor which Valter decorated himself, some w/views, #9 is the best rm., #6 is large, rooftop view, bar, no elevator, 3 flrs. Owned/managed by Valter Scarpa. **Vaporetto:** San Toma. Located in the university quarter. Walk up to Calle Campaniel, turn left, go across the first small canal, turn left and make a quick right onto Fondamenta Frescada, then left onto Calle Marcona. The hotel is in an alley on Calle Frescada which is at the foot of Calle Crosera where it meets Calle Marcona. (Closed mid-Nov.-Jan. 15)

HOTELS OVER $100 A NIGHT FOR TWO
These hotels may have rooms under $100 a night for two because it is low season or the rooms do not have private bathrooms.

ALLA SALUTE CICI: Fondamenta Ca' Bala 222. **Tel:** 041-5235404. **Tel/Fax:** 041-5222271. (60 rms., 25 w/toilet & bath or shower.) 125,000-165,000L (64-85E) single; 145,000-215,000L (74-110E) double; 220,000-290,000L (113-149E) triple. Breakfast (8-9:30am) is included in the rates but can be deducted to reduce room price. Cash only. English spoken (Sebastano), 17th-century palazzo w/nicely furnished comfortable rms. which vary in size, high ceilings & huge windows, the 10 rms. with a view of the canal don't have bathrooms, the rms. w/bathrooms don't have views of the canal, 4 rms. w/balconies, central heating, quiet location, bar (summer only), small terrace, garden, no elevator, 4 flrs. There are shower stalls inside some rooms that have no toilets and there is no door to separate the shower stall from the room. Owned/managed by Renato & Sebastano Cici. **Vaporetto:** Salute. As you exit the boat facing the La Salute Church, turn right paralleling the canal, walk straight ahead to the first small bridge through the tunnel, continue straight through Campo San Gregorio, continue straight on Calle Gregorio, just before you get to the next canal turn left onto Fondamenta Ca' Bala. (Closed mid-Nov.-Jan.)

CALCINA (LA): Fondamenta Zattere Gesuati 780. **Tel:** 041-5206466. **Fax:** 041-5227045. **E-mail:** la.calcina@libero.it (29 rms., 26 w/toilet & bath or shower.) 125,000-175,000L (64-90E) single; 195,000-295,000L (100-151E) double. Breakfast (7-10am) is included in the rates & cannot be deducted but can be served in the room (4,500L extra pp). Breakfast is served in the garden in warm weather. Visa, MC, AX, DC. English spoken, direct-dial phone, wonderful charming hotel w/antique furnished large comfortable rms., lots of Italian ambiance, all the rooms w/view of canal cost more than those w/o a view, 4 rms. w/terraces, #2, 4, 22 & 32 (corner view of canal) are the best rms., #38 charming rm. w/terrace & bathroom but no view, wooden flrs., #33 w/bathroom & wonderful view of canal, double-paned windows, central heating, air-conditioned, floating deck-terrace in front of hotel, some rms. w/views of the front & side canal, fabulous sunset, you have to make an advance reservation to enjoy the great rooftop terrace w/ view of canal because they don't want a lot of people on it at one time (no charge), quiet location, bar, no elevator, 5 flrs. Owned/managed by Debora & Alessandro Szemere. **Vaporetto:** Zattere. From the boat stop, turn right onto Fondamenta Zattere. (Closed Jan. 9-Feb. 4.)

GALLERIA: Rio Terra Antonio Foscarini 878/A. **Tel:** 041-5232489. **Tel/Fax:** 041-5204172. **E-mail:** galleria@tin.it (10 rms., 6 w/toilet & bath or shower.) 100,000-135,000L (51-69E) single; 145,000-

200,000L (74-103E) double. Call for triple & quad rates. Breakfast (8-9:30am) is included in the rates & cannot be deducted. Visa, MC, AX, DC. English spoken (Luciano & Stefano), direct-dial phone, 17th-century wonderful elegant palazzo w/old-fashioned furnished comfortable rms., beautiful doors, some w/frescoed or carved ceilings, lots of Italian ambiance, #8 is a magnificent rm. w/bathroom, sitting rm. & view of the canal, #10 is a large beautiful antique furnished rm. w/2 windows w/view of the canal & bathroom, #5 is a wonderful corner room w/2 windows & view of the canal but no bathroom, #9 is small but has a bathroom & view of the canal, #2 w/bathroom & view of the square/bridge, narrow spiral staircase, central heating, no elevator, 1 fl. Owned/managed by Luciano Benedetti & Stefano Franceschini. **Vaporetto:** Accademia. Located at the foot of the Ponte dell'Accademia (bridge), to the left of the Campo Carita. (Closed Dec. 23-27.) Luciano also owns the Hotel Locanda Leon Bianco, at corte Leon Bianco 5629, which I didn't get a chance to see. 7 rooms all with private bathrooms. 6 rms. overlook the canal. 210,000-400,00L double-quad. These special prices are for readers of this book. **Tel:** 041-5233572. **Fax:** 041-2416392. **E-mail:** leonebi@tin.it **Vaporetto:** Ca' d'Oro. Because of the floods, I also didn't have a chance to look at the rooms inside Hotel Algi Alboretti located a couple of doors down from Hotel Galleria, but it looked liked a wonderful charming quaint hotel. **ALGI ALBORETTI:** Rio Terra Antonio Foscarini 884. **Tel:** 041-5230058. **Fax:** 041-5210158. **E-mail:** albrett@gpnet.it (19 rms., all w/toilet & bath or shower.) 170,000L single; 210,000-250,000L double; 310,000L triple. Breakfast is included in the rates & cannot be deducted. Visa, MC. English spoken.

MESSNER: Fondamenta Ca' Bala 216/217.
Tel: 041-5227443/5288945. **Fax:** 041-5227266.
E-mail: a.nardi@flashnet.it (32 rms., all w/toilet & bath or shower.) 115,000-155,000L (60-79E) single; 135,000-225,000L (69-115E) double; 170,000-280,000L (87-144E) triple; 210,000-310,000L (108-159E) quad. Buffet breakfast is included in the rates & cannot be deducted but can be served in the room (5,500L extra pp). Breakfast is served in the garden in warm weather. MC, Visa, AX, DC. Two hotels in one (main house & annex), the *casa principale* (main house), a 14th-century grand palazzo, has 11 rms. and 15th-century annex has 20 rms. close by. The rates in the annex are usually cheaper but

the rms. in the main house are nicer, English spoken (Alex), direct-dial phone, 50% rms. have satellite TV w/English channel, beautiful charming hotel w/nicely furnished comfortable well-decorated rms. & modern bathrooms, lots of Italian ambiance, carpeted flrs., #1, 3, 7 (view of canal), 9 (view of canal) & 28 are the best rms., #8 has a balcony & view of canal, 3 rms. have handicapped access, double-paned windows, central heating, air-conditioned, wonderful garden/ courtyard, bar, restaurant, no elevator, 3 flrs. *10% rm. discount when you show owner/manager Bruno Nardi or staff this book.* They offer half- (30,000L extra pp) and full-board (60,000L extra pp) rates. The hotel has 2 entrances in case the canals overflow into the main entrance. **Vaporetto:** Salute. For directions, see Hotel Alla Salute Cici. (Closed mid-Nov.-mid-Dec.)

PAUSANIA: Rio San Barnaba/Fondamenta Gherardini 2824. **Tel:** 041-5222083. **Fax:** 041-5222989. (26 rms., all w/toilet & bath or shower.) 115,000-235,000L (60-121E) single; 195,000-340,000L (100-174E) double; 250,000-425,000L (128-218E) triple; 270,000-520,000L (138-267E) quad. Children under 3 free. Breakfast (7-10:30am) is included in the rates & cannot be deducted but can be served in the room (4,500L extra pp). Breakfast is served in the garden in warm weather. MC, Visa, AX. English spoken (Carlo), direct-dial phone, satellite TV, 14th-century modern palazzo w/elegantly furnished comfortable large rms., the rms. usually face the canal or the garden, #210 & 211 have views of the canal, #306 is a wonderful suite w/balcony & view of the canal, #209 is huge w/view of garden, minibars, hair driers, double-paned windows, air-conditioned, central heating, grand staircase, bar, no elevator, 3 flrs. To enter the lobby you pass through a magnificent medieval garden terrace. The hotel is not family-owned but is managed by Guido Gatto. *5% rm. discount when you show him or staff this book.* **Vaporetto:** Ca' Rezzonico. Walk down Calle Traghetto, turn right onto Campo San Barnaba, continue straight through the square, the hotel is around the corner to the left of the toy store on the canal.

SEGUSO: Fondamenta Zattere Gesuati 779. **Tel:** 041-5286858. **Tel/ Fax:** 041-5222340. (36 rms., 19 w/toilet & bath or shower.) 125,000-175,000L (64-90E) single; 185,000-250,000L (95-128E) double. Breakfast (8-10am) is included in the rates. MC, Visa, AX. English spoken, charming grand old hotel w/nicely furnished rms., the large rms. w/views of the canal have no private baths, #41 (no bathroom) & 40 (shower only) have wonderful views, some balconies, tiny terrace in front, quiet location, bar, restaurant, elevator. They offer half- and full-board rates. Not the warmest manager I've met but this charming hotel has a great location on the canal unless the canals overflow. This is one of the hotels that only has one entrance which is off the canal. **Vaporetto:** Zattere. From the boat stop, turn right onto Fondamenta Zattere. (Closed Dec. to Feb.)

TIVOLI: Crosera S. Pantalon 3838. **Tel:** 041-5242460/5237752. **Fax:** 041-5222656. (22 rms., 19 w/toilet & bath or shower.) 105,000-185,000L (54-95E) single; 145,000-225,000L (74-115E) double; 180,000-310,000L (92-159E) triple; 215,000-320,000L (110-164E) quad. Children under 3 free. Visa, MC. Breakfast (8-10am) is included in the rates & cannot be deducted but can be served in the room (9,500L extra pp). Breakfast is served on the terrace in warm weather. English spoken (Andrea), direct-dial phone, TV, nice hotel w/simply furnished rms. & modern bathrooms, #25 (large) & 26 have balconies, #34 has a terrace, 2 rms. have handicapped access after 2 steps, double-paned windows, central heating, garden, bar, no elevator, 3 flrs. *5% rm. discount when you show owner/manager Renato Gardin or staff this book.* **Vaporetto:** San Toma. Walk down Calle Traghetto Vecchio, turn left onto Calle Campaniel, turn right onto Fondamenta Forner, left onto Calle Donna Onesta, turn right onto Crosera S. Pantalon. Closed Dec. 20-27.)

Hotels in/near San Marco
(St. Mark's Square)
Considered to be the most crowded and expensive part of Venice. It is the cultural and commercial center of Venice, and Piazza San Marco with the Basilica San Marco is its heart. Nothing but tourists in heavy foot traffic area and lots of noise.

ALLA SCALA: Campo Manin (Corte Contarini Bolovo) 4306. **Tel:** 041-5210629. **Fax:** 041-5228958. (5 rms., all w/toilet & bath or shower.) 125,000-145,000L (64-74E) double; 185,000L (95E) triple. Breakfast (8:30-10am) at 11,500L pp is not obligatory & can be served in the room. Cash only. English spoken (Andrea), quaint charming basic hotel/simply furnished cozy pretty rms. w/small bathrooms, #2 & 3 are large, 1 rm. has handicapped access, one rm. has the smallest bathroom I have ever seen, the sink moves over the toilet so you can take a shower but it is a private bathroom, famous spiral stairway, central heating, quiet location, no elevator, 1 fl. Owned/ managed by Andreina Della Fiorentina. **Vaporetto:** Rialto. Walk to your right along the waterfront, turn left onto Calle Carbon to Campo San Luca, turn right onto Salizzada San Luca, follow it to Campo Manin, take Calle Vida from the square to Calle Locande, turn left, then a quick right onto Corte Contarini Bolovo. (Closed Aug.)

CASA PETRARCA: Calle Schiavine 4386. **Tel/Fax:** 041-5200430. (7 rms., 3 w/toilet & bath or shower.) 105,000L (54E) single (sinks only); 130,000-160,000L (67-82E) double. Call for triple rates. Breakfast (8-10am) at 11,500L pp is not obligatory & can be served in the room. Cash only. English spoken (Nellie & Alexandra), basic hotel w/simply furnished small rms. & nice bathrooms, some w/views of the canal, #1 has the best view but no private facilities, no elevator, 2 flrs. Owned/managed by Tramontin. **Vaporetto:** Rialto. Walk along the Grand Canal, turn left onto Calle Carbon which runs directly into Campo San Luca, go through the small square, walk down Calle Fuseri, take 2nd left onto Calle Ungheria, then quick right onto Calle Schiavine. Hotel door is on the left under the sign.

FIORITA: Campiello Novo 3457/A. **Tel:** 041-5234754. **Tel/Fax:** 041-5228043. **E-mail:** locafior@tin.it (10 rms., 8 w/toilet & bath or shower.) 110,000-135,000L (56-69E) single; 165,000-185,000L (85-95E) double; 240,000L (123E) triple; 280,000L (144E) quad. Breakfast (8-10am) is included in the rates & can be served in the room but can be deducted to reduce room price. Breakfast is served on the terrace in warm weather. Visa, MC, AX. English spoken (Peter), direct-dial phone, 15th-century wonderful hotel w/simply furnished rms. & modern bathrooms, some w/wood-beamed ceilings, #1 (no bathroom), 10 (private entrance), 8 & 9 are the best rms. & have TVs, hair driers, double-paned windows, central heating, air-conditioned (25,000L extra per day), terrace, no elevator, 1 fl. They also have an annex w/8 rms: 3 of the rms. have views of canal, a/c, satellite TV/CNN & 1 jr. suite. Prices range from 235,000-260,000L. *5% rm. discount when you show manager Renato Colombera or staff* *this book.* Located in a sunny little square. **Vaporetto:** Accademia or San Angelo. From Accademia, cross the Accademia Bridge, continue north to the large Campo Santo Stefano, cross the Campo, at the far northern end after the church, take a left at the flower stand. Go up three steps to reach the raised Campiello to find the hotel. (Closed Jan. 8-Feb. 8.)

SAN SAMUELE: Salizzada San Samuele 3358, 1st fl. **Tel/Fax:** 041-5228045. (10 rms., 2 w/toilet & bath or shower.) 55,000-85,000L (28-44E) single; 95,000-155,000L (50-79E) double. Call for triple rates. Breakfast (8:30-11am) at 8,500L pp is not obligatory & is served in the room. Cash only. English spoken (Dominic), basic hotel w/ simply furnished large bright rms., #9 & 10 have the bathrooms, #3 & 4 (w/2 windows) are huge, #8 has a romantic decor, quiet location, no elevator, 2 flrs. Located 1 flight up in an old business bldg. They may renovate in Dec.'99 to add telephones & 5 more bathrooms to rooms #1-4 & 8. Owned/managed by Dominic Verdino. **Vaporetto:** San Angelo or San Samuele. From San Samuele boat stop, take Calle Carrozze from Campo San Stefano straight to Salizzada San Samuele. (Closed 2 or 3 wks. in Jan.)

HOTELS OVER $100 A NIGHT FOR TWO
These hotels may have rooms under $100 a night for two because it is low season or the rooms do not have private bathrooms.

AI DO MORI: Calle Larga San Marco 658. **Tel:** 041-5204817/ 5289293. **Fax:** 041-5205328. (11 rms., 8 w/toilet & bath or shower.) 80,000-165,000L (41-85E) single; 135,000-195,000L (69-100E) double; 185,000-245,000L (95-126E) triple; 240,000-320,000L (123-164E) quad. Children under 6 free. No breakfast served. Visa, MC. English spoken (Antonella), direct-dial phone, satellite TV w/English channel, wonderful pleasant hotel w/bright rms., some w/views of rooftops, #11 is a small top-floor room w/wood-beamed ceiling, bathroom & a private rooftop terrace with view of basilica & clock tower, larger rooms are on the lower flrs., #6 & 7 have views, #45 is a suite w/2 bedrooms & bathrooms, double-paned windows, central heating, air-conditioned, bar, no elevator, 4 flrs. *5% rm. discount when you show owner/manager Antonella Bernardi or staff this book and pay in cash.* **Vaporetto:** San Marco. Located just off the Piazza

San Marco. From San Marco square, walk under the Torre l'Orologio clock tower, turn right as soon as you can and the hotel is on the left just before Wendy's. Walk up 2 flights of stairs to get to the gated door of the hotel.

AL GAMBERO: Calle Fabbri 4687.
Tel: 041-5224384/5201420. **Fax:** 041-5200431.
E-mail: gambero@tin.it or hotgamb@tin.it (27 rms., 15 w/toilet & bath or shower.) 100,000-180,000L (51-92E) single; 155,000-225,000L (79-115E) double; 209,000-303,000L (107-155E) triple; 258,000-377,000L (132-193E) quad. Children under 2 free. Buffet breakfast (7:45-9:30am) is included in the rates & cannot be deducted. Visa, MC. English spoken, direct-dial phone, recently renovated hotel w/rms. that vary in comfort from basic to fully equipped, #204 is nicely furnished rm. w/bathroom, TV, a/c, minibar & view of canal, there are 14 rms. that are identical to #204, #43 is a wonderful simply furnished bright rm. w/minibar, bathroom & 2 windows, #43, 45, 46, 47 & 48 all have a view of the canal but not all have bathrooms, #203 has a balcony, #401 has a terrace, if you get a room facing the street be aware that it is over a restaurant and you may smell fish, 1 rm. has handicapped access, double-paned windows, central heating, air-conditioned, bar, restaurant (discount if you eat there), no elevator, 4 flrs. Owned/managed by Sandro Rossi. **Vaporetto:** Rialto. Walk right along the canal, cross over the small footbridge, turn left turn onto Calle Fabbri. Hotel is on the right about 5 blocks up.

AL GAZZETTINO: Calle Mezzo 4971. **Tel:** 041-5286523. **Fax:** 041-5223314. (12 rms., all w/toilet & bath or shower.) 75,000-95,000L (38-50E) single; 165,000-195,000L (85-100E) double; 220,000-240,000L (113-123E) triple; 250,000-260,000L (128-133E) quad. Breakfast (8-10am) is included in the rates & cannot be deducted but can be served in the room (6,500L extra pp). Visa, MC, AX. Limited English spoken (Mario), direct-dial phone, nice hotel w/simple furnished rms., #12 & 16 (large rm. & bathroom) w/balconies & views of the canal are the best rms., central heating, air-conditioned, bar, restaurant (10% discount), no elevator, 5 flrs. *5% rm. discount when you show owner/manager Mario Lazzari or staff this book.* **Vaporetto:** Rialto. Walk straight ahead on Calle Larga Mazzini which becomes Calle San Salvatore Merceria, take it to the end, turn right onto Calle Ballotte, turn left onto Calle Mezzo. Ask hotel to fax you a map. (Closed Dec.-Feb.)

DO POZZI: Via XXII Marzo (Calle Do Pozzi) 2373. **Tel:** 041-5207855. **Fax:** 041-5229413. (29 rms., all w/toilet & bath or shower.) 145,000-205,000L (74-105E) single; 215,000-295,000L (110-151E) double. Call for triple/quad. Breakfast (7-10:30am) is included in the rates & can be served in your rm. Breakfast is served in the courtyard garden in warm weather. Visa, MC, AX, DC. English spoken (Enrica), direct-dial phone, TV, wonderful charming modern hotel w/elegantly furnished comfortable rms. & bathrooms that vary in size, some rms. w/bathtubs, about 12 rms. overlook the charming courtyard garden, minibars, some w/hair driers, lovely chandeliers, air-conditioned, central heating, laundry service, romantic courtside restaurant, elevator, 4 flrs. They offer half- and full-board rates. **Vaporetto:** Giglio. Walk down the long dark alley onto the Campo Santa Maria Zobenigo, turn right in the middle of the square onto Calle Ostreghe, follow it over the bridge to Via XXII Marzo. Located on a cul-de-sac behind the Museo Correr. (Closed Jan.)

GALLINI: Calle Verona 3673. **Tel:** 041-5204515/5489020. **Fax:** 041-5209103. (50 rms., 40 w/toilet & bath or shower.) 145,000-205,000L (74-105E) single; 200,000-255,000L (103-131E) double; 250,000-340,000L (128-174E) triple; 320,000-420,000L (164-215E) suites. Breakfast (7:30-10am) is included in the rates & cannot be deducted but can be served in the room (3,000L extra pp). MC, Visa, AX. English spoken (Adriano & Alberto), direct-dial phone, 10 rms. w/TVs, pleasant hotel w/nicely furnished large bright rms. & modern bathrooms, wooden flrs., some rms. are equipped w/air-conditioning (cost extra), about 10 rms. overlook the canal, #352 is wonderful w/wood-beamed ceilings, minibar, a/c and a view of the canal, #300 (a/c, TV, minibar) & 308 are large rms., #105 has TV & minibar, some rms. have double-paned windows & chandeliers, 10 rms. w/air-conditioning & minibars, central heating, bar, no elevator, 3 flrs. *10% rm. discount (15% in July & Aug.) when you show owner/manager Adriano & Ceciliati Gabriella or staff this book.* **Vaporetto:** Rialto or San Angelo. Walk the wavy road passing through

Campo San Angelo onto Calle Mandola, take a right onto Calle Assasini, which becomes Calle Verona. (Closed Nov. 15-Carnevale.)

SAN GIORGIO: Calle Mandola 3781.
Tel: 041-5235835/5289481. **Fax:** 041-5228072. (16 rms., all w/toilet & bath or shower.) 115,000-165,000L (50-85E) single; 155,000-240,000L (79-123E) double; 200,000-290,000L (103-149E) triple. Buffet breakfast (7:30-9:30am) is included in the rates & cannot be deducted but can be served in the room (4,500L extra pp). Visa, MC. English spoken (Manuela), direct-dial phone, TV, recently renovated classy hotel w/elegantly Venetian-style furnished comfortable large rms., #16 is the smallest but still very pretty, chandeliers in rms., hair driers, minibars, nice flrs., 2 rms. w/balconies, central heating, air-conditioned, no elevator, 3 flrs. In 1999, the hotel will be renovating the roof and making it into 2 suites: One w/a Venetian-style terrace & one w/normal-size terrace. *10% rm. discount (15% low season) when you show owner Renzo Cristofoli, manager Gabriella Gazzola or staff this book.* **Vaporetto:** San Angelo. Walk to your left along the waterfront, turn right onto Calle Traghetto through Campo San Benedetto, turn right onto Calle Magazen, turn left onto Rio Terra Mandola, turn left Calle Mandola. (Closed Jan.)

SAN SALVADOR: Calle Galiazzo 5264. **Tel/Fax:** 041-5289147. **Fax:** 041-5208658. (9 rms., all w/toilet & bath or shower.) 145,000-245,000L (74-126E) single; 165,000-295,000L (85-151E) double; 300,000-380,000L (154-195E) triple; 320,000-480,000L (164-246E) quad. Children under 9 free. Breakfast (8am) at 16,500L pp is not obligatory & can be served in the room (11,500L extra pp). Breakfast is served in the terrace in warm weather. Visa, MC. English spoken (Claudio & Ambra), direct-dial phone, satellite TV w/English channel, charming newly renovated hotel w/elegantly furnished pretty comfortable rms., nice flrs., the doors are made to fit the room (some slide & some open out), #19 has a private bathroom in the hall, minibars, hair driers, double-paned windows, central heating, air-conditioned, no elevator, 2 flrs. *5% rm. discount when you show owner/manager Franco Convilli or staff this book.* **Vaporetto:** Rialto. Walk straight ahead on Calle Larga Mazzini, turn left onto Calle Aprile 2 Merceria, turn right onto Calle Galiazzo opposite the McDonald's on the Campo San Bartolomeo.

SAN ZULIAN: Calle San Zulian 535.
Tel: 041-5225872/5232265. **Fax:** 041-5232265.
E-mail: h.sanzulian@iol.it (22 rms., all w/toilet & bath or shower.)
115,000-135,000L (60-69E) single; 135,000-335,000L (69-172E)
double; 180,000-420,000L (92-215E) triple; 220,000-470,000L (113-
241E) quad. Children under 5 free. Breakfast (7:30-10am) is included
in the rates & cannot be deducted but can be served in the room.
Visa, MC, AX, DC. English spoken (Mauro), direct-dial phone, satellite TV w/English channel, wonderful elegant hotel w/beautifully
furnished rms., #104 & 203 are the best rms., #304 has a terrace, hair
driers, minibars, double-paned windows, central heating, air-conditioned, 4 flrs., no elevator but in 1999 the hotel will shut down for a
couple months to renovate the rooms which will also include install-
ing an elevator. Owned by Tegon & managed by Mauro Girotto.
Vaporetto: San Marco or Rialto. From San Marco square, walk under the Torre l'Orologio clock tower, continue straight on Calle
Spadaria pass Calle Larga San Marco, pass the San Zulian church
onto Calle San Zulian.

SERENISSIMA: Calle Carlo Goldoni 4486. **Tel:** 041-5200011. **Fax:**
041-5223292. (37 rms., all w/toilet & bath or shower.) 148,000-
185,000L (76-95E) single; 193,000-265,000L (99-136E) double;
250,000-345,000L (128-177E) triple; 295,000-390,000L (151-200E)
quad. Children under 2 free. Breakfast (7-10am) is included in the
rates & cannot be deducted but can be served in the room (11,500L
extra pp). Visa, MC, AX. English spoken, direct-dial phone, wonderful charming w/nicely furnished comfortable rms., #252 is wonderful & elegantly furnished, #156 is nice w/bathtub, hair driers, double-
paned windows, central heating, air-conditioned, bar, no elevator, 5
flrs. *10% rm. discount when you show owner Maria Giust, manager
Roberto DalBorgo or staff this book.* The hotel is regularly visited
by famous artists. The young blond woman in the fabulous paintings
on the wall is Roberto's mother. You may recognize her as she serves
you your breakfast. I stayed at this hotel and it was a relaxing experience. Roberto is extremely helpful and charming. If you are an
artist, ask to see his treasured book of artwork sketched by various
artists from all over the world. 5 minutes from St. Mark's square and
the Rialto bridge. **Vaporetto:** Rialto. Walk to your right along the

waterfront, turn left onto Calle Carbon straight through Campo San Luca passing McDonald's to Calle Carlo Goldoni. (Closed Nov. 15-Carnevale.)

No options left. Use Venetian Hoteliers' Assoc. (VHA) for hotel information. **Tel:** 041-715016. Located on the right side near the front entrance of the train station. Or listen carefully to what some of the hotel agents in front of the station are saying as they try to convince you to stay at their hotels.

For a calendar of events, see Appendix V.

MONEY
Try to change your money before you get to Venice, but if you can't then try **Banco di Silvo:** San Marco 5051. **Tel:** 041-5219730. Located near C. S. Bartolomeo. Hrs.: Mon.-Fri. 8:30am-1:30pm and 2:35-3:35pm. Check for commission rates. Cirrus machines are everywhere but the only machine that accepts Plus cardholders is the Banca Nazionale Lavoro on Campo Rusolo/San Gallo.

LAUNDROMATS (Lavanderia)
I suggest you get to these places as soon as they open, otherwise it could be a long wait.

Gabriella: Rio Terra Colonne 985, San Marco. **Tel:** 041-5221758. Mon.-Fri. 8am-7pm. 23,500L for wash, dry and soap. Drop off clothes and pick up later that day.

Gettone SS. Apostoli: Salizzada Pistor 4553/A, Cannaregio. **Tel:** 041-5226650. Mon.-Sat. 8:30am-12pm and 3-7pm. 18,000L for 9 lbs. of wash, dry and soap. Drop off clothes and pick up later that day. Located off Campo S.S. Apostoli, close to the Rialto bridge.

Lavaget: Fondamenta Pescaria 1269, Cannaregio. **Tel:** 041-715976. Mon.-Fri. 8:30am-12:30pm and 4-6:30pm. 23,500L for 9 lbs. of wash, dry and soap. Drop off clothes early and pick up later that day. Located off Rio Terra San Leonardo. Take a left from the train station, cross first bridge, turn left along the canal.

RESTAURANTS

Please check page 20 for my criteria for selecting restaurants.

TRATTORIA DA REMIGIO: Calle Bosello/Salizzada Greci 3416, Castello. **Tel:** 041-5230089. Italian/Venetian. Hrs.: Lunch 12:30-2:30pm and dinner 7:30-10:30pm. Closed Monday evenings and Tuesday. Visa, MC, AX, DC. The minute you arrive in Venice make reservations at this family-style Venetian trattoria. This place is booked weeks in advance. About 55,000L pp including a 12% gratuity which is added to your check. English spoken, small wonderful restaurant that offers fresh fish sold by weight, homemade pasta and lots of meat choices. Take some of that money you saved on your room and splurge on this great food. *Show Fabio Bianchi this book and get a complimentary after-dinner drink.* **Vaporetto:** San Zaccaria. Turn right and walk along the waterfront until you come to the white Chiesa Santa Maria Pieta, turn left onto Calle Pieta, which becomes Calle Greci, continue straight onto Salizzada Greci. Restaurant is on the right.

ANTICA MOLA: Fondamenta Ormesini 2800, Cannaregio. **Tel:** 041-717492. Hrs.: Daily 12pm-11pm. Visa, MC, AX, DC. Lots of locals eat at this simple neighborhood trattoria which serves good food at decent prices. The risotto is wonderful. Homemade desserts. Owned by Antonio, whose wife is the cook. Sandra, Sara & Francesca, three English -speaking waitresses/students who live together take turns working the restaurant in the evenings. *Show Antonio, Giorgio the waiter or Sandra, Sara & Francesca this book and they will give you a complimentary after-dinner drink.* From the train station, turn left onto Lista Spagna, walk straight up Lista Spagna, continue straight through Campo San Geremia onto Salazzada San Geremia over the bridge to Rio Terra San Leonardo, bear to the left as it becomes Rio Terra Farsetti, walk over the bridge, turn left onto Fondamenta Ormesini. **Vaporetto:** San Marcuola.

IL CAFFE: Campo Santa Margherita 2963, Dorsoduro. **Tel:** 041-5287998. Snacks/sandwiches. Hrs.: 7am-1am. Closed Sun. Cash only. Great fresh nice-size sandwiches. They will grill them for you. This sandwich place is always crowded w/young people (no tourists) and lots of cigarette smoke. Better to eat your food outside in the square.

VENICE

As always, the food is cheaper if you stand than if you sit at a table. **Vaporetto:** Ca' Rezzonico. Located opposite Hotel Antico Capon.

CASA GRAPPA: San Polo 779/a, Rialto. **Tel:** 041-5236578. My friends Jeff Fischgrund and Geovanni Brewer think this is the best gourmet delicatessen in all of Venice. They have the best Parma ham and cheese, grappa and lots of Venetian specialties you'll want to take home. Ask for Luciana or Nicola, his son who speaks English, they will be happy to help you with your selections.

VERONA
Veneto, zip code 37121
Area code 39, city code 045

Orientation: Verona is a beautiful romantic city made for walking. **Porta Nuova** train station is located south of the **Piazza Brå**, the center of the city (the gate with a clock.) Piazza Brå is on the south side of the **Adige River**, between **Piazza Erbe** (picturesque market square) and the **Arena**. Catch bus #11, 12, 13, 14 weekdays or 91, 92 & 93 holidays/Sundays to Piazza Brå. First buy your bus ticket at the newsstand inside the train station. Then look for the bus station marked "A" directly in front of the train station. There will be a display listing several bus numbers departing for Piazza Brå. You'll know you reached Piazza Brå when you see a large round clock displayed on the arched gate. To walk from the station, walk to the right past the bus station, cross the river, and walk (20 min.) along the boring **Corsa Porta Nuova** until you arrive into Piazza Brå. From Piazza Brå, take the pedestrian **Via Mazzini**, turn left at **Via Cappello** to reach Piazza Erbe, **Piazza Dante** and its adjacent **Piazza Signori** (also centers of activities). The area surrounding the train station is not safe.

Verona's Tourist Information Centers
1.) Via Leoncino 61. **Tel:** 045-592828. **Fax:** 045-8003638. **Hrs.:** Mon.-Sat. 8am-7pm. Sun. 9am-12pm. Later hrs. in-season. Located on the corner of Piazza Brå, facing the Arena. **2.)** Porta Nuova train station. **Tel:** 045-800861. **Hrs.:** Daily 9am-6pm. Later hrs. in-season. **3.)** Piazza Erbe 42. **Tel:** 045-8000065/8006997/8030086. **Fax:** 045-8010682/8010632. **Hrs.:** Daily (summer only) 9am-12:30pm and 2:30-7pm.

High season is opera season: July-Sept.; Easter & Christmas.

Hotels near Piazza Brå
See directions listed under orientation. Taxi 15,000L.

AL CASTELLO: Corso Cavour 43. **Tel/Fax:** 045-8004403. (10 rms., 8 w/toilet & bath or shower.) 105,000L (54E) single; 155,000L (79E) double. Call for triple rates. Breakfast (8:30-10am) is included in the rates & cannot be deducted but can be served in the room (4,500L extra pp). Visa, MC, DC. English spoken (Katia), direct-dial phone,

TV, basic hotel w/simply furnished rms., ceiling fans, #21, 19 & 30 have balconies which face the noisy street, no atmosphere, bar, restaurant, no elevator, 3 flrs. Noisy location. They offer half- (130,000L pp) and full-board (165,000L pp) rates. Owned/managed by Clara Dal Corse. As you walk through the gate into Piazza Brå, walk to your left on Via Roma, turn right onto Via Cattaneo, turn left onto Via Brusco. Hotel is on the corner of Via Brusco & Corso Cavour.

CATULLO: Via Valerio Catullo 1. **Tel:** 045-8002786. (21 rms., 4 w/toilet & bath or shower.) 85,000L (44E) single (no toilets); 105,000-125,000L (54-64E) double, 145,000-175,000L (74-90E) triple; 220,000L (113E) suite. No breakfast is served. Cash only. English spoken (Erica & Cristina), 19th-century basic hotel w/simply furnished large rms. & high ceilings, French doors, marble parquet flrs., #11 & 29 both w/bathrooms & balconies are the best rms., #9 & 28 also have bathrooms, #3, 4, 24 & 23 have balconies, they turned rooms #26 & 27 into a suite w/one bathroom, central heating, no elevator, 4 flrs. If you make advance reservations, it's a minimum-stay requirement of 3 nights. Owned/managed by Lorentini Pollini. Located right in the middle of all the action. From Piazza Brå, walk along Via Mazzini, left onto Via Catullo, walk down the alley between 1D and 3A on Via Valerio Catullo. Taxi 22,000L.

CAVOUR: Vicolo Chiodo 4. **Tel:** 045-590166. **Tel/Fax:** 045-590508. (22 rms., all w/toilet & bath or shower.) 103,000-133,000L (53-68E) single; 125,000-173,000L (64-89E) double; 182,000-228,000L (93-117E) triple. Breakfast (8-10am) at 16,500L pp is not obligatory & can be served in the room (6,500L extra pp). Cash only. English spoken (Patricia), direct-dial phone, some rms. w/TVs, classy 19th-century wonderful charming hotel w/nicely furnished comfortable rms., 5 rms. w/balconies & 2 rms. w/terraces, #39, 37 & 42 (jr. suite) are some of the best & largest rooms w/huge balconies, wooden ceilings & 15th-century wall inside the rooms @ 220,000L; #24 (large bathroom) & 21 both w/balconies are wonderful, 3 rms. have handicapped access, central heating, air-conditioned, inner-courtyard elevator next to a 15th-century Roman wall, 3 flrs., parking (30,000L per day). Owned/managed by Carolina Giovanni. As you walk through the gate into Piazza Brå, walk to your left on Via Roma, turn right onto Via Cattaneo, turn left onto Vicolo Chiodo. (Closed Jan. 15-Feb.)

VERONA

EUROPA: Via Roma 8. **Tel:** 045-594744/8002882. **Fax:** 045-8001852. (46 rms., all w/toilet & bath or shower.) 130,000-175,000L (67-90E) single; 165,000-255,000L (85-131E) double; 200,000-300,000L (103-154E) triple. Call for suite prices. American buffet breakfast (7:30-10am) is included in the rates & cannot be deducted but can be served in the room (3,500L extra pp). Visa, MC, AX, DC. English spoken (James), direct-dial phone, TV w/English channel, charming modern hotel w/nicely furnished nice-size pretty airy rms. & most w/modern bathrooms, they renovate 5 bathrooms a year, #106 w/2 windows & bathtub is bright & airy, no-smoking rooms available, 4 suites available, rms. vary in size & brightness, 10 rms. w/balconies, minibars, central heating, air-conditioned, elevator, 4 flrs., parking (25,000L per day). Owned/managed by Luigi Chiecchi Dott. As you walk through the gate into Piazza Brå, walk to your left on Via Roma to the hotel.

TORCOLO: Vicolo Listone 3. **Tel:** 045-8007512. **Fax:** 045-8004058. (19 rms., all w/toilet & bath or shower.) 103,000-130,000L (53-67E) single; 115,000-175,000L (60-90E) double. Call for triple rates. Children under 2 free. Breakfast (7:30-10:30am) at 13,500-19,500L pp is not obligatory & can be served in the room. Breakfast is served on the terrace in warm weather. Visa, MC, AX, DC. English spoken (Marina), direct-dial phone, satellite TV w/English channel, pleasant old-fashioned hotel w/nicely furnished rms. which vary quite a bit in style & size from 18th-century to modern, hair driers, minibars, double-paned windows, central heating, air-conditioned, #24 & 36 are the best because they are the only ones w/bathtubs, excellent & quiet location, a favorite w/opera crowd, terrace, elevator, 4 flrs. *5% rm. discount when you show owner/manager Silvia Pomari or staff this book except in July & Aug.* Silvia is wonderful and very accommodating. She will help you with all your questions. Located just off Piazza Brå, near the Arena. As you walk through the gate into Piazza Brå, walk straight ahead on the left side of the Arena, turn left at the restaurant Tre Corone, hotel is on the left side of the street . (Closed Jan. 10-30th.)

Hotels near Piazzas Erbe & Signori
AURORA: Piazza Erbe 4a/Via Pelliciai 2. **Tel:** 045-594717/597834. **Fax:** 045-8010860. (20 rms., 18 w/toilet & bath or shower.) 95,000-

130,000L (50-67E) single (no bathrooms); 175,000-205,000L (90-105E) double; 240,000-320,000L (123-164E) suites. Buffet breakfast (7:30-10am) is included in the rates & cannot be deducted but can be served in the room (6,500L extra pp). Visa, MC, AX, DC. English spoken (Eleanor), direct-dial phone, satellite TV w/English channel, newly renovated old-fashioned charming hotel w/nicely furnished comfortable rms., 3 rms. have views of the square, one of these rooms have a balcony but Eleanor wouldn't give me the room number, triple rms. have bathtubs, central heating, some rms. w/air-conditioning, charming terrace w/view of the square, walk up 1 flight to the elevator, 4 flrs. Owned/managed by Olivieri Bepino. Great location in the middle of the pedestrian area. Bus #72/73. Taxi 23,000L.

MAZZANTI: Via Mazzanti 6. **Tel:** 045-591370/8006813. **Fax:** 045-8011262. (23 rms., 18 w/toilet & bath or shower.) 105,000-130,000L (54-67E) single; 165,000-185,000L (85-95E) double; 190,000-230,000L (97-118E) triple. Visa, MC, AX, DC. Buffet breakfast (7:30-10am) is included in the rates & cannot be deducted but can be served in the room (6,500L extra pp). English spoken (Benedetto), direct-dial phone, TV, basic old hotel w/simply furnished small rms., #22 has balcony but no bathroom, #16 & 7 are the best rms., central heating, air-conditioned, bar, restaurant, no elevator, 3 flrs. Owned/managed by Flavia Raspino. Good location off Piazza Signori. Facing the white female statue in the middle of the Piazza Signori, look to your far left at the 3rd arch, hotel will be on the right. Taxi 23,000L.

Hotel far right of the Piazza Brå
ARMANDO: Via Dietro Pallone 1. **Tel:** 045-8000206. **Tel/Fax:** 045-8036015. (20 rms., 10 w/toilet & bath or shower.) 125,000-155,000L (64-79E) double; 170,000-190,000L (87-97E) triple; 200,000-220,000L (103-113E) quad. Breakfast (7-10am) at 14,500L pp is not obligatory. Visa, MC. English spoken (Alberto & Diana), direct-dial phone, TV, newly renovated pretty hotel w/simply furnished comfortable nice-size rms., modern bathrooms, tiled flrs., #56, 51 & 52 are the best rms., 2 rms. w/balconies, bar, elevator, 2 flrs., street parking. Quiet residential location. Owned/managed by Diana Cornaehini-Marini. As you walk through the gate into Piazza Brå, walk to your right along Via Pallone paralleling the wall, cross the street, turn left onto Via Dietro Pallone. Taxi 18,000L. (Closed Dec.-Jan.)

Hotel between the train station & Piazza Brå

SCALZI: Via Carmelitani Scalzi 5. **Tel:** 045-590422. **Fax:** 045-590069. (23 rms., 20 w/toilet & bath or shower.) 95,000-143,000L (50-73E) single; 115,000-193,000L (60-99E) double; 180,000-242,000L (92-124E) triple. Breakfast (7:20-10:30am) is included in the rates & can be served in the room (3,500 extra pp) but can be deducted to reduce room price. Visa, MC. English spoken (Tiziano), direct-dial phone, TV, newly renovated hotel w/simply furnished comfortable rms., #20 & 16 are the best rms., 2 rms. w/balconies, central heating, double-paned windows, air-conditioned, bar, no elevator, 2 flrs., parking (20,000L per day). Owned/managed by Graziano Leoni. A 10-minute walk from the train station. (Closed Dec. 23-Jan. 12.)

There is a Hotel Booking Service, Via Patuzzi 5. **Tel:** 045-8009844. **Fax:** 045-8009372. Mon.-Fri. 9am-6pm. Via Patuzzi runs parallel to Via Leoncino off Piazza Gallieno on the corner of Piazza Brå.

VICENZA
Veneto, zip code 36100
Area code 39, city code 0444

Orientation: I think Vicenza is a best-kept secret with its tranquil beauty and lovely quiet evenings. I made Vicenza my base to explore the Veneto after tiring of the Venice crowds. It is an hour away by train from Venice. Vicenza train station is located in **Piazzale Stazione** at the southern end of **Viale Roma**. Bus station on **Viale Milano** 7 is next to the train station. It is about a 10-minute walk from the station to **Piazza Signori**, the center of town. Walk straight ahead along **Viale Roma** into **Piazzale Gasperi**, turn right onto **Corso Andrea Pallidio**, Vicenza's main street. **Corso Palladio** cuts right through the old center from the **Piazza Castello** to the **Piazza Matteotti** which is at the other end of Corso Pallidio. Buses run to the center and Piazza Matteotti.

Vicenza Tourist Information Center
Piazza Matteotti 12. **Tel/Fax:** 0444-320854. **Fax:** 0444-325001. Hrs.: Mon.-Sat. 9-12:30pm & 2:30-5:30pm, Sun. 9am-1pm. Catch bus #1 from the train station to Piazza Matteoti. Next to Teatro Olimpico (Olympic Theater) at end of Corso Palladio.

Hotel near the train station
ITALIA: Via Risorgimento 2. **Tel:** 0444-321043/327863. **Fax:** 0444-230455. (17 rms., all w/toilet & bath or shower.) 155,000L (79E) single/double; 180,000L (92E) triple. Breakfast (7-10am) at 13,500L pp is not obligatory & can be served in the room (23,500L extra pp). Breakfast is served in the garden in warm weather. Cash only. English spoken (Monia), direct-dial phone, basic hotel w/simply furnished rms., #6 & 7 have balconies, 1 rm. has handicapped access, double-paned windows, central heating, noisy location (trains & cars), bar, no elevator, 2 flrs., parking (10,000L per day). From the train station, follow Viale Venezia to your right, turn right onto Viale X Giugno, then a left onto Via Risorgimento. 10-minute walk to the train station & the center.

Hotels in the center

DUE MORI: Contra Do Rode 26. **Tel:** 0444-321886. **Fax:** 0444-326127. (26 rms., 23 w/toilet & bath or shower.) 80,000-90,000L (41-46E) single; 115,000-135,000L (60-69E) double; 150,000L (77E) triple. Breakfast (7:30-10:30am) at 11,500L pp is not obligatory. Visa, MC, AX. English spoken (Massimo & Alexandro), direct-dial phone, wonderful charming hotel w/antique furnished bright comfortable nice-size rms., all the rooms vary in size & decor, 5 rms. w/balconies (#5, 6 & 7 overlook the street, I couldn't get the numbers to the other 2 rooms), #10 has a romantic feel, some rms. still have the 19th-century furnishings, great ambiance, ceiling fans, quiet location, no elevator, 2 flrs. The hotel is not family-owned. Located in the heart of the city, around the corner from the Hotel Vicenza, just off Piazza Signori. Taxi 13,000L.

PALLADIO: Via Oratorio Servi 25. **Tel:** 0444-321072. **Fax:** 0444-547328. (24 rms., 15 w/toilet & bath or shower.) 90,000L (46E) single; 135,000L (69E) double; 170,000L (87E) triple; 200,000L (103E) quad. Buffet breakfast (8-10am) at 16,500L pp is not obligatory. Visa, MC, AX, DC. English spoken (Paolo), direct-dial phone, satellite TV w/English channel, wonderful charming hotel w/modern furnished bright comfortable rms., lots of ambiance, plenty of storage space, #22 has 2 balconies, 5 rms. w/terraces, double-paned windows, central heating, bikes available for rent, quiet location, no elevator, 4 flrs., parking (10,000L per day). Owned/managed by 2 wonderful women, Diana Vincenzi & Victoria. Located close to Piazza Signori & Piazza Matteotti. Taxi 13,000L. (Closed Aug. 8-15.)

VICENZA: Stradella Nodari 5/7. **Tel/Fax:** 0444-321512. (37 rms., 30 w/toilet & bath or shower.) 90,000L (46E) single; 125,000L (64E) double; 170,000L (87E) triple; 200,000L (103E) quad. Breakfast (9-10:30am) at 9,500L pp is not obligatory. Cash only. English spoken (Marie & Vittorio), direct-dial phone, TV, old hotel w/simply furnished small dark rms., nothing special, 15 rms. w/balconies, noisy location, central heating, elevator, 4 flrs., free parking. Located close to Piazza Signori. From Piazza Signori, take Contra Cavour to Corso Palladio, make a left turn onto Stradella Nodari. The hotel might start taking credit cards in '99. The hotel is across from Ristorante Garibaldi. Taxi 13,000L. (Closed Aug. 1-Aug. 16.)

Hotels outside the center

CONTINENTAL: Viale Giangiorgio Trissino 89. **Tel:** 0444-505476/ 505478. **Fax:** 0444-513319. (55 rms., all w/toilet & bath or shower.) 75,000-170,000L (38-87E) single; 135,000-225,000L (69-115E) double; 160,000-295,000L (82-151E) triple; 180,000-360,000L (92-185E) quad. Children under 11 free. Buffet breakfast (7-10am) at 16,500L pp is not obligatory & can be served in the room (6,500L extra pp.) Visa, MC, AX, DC. English spoken (Andrea Dona), direct-dial phone, satellite TV w/English channel, nice hotel w/modern furnished comfortable rms., #108 & 202 both w/balconies are the best rms., 25 rms. w/balconies, 8 rms. have handicapped access, hair driers, double-paned windows, panoramic view from solarium terrace, minibars, central heating, air-conditioned, bar, elevator, free parking. *15% rm. discount or free breakfast when you show part-owner/manager Renato Bonotto or staff this book.* Located in front of the stadium not far from the center of town. Catch bus #3 or 1 from train station to hotel. Tell bus driver you want the hotel. This hotel is not conveniently located to the center. 25-minute walk to the center. Taxi to train station 14,000L.

GIARDINI: Via Giuriolo 10. **Tel/Fax:** 0444-326458. I didn't have a chance to re-visit this wonderful 3-star hotel. 200,000L (103E) including breakfast for a double. Visa, MC, AX, DC. English spoken. Via Giuriolo runs off Piazza Matteotti where the tourist office is located.

RESTAURANT

Please check page 20 for my criteria for selecting restaurants.

AL BERSAGLIERE: Via Pescaria 11. **Tel:** 0444-323507. Hrs: Mon.-Sat. Lunch 12-2:30pm; dinner 7pm-10:30pm. Closed Sun. A full dinner complete with a liter of house wine and dessert will cost about 55,000L for two people. Cash only. Limited English spoken (Angelo). Better to make reservations, only 10 tables. Wonderful little local family restaurant that serves fabulous traditional recipes including homemade pasta and fresh fish (not every day). The father is chef/owner Sergio (long white-haired ponytail), son Sergio Jr. works behind the bar and daughter Vanessa is the waitress. Ask Angelo (who usually arrives about 7:30pm) to make you his special *fragola deserto caslingo* (in-season strawberry dessert). The restaurant caters to the locals. Don't forget to bring your *Eating and Drinking in Italy* menu reader or ask Angelo for the specials. Located off Piazza Erbe. *Show the family this book and they will give you a complimentary limoncello.* Whenever I stay in Verona or Venice, I include Vicenza as a day trip and make sure I have dinner here. I arrive at the restaurant exactly at 7pm, eat a wonderful meal & catch the train back to Verona or Venice.

APPENDIX I

PACKING THE UNUSUAL

Alarm clock radio: Helps you to catch those early-morning trains.

Apple slicer/peeler: Fruit makes a great snack. Assume the fruit has not been washed and you have no place to wash it. The slicer and peeler are handy when you are traveling on the train where the warning signs over the sink say "Do Not Drink the Water."

ATM: Please refer to the section "Before You Leave Home" in the front of this book for detailed information on this subject.

Batteries: For alarm clock, radio, flashlight, camera and tape recorder. Don't forget lots of film which usually costs more in Europe.

Cable lock: A lightweight adjustable-length cable lock. Great for locking your bags on trains and ships. I travel alone by train to do my research so I lock my bags to the overhead rack.

Calculator: Perfect for figuring out exchange rates.

Clothesline, clothes-pegs, sink stopper and soap: Take advantage of those sinks and don't forget the soap suds!

Earplugs: A lifesaver when your roommate's snoring becomes unbearable. They also come in handy for those rooms that sound like they're in the middle of a highway. Include an eye mask to help you sleep in hotels, on planes or trains.

Eyeglasses: Bring a backup pair of sunglasses/eyeglasses, photocopy of the prescription and a retainer cord. I have had to replace lost eyeglasses more than once.

Facecloths: Italy's hotels do not supply them.

Flashlight (purse-size): You never know when you will need this.

PACKING THE UNUSUAL

Guidebooks: Travel guide (your favorite), language book and, of course, do not forget this one! Please refer to the section "Before You Leave Home" in the front of this book for detailed information about why it is important to purchase certain books prior to leaving home. (We also use a European-language translator that doubles as a foreign-currency converter.)

Hand sanitizers or towelettes: You can never pack enough of these.

Highlighter: Handy to use for highlighting maps and sections in your travel guide.

Inflatable neck cushion: Handy for planes, trains, buses and resting your head while on the beach.

Magnifying glass: Great for reading maps. Even better if it comes with a light.

Maps: Please refer to the section "Before You Leave Home" in the front of this book for a detailed explanation about why it is important to purchase your maps prior to leaving home.

Mosquito spray & citronella candles: Window screens are rare. A definite must for the summer.

Night-light (international voltage): Comes in real handy when you are trying to find your toilet in the middle of the night, especially if you change hotel rooms as often as we do.

Notebook (small, spiral): Perfect for recording your memories. The notebook also comes in handy when negotiating room prices and taking down train information. I also pack a microcassette recorder to record my trip.

Novels (paperbacks): They help pass the time when you encounter the inevitable long train lines. When you finish reading them, give them away to other English-speaking tourists. They are five times the cost in Italy. It's a great way to introduce yourself.

PACKING THE UNUSUAL

Photocopies: Make copies of your passport, credit card numbers (including their domestic and international numbers in case they are stolen or lost), a record of traveler's checks and airline tickets. Also, make copies of medication and eyeglass prescriptions. Leave two copies at home with friends/family and take two with you. Remember to pack the copies separate from the originals.

Photo ID: You can use theese photos if you have to replace your passport.

Plastic bags: Small, medium and large resealable plastic bags to be used for carrying food, stuff, wet or dirty clothes and brochures you pick up along the way. Also use them as hot or cold compresses, as well as for the plastic bottles filled with liquid in your suitcase.

Pre-printed address labels: Makes your life so much easier when you can just stick a pre-printed or handwritten address label on a postcard to friends back home. This is great if you are traveling with children. You can have their friends names on pre-printed address labels.

Prunes, figs or something similar: Fiber is not big on Italian menus, and all that pasta do not exactly help your digestive system. Sometimes it needs a little assistance. Whatever works.

Reading light: Perfect for reading books on planes, trains or in hotels. Also, not all hotels have overhead reading lights or they are not bright enough. I recommend the *Light Voyager Booklight* because it is convenient to pack and gives off a lot of light.

Security undercover wallets: Invest in a deluxe undercover wallet that is worn underneath your clothes. They come in different shapes and styles to be worn around your waist, shoulders, legs or neck. Buy whatever is comfortable for you but get one. Also get a small pouch with a loop in the back that slips onto your belt. I use the Eagle Creek's *Departure Pouch*. Use this pouch to carry your day's money, train tickets and the one credit card to avoid having to go into your secured undercover wallet. Look in the section under "Before You Leave Home" to get more information on pickpockets.

Sea bands: Wear them on your wrists and use them for traveling by buses or cars while they are navigating scary narrow roads. Even short boat rides can be bumpy going across the water.

Self-adhesive labels: Stick small labels (1/2" x 3/4") on used rolls of film to identify the city you are currently shooting. This will assist you when you develop all those rolls of film and cannot remember which city you were in when you shot the pictures.

Survival kit: Combination of rubber bands, safety pins, shoelaces, sewing kit, bobby pins, transparent tape, pens, compact scissors, Bandaids™ and Visine™ eye drops (for those late nights).

Toilet paper (1 roll): European toilet paper has become a lot softer, but it may not always be available when you use the public toilets. There are times when you have to pay for sheets of toilet paper in public restrooms and sometimes a pack of tissues is just not enough. Some toilets on trains don't have toilet paper.

Toilet seat covers: When you finally find a public toilet bowl that has a seat on it, you may not always have the strength to bend your knees and hold yourself up. After hiking for 5 hours, a friend of mine did not care what type of disease she caught from sitting on the toilet. Perfect for toilets on trains.

Umbrella (collapsible): Just when you think you don't need one, it rains.

Utility web straps (3/4" x 24"): Great for tying your jacket to your purse straps.

Vaseline™: Use it to rub on the bottom of your feet to cut down on friction and to avoid getting blisters from all that walking on cobble streets. Add baby powder, blister/corn pads, inner cushion soles, moleskin and Second Skin™ to your list.

Water bottle carrier: So you can always have fresh water handy.

Wine bottle opener/corkscrew/wine cap: We eat a lot of our dinners on late-night trains and a bottle of wine complements the meal. We also like to bring a bottle back to our room at night. Also carry a set of camping utensils.

Most of these items are carried by your local favorite travel bookstore or drugstore. If you have difficulty locating these items, you can contact Magellan's at (800) 962-4943 or **Web site** http://www.magellans.com/ They extend a one-time 15% discount on your first order to readers of this book. Code TO1.

APPENDIX II

TOURIST OFFICES OF ITALY IN THE U.S.

Tourist Offices of Italy Web site:
http://www.italiantourism.com/ or http://www.enit.it.com/

New York: 630 Fifth Avenue, Suite 1565, New York, NY 10011, Tel: (212) 245-4882, Fax: (212) 586-9249.

Los Angeles: 12400 Wilshire Blvd., Suite 550, Los Angeles, CA 90025, Tel: (310) 820-0098 Fax: (310) 820-6357.

Chicago: 500 N. Michigan Ave., Suite 2240, Chicago, Il 60611, Tel: (312) 644-0996; Tel: (312) 644-0990 brochures only; Fax: (312) 644-3019.

When contacting the tourist offices via mail, fax or e-mail, please include your mailing address so they can forward their travel brochures to you. Should you need to speak to somebody about specific questions regarding travel and tourism in Italy, please call, write, fax or e-mail one of the above Tourist Offices of Italy nearest you.

Italian Embassy in U.S.: http://www.italyemb.org/

Customs: http://www.info-italy-usa.org/america/embassy/customs/cover.htm

For each city in this book, I have included the phone, fax numbers and most Web sites of the city's local tourist office. Take advantage of this and write, fax or e-mail them prior to your leaving home. Request that they send you information on the city, a detailed list of local events for the month you plan to visit the city, a list of hotels and, most important, a map of the city.

APPENDIX III

TELEPHONES/FAXING/TIME DIFFERENCES

Italy's telephone system is very efficient. Most public (street phone box) phones are now operated by prepaid phone cards (*carte telefoniche*) which you can purchase from post offices, train stations, newsstands and tobacco shops. They cost 5,000, 10,000 or 15,000L. To make a call, take the phone off the hook, insert the phone card into a slot on the phone, then dial your number slowly. 800 numbers do not work from Italy.

Calling from United States to Italy: Dial 011 (U.S. international access code), 39 (Italy's country code), the city's code including the zero (listed under each city in this book), then dial the remaining local telephone number listed for each hotel. For example, to call hotel Campo Fioro in Rome from the US, dial 011-39-06-68806865.

Faxing & e-mailing hotels in Italy from the U.S.: Everything that is stated above for calling also applies to faxing, except many of the hotels do not have a dedicated fax line. I used to fumble my way through a conversation requesting a fax tone so that I could fax that person's hotel. I was successful less than 50% of the time. I would hang up out of frustration and mail the hotel a letter requesting the information I was trying to get by fax. I have now discovered an easier way to fax Italy. I dial the fax number listed for the hotel in this book on the keypad of my fax machine without using the speaker phone. After I dial the number, I press "start." If it doesn't go through the first time, the machine automatically redials the fax number and the fax will go through the 2nd time. I have a 95% success rate using this method of faxing. As far as e-mailing the hotels, I have verified all Web sites and e-mail addresses for the hotels listed in this book. However, every now and then I get an e-mail error message when I try to e-mail a hotel in Italy. I was told it had something to do with the phone lines in Italy. I have included a convenient hotel fax form at the end of this book and on my **Web site:** www.HelloEurope.com/ See hotel reservations in "Tips on Hotels Accommodations" for more details on faxing hotels.

TELEPHONES

Cellular Phone: Please see "Before You Leave Home" on the advantages of renting a cellular phone for abroad.

Calling card from Italy to United States: Just dial the toll-free access codes listed below to reach the U.S. operator. Always check the hotel's policy for making local and long-distance calls before placing any phone calls from your hotel room or the hotel switchboard. Rates are lower from 12:00pm to 2:00pm & 8:00pm to 2:00am Monday through Friday and Sunday afternoon.

Telephone access codes for calling cards to U.S.:
AT&T = 172-1011; Sprint = 172-1877; MCI = 172-1022.

Dialing direct from Italy to United States (without a calling card): Insert a phone card, dial 00 (Italy's international access code), then 1 (U.S.A.'s country code), then area code and number. For example, Rome to my Los Angeles office is: 00-1-323-939-0821. Calling from a public pay phone is more expensive than a regular phone but with a prepaid phone card it turns out to be about the same rate. A more economical and comfortable alternative is to use your AT&T, Sprint or MCI local access numbers listed above. You can use a phone card or a 200L coin to make a call back home when you use access codes.

Calling long distance within Italy: Dial the city code (listed under each city in this book), then the local number. For example, Rome to hotel Centrale in Florence: dial 055 (Florence's city code), 215761 (tel. # for hotel Centrale in Florence).

TIME DIFFERENCES
Time zones: Italy is 6 hours ahead of the East Coast of the United States except for a few days each spring (7 hrs.) and fall (5 hrs.). I almost missed my train once because I was unaware Italy had forwarded the clocks an hour just before Easter Sunday. The United States did not "spring forward" until a week later.

Clock time: Europe uses the 24-hour clock.
Noon is 1200 hrs., 6pm is 1800 hrs., midnight is 2400 hrs.

Website for World Clock
http://www.stud.unit.no/USERBIN/steffent/verdensur.pl/

APPENDIX IV

ITALIAN PHRASES FOR CHECKING IN

Good morning!
Buon giorno!
boo-OHn jee-OHr-noh!

Good afternoon!
Buon pomeriggio
boo-OHn poamayREEDjoa

Good evening (night)!
Buona sera (notte)
boo-OH-nah sAY-rah (nOHt-teh)

Hello! (telephone) Good-bye
pronto!   **Arrivederci**
prOHn-toh!   *ahr-ree-veh-dAYr-chee*

Sir   Madame   Miss
Signore   **Signora**   **Signorina**
see-ny-OH-reh see-ny-OH-rah see-ny-oh-rEE-nah

Please
Per piacere
pEHr pee-ah-chAY-reh

Thank you (very much)!
(Mille) grazie!
(mEEl-leh) grAH-tsee-eh!

You're welcome
prego (They say *prego, prego* for almost everything.)
PRAYgoa

ITALIAN PHRASES FOR CHECKING IN

My name is ...
Mi chiamo ...
mee kee-AH-moh ...

Do you speak English?
Parla inglese?
pAHr-lah een-glAY-seh?

Yes or no?
Si o no?
see oh noh?

I don't speak Italian.
Io non parlo italiano.
EE-oh nohn pAHr-loh ee-tah-lee-AH-noh.

I understand.
Capisco.
kah-pEE-skoh.

Do you understand?
Capisce?
kah-pEE-sheh?

I don't understand.
Non capisco.
nohn kah-pEE-skoh.

Do you have any vacancies?
Avete camere libere?
ahVAYtay KAAmayray LEEbayray?

I would like a single (double) room tonight.
Vorrei una camera singola (dopia) per stanotte.
*vohr-rEH-ee oo-nah kAH-meh-rah sEEn-goh-lah
(dOHp-pee-ah) pehr stah-nOHt-teh.*

ITALIAN PHRASES FOR CHECKING IN

for two people
per due persone
pehr DOO-ay pehr-SOH-nay

---

with (without)
con (senza)
kohn (sEHn-tsah)

---

with a toilet
con toilette
kohn too-ah-lEHt

---

with a shower/with a bathtub
con doccia/con vasco da bagno
kohn dOH-chee-ah/kohn VAH-skoh dah bAH-ny-oh

---

with a private bath
con bagno propio (privato)
kohn bAH-ny-oh prOH-pee-oh (pree-vAH-toh)

---

with (without) breakfast
con (senza) colazione
kohn (sEHn-tsah) koh-lahtsee-OH-neh

---

with twin beds
con due letti singoli
kon DOOay LEHTtee SEENG-goh-lee

---

with double bed
con letto matrimoniale
kon LEHTtoa mahtreemoaneeAAlay

---

with balcony
con balcone
kon bahl-KOH-nay

May I see the room?
Potrei vedere la camera?
poh-trEH-ee veh-dAY-reh lah kAH-meh-rah?

ITALIAN PHRASES FOR CHECKING IN

How much is the room?
Quanté la camera?
koo-ahn-tEH lah kAH-meh-rah?

Do you have something cheaper?
Ha qualche cosa meno costoso?
ah koo-AHl-keh kOH-sah mAY-noh koh-stOH-soh?

Is everything included?
E tutto compreso?
EH tOOt-toh kohm-prAY-soh?

Is it cheaper if I stay _____ nights?
E piu economico se mi_____ notti?
eh pew ay-koh-NOH-mee-koh_____NOTti

The room is very nice. I'll take it.
La camera é molto bella. La prendo.
lah kAH-meh-rah EH mOHl-toh bEHl-lah.
Lah prAYn-doh.

We'll be staying one (1) night.
Resteremo una notte.
rehs-teh-rAY-moh OO-nah nOHt-teh.

---

for tonight
per stanotte
pehr stah-NOT-tay

---

two (2) nights
due notti
dOO-eh nOHt-tee

3
tre
trEH

4
quattro
koo-AHt-troh

5
cinque
chEEn-koo-eh

6
sei
sEH-ee

7
sette
sEHt-teh

8
otto
OHt-toh

9
nove
nOH-veh

10
dieci
dee-EH-chee

11
undici
OOn-dee-chee

12
dodici
dOH-dee-chee

13
tredici
trEH-dee-chee

One thousand (1,000)
mille
mEEl-leh

20
venti
vAYn-tee

30
trenta
trEHn-tah

40
quaranta
koo-ah-rAHn-tah

50
cinquanta
cheen-koo-AHn-tah

60
sessanta
sehs-sAHn-tah

70
settanta
seht-tAHn-tah

80
ottanta
oht-tAHn-tah

90
novanta
noh-vAHn-tah

100
cento
chEHn-toh

APPENDIX V

ANNUAL SCHEDULE OF HOLIDAYS, FESTIVALS AND EVENTS

Call, write or fax the Tourist Office of Italy (see Appendix II) for more information because some of the dates vary from year to year. Also, some of the events continue into the next month.

JANUARY
Jan. 1: "Primo dell A' Anno" (New Year's Day) national holiday

Jan. 6: Epiphany Celebrations (national holiday). All the towns and villages in Italy stage Roman Catholic Epiphany observances.

FEBRUARY
Two weeks before Lent: **Venice** Carnevale (Carnival)

MARCH
Check April for Easter celebrations.

Two weeks before Lent: **Venice** Carnevale (Carnival)

March 19: **Rome** celebrates "Festa di Giuseppe" in the Trionfale Quatrer, north of the Vatican.

APRIL
April: **Rome** celebrates "Festa della Primavera." The Spanish steps are layered with azaleas.

Good Friday: **Rome**, Pope leads a candlelighted procession at 9pm in the Colosseum.

Easter week/Sunday: Easter national holiday. Something special is happening all over Italy.

Easter Sunday: **Rome**, Pope gives a televised annual blessing from the St. Peter's balcony at 12pm. **Florence** celebrates "Scoppio del Carro" (Explosion of the Cart).

Venice hosts "La Vogalonga" on the 1st Sunday after Ascension day. Anybody with an oar who can row can participate.

April 25: Liberation Day national holiday

April 25: **Venice** honors St. Mark (its patron saint).

MAY
Florence celebrates "Maggio Musicale Fiorentino" (Musical May Florentine).

May 1: "Festa del Lavoro" (Labor Day) national holiday

May 6: **Rome**, swearing-in of the new guards at the Vatican in St. Peter's square.

2nd Sunday in May: **Camogli** celebrates "Sagra del Pesce" (Fish Feast).

Last Sunday in May: **Orvieto** celebrates "Festa della Palombella."

JUNE
June 2: Some cities celebrate Proclamation of Republic.

1st Sunday in June: **Pisa** celebrates "Gioco del Ponte" (Battle of the Bridge). **Milan** hosts "Festa dei Navigli," a folklore celebration in the Ticinese section.

1st or 2nd week: **Orvieto** celebrates "Corpus Domini" (Corpus Christi), a 1264 miracle.

June 24: **Florence** honors St. John the Baptist (their patron saint).

June 24 & 28: **Florence** celebrates "Gioco del Calcio" (Soccor Match).

June 29: **Genova** celebrates "Palio Marinaro dei Rioni" (Rowing Race).

June 29: **Rome** and **Genova** honor Sts. Peter and Paul (their patron saints).

ANNUAL SCHEDULE OF HOLIDAYS, FESTIVALS & EVENTS

End of June: **Orvieto** & **Perugia** celebrate Rockin' Umbria (rock festival).

JULY
July: **Rome** hosts "Tevere Expo" arts & crafts booths, fireworks and folk music festivals.

July 2: **Siena** celebrates "Il Palio delle Contrade" (Palio horse race) and Aug. also.

Mid-July: **Perugia** hosts the "Umbria Jazz Festival" for 2 weeks in July.

3rd Sunday in July: **Venice** commemorates "Il Redentore" (Feast of the Redeemer).

Last week of July: The Trastevere neighborhood in **Rome** turns into "Festa de Noantri" (village fair).

Verona hosts the "Arena Outdoor Opera Season."

AUGUST
1st Sunday in August: **Camogli** celebrates "Stella Maris" (Our Lady of the Sea).

Aug. 15: "Ferragosto Assumption of the Virgin" national holiday.

Aug. 16: **Siena** celebrates "Il Palio delle Contrade" (Palio horse race).

Venice hosts International Film Festival, late August to early September.

SEPTEMBER
1st Sunday in September: **Venice** participates in "Regata Storica" (historical regatta) horse races preceded by a spectacular procession of period boats on the Grand Canal.

Mid-Sept.: **Perugia** hosts the "Sagra Musicale Umbria" (Umbrian Festival of Sacred Music).

ANNUAL SCHEDULE OF HOLIDAYS, FESTIVALS & EVENTS

Sept. 19: **Naples** honors St. Gennaro (its patron saint).

OCTOBER
Oct. 4: **Bologna** honors St. Petronio (its patron saint).

Oct. 10: **Genova** hosts a 10-day boat show.

Oct. 24-Nov.: **Perugia** hosts the "Antique Trade Fair" last week in Oct & 1st week of Nov.

NOVEMBER
Nov. 1: "Ognissanti" (All Saints' Day) national holiday.

Nov. 4: Some cities celebrate national unity day.

DECEMBER
Dec. 7: **Milan** honors St. Ambrose (its patron saint).

Dec. 8: "Festa dell Madonna Immacolata" (Immaculate Conception of the Virgin Mary) national holiday.

Mid-Dec.: **Rome** hosts start of the Epiphany Fair in Piazza Navona.

Dec. 25: "Natale" (Christmas) national holiday. **Rome**, Pope gives a televised annual blessing from the St. Peter's balcony at 12 noon.

Dec. 26: "Saint Stefano" national holiday.

Dec. 31: New Year's Eve.

Dec. 30-Jan. 3: **Orvieto** hosts the "Umbria Jazz Winter."

For the Umbria region, **Web site:** http://www.rai.it/ or http://www.regione.umbria.it/

Starting Dec. 1, 1999 through the entire year of 2000, Rome will be celebrating "Giubileo 2000". A celebration that takes place once every 25 years involving the Pope and pilgrims coming in from all over the world. Lots of events are planned for the year so rooms will

be scarce. For more info contact their office at **Tel:** 06-681671.
Fax:06-6864673. **Web site:** http://www.romagiubileo.it/
E-mail: agenzia@romagiubileo.it.

Note: If a public holiday falls on a Tuesday or Thursday, many businesses also close on the nearest Monday or Friday for a long weekend.

Pronto! **I am a reader of the travel book "Hello Italy! A Hotel Guide to Italy $50-$99 (45-90 Euro) a night ."**

I am interested in information on the availability of rooms at your hotel. Please fill in the answers, sign the form and fax it back to me. I will fax the form back to you with my signature.

Date of Fax:_____ From (print):_____

Telephone #:_____ Fax #:_____

(Don't forget to include your access code & country code)

E-mail address:_____Country:_____

My address:_____

_____

Name of Hotel:_____City:_____

Telephone #:_____Fax #:_____

Hotel's e-mail address:_____

Hotel's address:_____

Date of reservations: Arrival_____ Departure_____

(To avoid any confusions, write day/month/year in this order)

# of people:___ # of children:__ ages___ # of nights:__ # of rooms:___

Type of bed (s) I prefer: Twin_____ Double_____ Queen/King_____

Type of bathroom inside room: Toilet_____Shower_____ Bathtub_____

Balcony/Terrace _____ View_____ Cheapest room_____

Back or Front of hotel_____ Parking (cost per day)_____

Breakfast (si/no)_____ Served in room (si/no)_____Cost_____

Cost of room per night with tax and breakfast (lire/euro)_____

Cost of room per night with tax without breakfast (lire/euro)_____

Method of paying: Cash (or euro)_____ Visa__ MC__AX__DC__

I will mail a check ____or use my credit card ____ for __night(s) deposit.

Credit card information:_____exp. _____

Name on card (print) _____Signature_____

Hotel manager's name (print)_____

Hotel manager's signature_____

The book mentions that _____ at your hotel will give a _____discount off the nightly cost of the room if I show this book to your staff when I arrive.

Will you be able to give me the discount? (si/no)_____

(This form is available on: http://www.HelloEurope.com/)

The following recipe is compliments of Carlo Cuomo, owner of Hotel Bougainville, Positano, Italy.

LIMONCELLO A CARLOS POSITANO

INGREDIENTS

> 7 lemons - one of them should be green/hot ripe. (This will make it taste stronger.)
>
> 1 liter of pure 100% grain alcohol
>
> 1 liter of water
>
> 600 grams of sugar

Skin the lemons - only using the top layer (yellow skin) of skin. The white flesh of the lemon must not be used.

Take the skin of the lemons and put it in the liter of pure alcohol. Let it sit for 6 days.

After the 6 days, boil a liter of water and add 600 grams of sugar while it is boiling. Allow the water to become room temperature.

When the water is room temperature, combine it with the alcohol and lemon skins and stir.

INDEX

INDEX

ADDITIONAL WEB SITES

Milano
Walking art tours: http://www.provincia.milano.it/
Hotels in Milan: http://www.mebs.it/hotels/
http://lascala.milano.it/
http://www.hellomilano.it/milaninfo.HTM/
http://www.rcs.it/inmilano/english/
Reservations via phone for Last Supper 02-89421146 before you leave home. Or while you are in Milan but it takes 5 days.

Cinque Terre
http://www.cinqueterre.it/
http://home.sunrise.ch/avong/cinque_terre/
Ferry shuttle: http://www.navigazionegolfodeipoeti.it/
Vernazza: http://www.fast.mi.it/eia/vernazza/
Lerici: http://www.village.it/lerici/
http://www.salonmagazine.com/wlust/pass/1997/12/22pass.html/
http://italianvillas.com/liguria/cinque.htm/

Lake Como
http://www.traveleurope.net/comolake.htm/
http://www.traveleurope.it/bellagio.htm/
http://www.lagodicomo.com/
http://www.highonadventure.com/Hoa98apr/Lakecomo/

Lake Garda
http://www.lagodigarda.it/lakegarda/
http://www.telmec.it/Uk/Arena_frame.htm/
Hotel Rock: http://www.hotelrock.com Zambiasi Renato

Sirmone
http://www.comune.sirmione.bs.it/index-en.html/

Venice
Welcome to Venice: http://www.port.venice.it/
Venice boats: http://www.venetia.it/boats/
Hotels in Venice: http://www.venicehotel.com/
Walks: http://pathfinder.com/travel/TL/801/venice1.html/

ADDITIONAL WEB SITES

Venice hotels: http://www.veniceinfo.it/
Texan in Venice: http://www.iuav.unive.it/~juli/
Guide to Venice: http://ucgi.venere.it/venezia/guida/
Grand Canal: http://www.gondolavenezia.it/
http://www.stb.dircon.co.uk/
http://www.venetia.it/
http://www.webcom.com/~italys/
http://www.tradenet.it/veniceworld/

Vicenza
http://www.ascom.vi.it/aptvicenza/

Padua
Brenta Canal: http://antoniana.it/mainuk.html/

Bologna
Hotels: http://www.venere.it/emilia_romagna/bologna/bologna.html/

Parma
http://www.parmaitaly.com/

Florence
Taste of Florence: http://www.divinacucina.com/
http://www.weekendafirenze.com/
Hotels in Florence: http://www.firenzealbergo.it/
Florence & Tuscany: http://www.fionline.it/
http://www.arca.net/
http://www.tiac.net/users/pendini/index.html/
http://www.vps.it/propart/
http://www.whatsuptuscany.com/
http://www.firenze.net/events/

Pisa
http://www.csinfo.it/PISA/

Siena
http://www.turismoverde.com/
http://www.sienaweb.it/territorio/

ADDITIONAL WEB SITES

San Gimignano
http://www.sangimignano.com/
http://www.firenze.net/events/itineraries/sangim.htm/

Umbria
Umbria index: http://www.argoweb.it/umbria/umbria.uk.html/
Umbria cities: http://www.umbria.org/

Orvieto
http://www.eng.uci.edu/~alberto/orvieto/
http://www.argoweb.it/orvieto/orvieto.uk.html/
http://www.eng.uci.edu/~alberto/

Perugia
http://www.perugiaonline.com/
Map: http://hppg04.pg.infn.it/images/hotelmap.gif/

Rome
Walking architectural Itineraries: http://www.scalareale.org/
Rome, walks, numbers, maps, events: http://www.romeguide.it/
Getting in/out of Rome: http://www.enjoyrome.it/
Papal audience: http://twenj.com/romewalk.htm#info/
Public Holidays: http://www.inforoma.it/romepage.htm/
Forum: http://library.thinkquest.org/11402/
History: http://www.ukans.edu/history/index/europe/

Papal Audience - Public audiences are held (almost) every Wednesday morning. One must reserve (free) tickets for these and other papal ceremonies from the Prefecture of the Pontifical House of the Vatican City (phone: 011-39-6-698-83017.) The entrance is through the Bronze Door (at the right of the entrance porch to St. Peter's) and is open weekdays from 9 a.m. to 1 p.m. It is reported that you may be able to make reservations now by e-mail to Bou.S.Vv@agora.stm.it All this information was taken from http://TWEnJ.com/ Ed & Julie.

Naples
http://www.itb.it/metroNA/english/home.htm

ADDITIONAL WEB SITES

Pompeii
http://www.marketplace.it/pompeionline/

Positano
http://www.starnet.it/positano/welcome.html/
http://www.positanonline.it/

Amalfi
http://www.starnet.it/onda_verde/
Amalfi coast: http://www.starnet.it/italy/amalfi/
http://www.ondaverde.it/

Ravello
http://www.starnet.it/italy/ravello/ingrawel.htm

Capri
Hotels: http://www.capriweb.com/Capri/hotels/
http://www.caprionline.com/
http://www.capri-island.com/

Sicily
http://www.osolemio.it/sicily/turismo/default.nclk

Taormina
Excursions: http://taol.taormina-ol.it/sunshine/
http://www.taormina-ol.it/host/aastao/aastao.htm

Ferries Italy to Greece: http://www.greekislands.gr/sff/

NOTES OR MEMORABLE EVENTS

NOTES OR MEMORABLE EVENTS

Margo Classé, author of *Hello France! A Hotel Guide to Paris & 25 Other French Cities $50-$99 A Night* and *Hello Spain! An Insider's Guide To Spain Hotels $40-$80 A Night For Two*, is a freelance marketing and sales promotion professional who turned her passion for traveling into a career. She and her husband have spent 10 years traveling extensively throughout southern Europe researching its most affordable, charming, and traveler-friendly hotels. She resides in Los Angeles, CA.